REPRESENTING MODERN ISTANBUL

REPRESENTING MODERN ISTANBUL

Urban History and International Institutions in Twentieth Century Beyoğlu

Enno Maessen

I.B. TAURIS

LONDON • NEW YORK • OXFORD • NEW DELHI • SYDNEY

I.B. TAURIS
Bloomsbury Publishing Plc
50 Bedford Square, London, WC1B 3DP, UK
1385 Broadway, New York, NY 10018, USA
29 Earlsfort Terrace, Dublin 2, Ireland

BLOOMSBURY, I.B. TAURIS and the I.B. Tauris logo are trademarks of
Bloomsbury Publishing Plc

First published in Great Britain 2022
This paperback edition published 2023

Series design by Adriana Brioso
Cover image: Karaköy Square at the foot of the Galata Bridge (Galata Köprüsü),
Istanbul, Turkey, ca 1960. (© Archive Photos/Getty Images)

A catalogue record for this book is available from the British Library.

A catalog record for this book is available from the Library of Congress.

ISBN: HB: 978-0-7556-3746-1
PB: 978-0-7556-3750-8
ePDF: 978-0-7556-3474-8
eBook: 978-0-7556-3748-5

Typeset by Deanta Global Publishing Services, Chennai, India

To find out more about our authors and books visit www.bloomsbury.com and
sign up for our newsletters.

CONTENTS

ILLUSTRATIONS

Map

Figures

Table

ACKNOWLEDGEMENTS

Over the years many friends and colleagues have contributed to this book. Without their support it would undoubtedly not have been realized. I thank Luiza Bialasiewicz, Guido Snel, Uğur Üngör and Paolo Girardelli, for their friendship, intellectual guidance and inspiration. My gratefulness also goes out to those in Istanbul whose particular support and friendship helped me through the complexities and practicalities of fieldwork, Fokke Gerritsen, Ata Gür and Nilay Özlü.

I have received much support from colleagues and friends at the University of Amsterdam, Utrecht University and Boğaziçi University. I especially and heartfully thank Boyd van Dijk, Dana Dolghin, Moritz Föllmer, Tim van Gerven, Milou van Hout, Josip Kešić, Ayşenur Korkmaz, Joep Leerssen, Hanna Muehlenhoff, Tymen Peverelli, Anna Secor and Tuna Taşan-Kok for their advice and comments to earlier versions of the manuscript. I am indebted to many for their advice, support and help: Asu Aksoy, Lorans Baruh, John Dyson, Kerem Eksen, Edhem Eldem, Ahmet Ersoy, Çiğdem Kafesçioğlu, the late Vangelis Kechriotis, Mehmet Kentel, Beate Kretzschmann, Jean-François Pérouse, Felix Pirson, Rosamund Wilkinson and Richard Wittmann. Many thanks also to the staff of the many research institutions and libraries in Istanbul and elsewhere, especially at the Atatürk Kitaplığı, Deutsches Archäologisches Institut Istanbul, Institut Français d'Études Anatoliennes, İstanbul Araştırma Enstitüsü, Nederlands Instituut in Turkije, Orient Institut, SALT Galata and the library of the Türk Mühendis ve Mimarlar Odaları Birliği at Istanbul.

A special word of thanks to the editors at I.B. Tauris & Bloomsbury Publishing, Yasmin Garcha and Rory Gormley, for guiding me through the process of publishing and answering my many queries. I would also like to express my gratitude to the anonymous reviewers for their careful assessment of the manuscript and many useful corrections.

Finally, I thank my friends and family who helped me stay in touch with a reality beyond the book. My special thanks goes to Thijs van Blitterswijk, Bahar Çakıroğlu, Roselyn Flach, Jon Heinrichs, Rick van Hemert, Mette Maessen, Frank Smolenaers, Hans Smolenaers, Zara Weijers. Most of all, my gratitude goes to my parents, Jan and Marina Maessen-Roelofsen, who always had my back. I dedicate this book to them.

INTRODUCTION

In a 2016 article in *The New York Times* entitled 'On Istiklal, Istanbul's Champs-Élysées, Symbols of a City's Malaise', the author offers a prosaic description of the central artery in one of Istanbul's historic districts, Beyoğlu, presenting it as a 'mile-long sea of humanity, with a quaint streetcar rumbling down the middle'. This 'quaint' scene is no more, he claims: 'These days, though, it is a symbol of the city's malaise.'[1] Extrapolating the situation of 'malaise' of the İstiklal Caddesi (İstiklal Avenue) to the district of Beyoğlu at large, the author quotes a prominent voice from Istanbul's urban activist scene who states:

> 'All the characteristic landmarks that made Beyoglu special disappeared one by one,' said Mucella Yapici, a member of Istanbul's Chamber of Architects. [. . .] And the neighborhood turned into a place that entirely lost its soul. Old taverns, bookstores, theaters, and especially movie theaters, shut down.[2]

The representation of Beyoğlu's perpetual demise, here presented in an international news outlet, is a recurrent historical trope about the area. It lies at the core of this book, which highlights the complexity of processes of place-making in Istanbul and problematizes popular representations of processes of continuity and discontinuity in Beyoğlu and Istanbul between 1950 and 1990. It will analyse how different communities made their place in Beyoğlu, while at the same time claiming space in local, national and international processes of education, cultural diplomacy and the cultivation of culture broadly conceived.[3] Perceptions of the district's change in terms of its sociocultural composition and built environment have resulted in discursive overdeterminations of the area's representations: cosmopolitanism, urban deterioration, sociocultural marginalism and a place where people fail to claim their rights to the city. The book's historical focus is the period between 1950 and 1990, four decades marked by Istanbul's development from a middle-sized city into a metropole, ending with the acceleration of gentrification processes in the area. Geographically, the book will focus on the area known as Beyoğlu, although that name should be considered as a geographic container primarily from a discursive point of view; what is associated with Beyoğlu as an area is a dynamic process subject to change over time.

Writing urban history on post-1940s Beyoğlu

The four decades following 1950 are particularly significant for Beyoğlu and Istanbul because they mark a period perceived as the era in which Beyoğlu lost its true 'cosmopolitan' self and ceased to be the vibrant and wealthy belle-époque setting that it had allegedly been some eighty years prior. Research on this period so far is limited. The district features explicitly or implicitly in publications examining tragic events, notably the pogroms of September 1955, yet beyond a few notable exceptions the burgeoning popular and academic literature on the history of Beyoğlu from the 1980s onwards has zoomed in nearly exclusively on the late nineteenth and early twentieth centuries.[4] When the post-1940s period is mentioned it is typically as an object of nostalgia. Beyond the boundaries of historiography, a wealth of research exists on the district's more recent evolution. Yet the years between 1950 and 1990 – a crucial period in Beyoğlu's transition marked by important shifts in its demography, society, cultural production, position in the city's economy and fundamental transformations in its urban landscape – barely feature in the rich literature on Istanbul.

Urban historiography has shown us that Beyoğlu is no exception, since modern urban history has been marked by a tendency to focus on the nineteenth and early twentieth centuries. Those studies that do focus on contemporary issues struggle to integrate their research into the broader range of topics featuring in the disciplines of social and cultural history, dealing mostly with issues of planning instead. Additionally, social and cultural historians still have difficulty in finding their way in urban contexts and, rather, focus on social movements, state formation or other topics related to social, political or intellectual trends.[5] Engaging this lacuna in the context of Istanbul, I will investigate the historical interplay between specific social institutions in Beyoğlu and their surrounding urban landscape. From a theoretical point of view, landscape is crucial to understand the social and cultural relations in the urban environment, as Denis Cosgrove has explained: '[landscape] is an ideological concept. It represents a way in which certain classes of people have signified themselves and their world through their imagined relationship with nature, and through which they have underlined and communicated their own social role and that of others concerning external nature.'[6] Landscape, he argues, is something that 'acts to "naturalize" what is deeply cultural'.[7]

Beyoğlu is, and has for centuries been, a very dynamic urban area, which in part is a catalyst for urban nostalgias about the area, particularly for times long passed. From that perspective I consider the comment by one of my informants, 'You have chosen the most uninteresting period for your research!' to be illustrative. I will indicate in more detail in Chapter 1 how nostalgia for 'convenient cosmopolitanisms' – narratives of Istanbul's social history that fit the goals of various urban actors (municipalities, the private sector, NGOs and private individuals) – have a tendency to colour our understanding of Beyoğlu's recent history, during which spaces and communities were ceaselessly marked by simultaneous stagnation and change. Nostalgia in Beyoğlu has oppressive qualities, similarly observed in the context of Alexandria by Della Dora.[8] The urban environment becomes an embellished, sanitized version of an imagined historical 'reality', with disregard for the 'uninteresting' episodes that somehow sully the supposed 'original' and its reproduction. Svetlana Boym famously ascribes a 'nostalgia for world culture' or a 'provincial cosmopolitanism', rather than a nostalgia for empire, to briefly take root in 1990s St Petersburg, making some of its citizens 'not nostalgic for the past it [the city] had, but for the past it could have had'.[9] In Istanbul, Edhem Eldem urges for the need to critically analyse its urban nostalgias, since the desire for 'authenticity' has the capacity to be as oppressive as the over-romanticized variations on nostalgia, particularly in the context of Beyoğlu.[10] With regard to Beyoğlu, one can therefore, for instance, consider whether opening an exhibition space or cultural institution in a historical building is inherently 'better' for the accessibility of that space than opening a hotel, restaurant or shopping mall.

I primarily intend to critically re-assess interpretations of Beyoğlu's and Istanbul's recent history by drawing attention to the complex and sometimes paradoxical relationship between the district's spatial and social continuities and discontinuities. It explores how five institutions and their physical locations have functioned between the 1950s and 1980s: a period commonly represented as one of change, demise and decay (see map 1 for an overview of the locations of these institutions). Some of the cases in part confirm this thesis, while others contradict it. The German club 'Teutonia', for instance, shows how a historically vibrant community struggled to survive and barely managed to hold on to its properties.

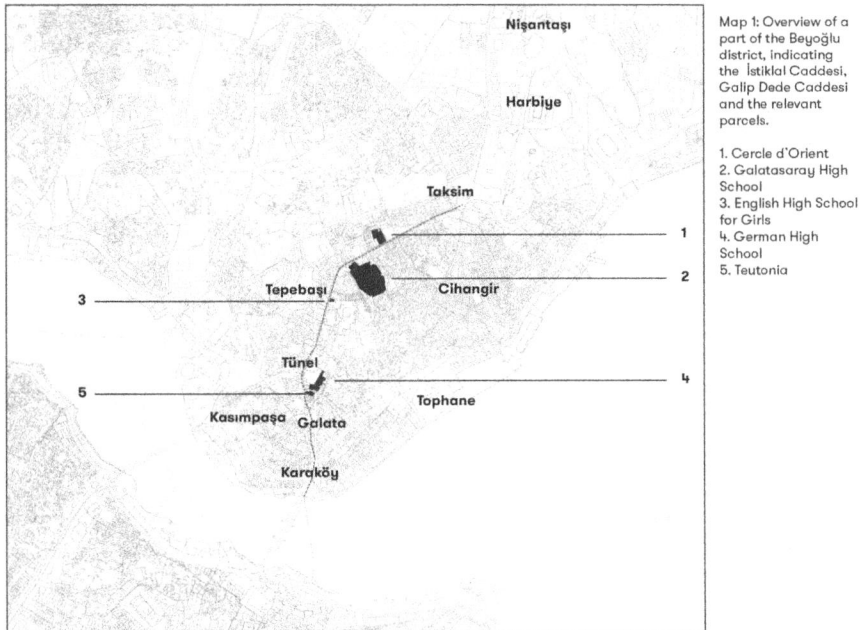

Map 1: Overview of a part of the Beyoğlu district, indicating the İstiklal Caddesi, Galip Dede Caddesi and the relevant parcels.

1. Cercle d'Orient
2. Galatasaray High School
3. English High School for Girls
4. German High School
5. Teutonia

Map 1 Hans Smolenaers & Enno Maessen (2019) – Map of Beyoğlu and relevant parcels.

The club's recent history shows how this was only in part caused by the shifting demographics and social functions of Beyoğlu, and much more by the institution's own troubled history, as well as decreasing interest in sustaining 'national' communities. From a different perspective, the case of Cercle d'Orient highlights how a building can become progressively dissociated from its namesake, an elite gentlemen's club, although its longer histories (and significance) are maintained in other ways. Indeed, as its relevance to the club declined, its significance as a hub for the booming film industry only grew. An English High School for Girls, on the other hand, reveals how a flourishing institution was much less affected by relatively positive local conditions as it was by neoliberal decision-making in London.

The local, national, international and transnational are intimately connected in Beyoğlu. Although Turkey's centre of politics had been moved to Ankara in the wake of the founding of the Republic of Turkey, Istanbul's prominent position in geopolitics remained self-evident due to its strategic position, connecting the Black Sea with the Mediterranean. Turkey's alignment with European and transatlantic alliances was relatively solid, while vehement anti-Communism in parts of the national elite, security apparatus and army was a pretext for fierce suppression of Turkey's left-wing groups, trade unions as well as Kurdish and Alevi organizations.[11] In this climate, foreigners sought to bring Turkey closer into their sphere of influence or at least sustain the existing impact they had in the country. The United States was an obvious player, incorporating Turkey into the Marshall Fund scheme, but also through claiming visibility through prominent representations of US-sponsored global capitalism such as the Istanbul Hilton Hotel.[12] European countries that had historically held a strong presence in Turkey or the Ottoman Empire, however, relied more significantly on their historical institutions to sustain their relevance in the country, exercising a significant form of soft power through them.[13] The English High Schools and German High School are clear representations of that paradigm. As will be shown in two chapters, both British and Germans at various temporal intervals considered the Beyoğlu-based schools historically linked to their respective countries as crucial in the cultural diplomatic efforts of the country. Educating elite students and cultivating sympathy for British or German culture was presented as an effective way to cultivating a positive attitude towards the UK and West Germany among the country's next generation's leadership.

Structure and composition

This book is divided into six chapters. The first chapter will provides a bird's-eye view of the historical development of Istanbul in general and Beyoğlu in particular. The chapter will zoom in on the issues of identity formation and place-making in Beyoğlu between the nineteenth century and the 1990s, contextualizing the area within Istanbul, the Ottoman Empire and Turkey. It will demonstrate the intricate relationship between Beyoğlu's physical environment and its communities in these processes and investigate the development, continuities and discontinuities, of representations on the district between the nineteenth century and the 1980s. It shows, moreover, how Beyoğlu was both a unique place in the Ottoman Empire and Turkey and a microcosm, mirroring social, political and economic processes that occurred on a citywide, national and international scale. The development of Beyoğlu can to a certain degree be seen in the broader perspective of urban development in Europe after the Second World War.[14] Istanbul is arguably the most dramatic example of rapid and massive urbanization in South-eastern Europe. The city, however, also provides additional room for reflection on an alleged dichotomous relation regarding urban development on both sides of the Iron Curtain. Turkey in post-war Europe may arguably have been institutionally anchored in the West European or North Atlantic 'bloc', yet the high degree of governmental centralization and fragility of its democracy further undermine a dichotomous representation of urban developments across capitalist versus collectivist Europe. Istanbul's development provides nuance to this representation as a case of hyper-urbanization that was a direct consequence of policies made at the national level.

In a local context this book also fits in a broader paradigm of critical studies that have argued against interpretations, for instance, of Beyoğlu and its urban landscape as an island of exceptionalisms in the late Ottoman Empire or as a case of general neglect of Istanbul after the foundation of the Turkish Republic. The case of Beyoğlu, however, notably shows how representations of post-war historic urban centres have overdetermined the dwindling of core functions. Ideas on Beyoğlu's revival through its 'rediscovery' and gradual gentrification from the late 1980s onwards, moreover, downplay the significance of Beyoğlu on a local, national and international scale. The enforced or voluntary departures of residents, on the other hand, also resonate in discourses of loss and challenges notions of continuity. From a functional point of view, for instance, it should be stressed that the district retained much of its significance and even witnessed an increase in pre-existing core functions. It was in Beyoğlu and its direct vicinity that experiments with high modernist architecture by local and international artists were executed in the 1940s and 1950s.[15] A high concentration of the country's reputable schools were located in this district or its direct surroundings, positioning it as an enduring centre for the education of the country's elite. The district had, and continues to have, a pivotal role in the social life of Istanbul's various local and foreign communities. Analysing these processes of building relations between actors and surroundings in the context of Beyoğlu undermines the overdetermined representations about the district's demise or corruption.

Chapters 2 and 3 discuss the buildings and communities connected to two club buildings in Beyoğlu. Chapter 2 will discuss the Teutonia club, a German social club founded in the nineteenth century and a pivotal meeting point for German-speaking residents in Istanbul until the Second World War. The chapter will begin with an overview of the club's historical roots, with particular attention to its surroundings and the building it owns in Galata since the late nineteenth century. It will proceed with a discussion of unique post-war archival material from the

Teutonia club to consider its development in Beyoğlu from the 1950s onwards. The Teutonia chapter demonstrates what provided the primary incentive for the club to keep itself alive at the end of the 1970s, when it was essentially facing its demise, was the desire to retain its building for an unspecified 'German purpose'. We see here, in fact, that the imagined community of Teutonia, which once held a pivotal role in the community of *Bosporusdeutschen* and other German speakers, had gradually fallen apart due to a variety of circumstances ranging from a lack of engagement, a troubled history, to the settlement of what in the past was its former member target group in different areas of the expanding city. Dynamics in Germany, moreover, from the rise of Nazism to the exodus of German academics and the Cold War's German East–West divide also resonated with the history and destiny of Teutonia. Had the club not been able to successfully reinvigorate and reorganize itself with the goal of reclaiming its building, it may have been well possible that Teutonia had ceased to exist over four decades ago rather than succeeding in maintaining itself as a point where the interests of German speakers could converge.

Chapter 3 will focus on a group of buildings that is known as the Cercle d'Orient parcel. This group of buildings got its name from an elite gentlemen's club which had its main premises in the main building until the 1960s. This chapter is different from the previous one in the sense that the discussion of the club's history constitutes a relatively minor part of the chapter. This group of buildings is primarily known for the formative position it held, in terms of place and memory, in cinema production and consumption between the 1960s and 1980s. This chapter will zoom in on this history and discuss it in relation to its contested usage and appropriation by Turkish governments and private actors. The significance of ownership of place is also exemplified by the case of the Cercle d'Orient. Demonstrating the duality and coexistence of narratives, one of an elite club and the other of a local and national hub for cinema production and viewing, this case shows the impact of rapid and chaotic urbanization on various levels, local as well as national. Since the Cercle d'Orient never owned the Beyoğlu building in which it resided, it was apparently easier for the club to abandon it, particularly since it already had access to an alternative location summer location on the Asian side of the city. More broadly speaking, the case of the Cercle d'Orient parcel demonstrates the complexity of place-making if ownership is legally established. The parcel became the spatial centre point of cinema production in Turkey, yet this significance was entirely disregarded during the process of leasing the building by a state organization to a private party. This demonstrates the limits of place-making in the district and, notably, the limits of informal place-making beyond that of institutional actors. Regardless, the Yeşilçam film industry shows how a particular locality can become a national symbol of cultural production. This industry has significantly added to Beyoğlu's reputation and reality as an urban and national centre, notably in the 1960s and 1970s.

The remaining three chapters will discuss three schools and their respective buildings. Chapter 4 will focus on the history of the Galatasaray High School, founded in the middle of Pera/Beyoğlu as the first of a projected imperial system of high schools in the late nineteenth century and transformed into a francophone Turkish state school in the 1920s. The chapter will dedicate particular attention to the sense of belonging that its alumni attribute to growing up and being educated in a francophone institution situated in Beyoğlu. It shows how Turkish French-speaking alumni of the school felt a strong connection with this district. This is further amplified by the connections that are built in the high school's narration of its own history, which harks back not only to its predecessor that was founded in the late nineteenth century but also to the Palace School from the late fifteenth century, an interesting case of an invented tradition. The strong feelings of attachment and sense of belonging to the school's site in Beyoğlu are actively cultivated by the various alumni associations connected to the Galatasaray High School. The alumni here cherish representations of their sense of belonging to Galatasaray and that of the school to Beyoğlu. The Galatasaray High School, apart from having its main student campus in the middle of historical Beyoğlu, periodically is the scene for gatherings of alumni, for instance, with the annually organized traditional alumni day, known as the Pilav Günü (Pilaf Day). The location in Beyoğlus thus hold a pivotal significance not only in the imagining of the community but also in the ritualized enactments of the embodied communities. The institution, moreover, makes its presence known to the outsiders, passers-by, through place names, symbolism and architecture, yet at the same time displays seclusion, through institutional traditions and tall fences, demonstrating that Beyoğlu belongs in part to Galatasaray, but that it is distinct from their surroundings as well.

In the final two chapters, the reader will see strong correlations between the histories an English and a German High School. Chapter 5 discusses the English High School for Girls, a grammar school based in a building directly along the İstiklal Caddesi and founded in the second half of the nineteenth century. This school, the girls section of the English High Schools, with its counterpart for boys based in Nişantaşı, was particularly popular among non-Muslim minorities until its closure and transferral to the Turkish state in the late 1970s. The final chapter engages the German High School, founded in the second half of the nineteenth century, which is still a reputable co-educational high school in Tünel. The cases of both the English High School for Girls and the German High School show the significance of educational institutions in the cultural diplomacy of the UK and West Germany and are as such apt cases to demonstrate not only the enduring significance of Beyoğlu but also the interconnectivity between local and international levels. The cases of the English High School for Girls and the German School both shed light on how place-making can also be a process that is partially enforced or established by faits accomplis determined at levels beyond the influence of the schools or their respective administrations. Both schools were severely obstructed by the Turkish state in developing plans to move their buildings to sites that they considered more suitable to facilitate accessibility and growth in the future. They therefore remained in Beyoğlu not necessarily because they felt a strong and heartfelt connection with the area and building, but rather since they had no other options to be re-established elsewhere without jeopardizing the school's future. The ongoing efforts of the British and German governments to keep these expensive schools open should be considered in the light of these countries' efforts to maintain good relations with Turkey. At various temporal intervals both schools are presented as the primary instruments of cultural diplomacy in Turkey of the UK and West Germany.

Following the six chapters, a synthesis of the findings is presented in the conclusions, the final part of this book.

Chapter 1

ISTANBUL AND BEYOĞLU IN HISTORICAL PERSPECTIVE

Beyoğlu or Galata/Pera has become the iconic site of Istanbul's imagined 'cosmopolitanism'. The settlement of the Genovese has been known as Galata since the eighth century, its borders formalized since 1303 with significant expansions of its territory in the fourteenth century. The settlement was lined with defence walls and watch towers, of which the Galata Tower from 1349 is the most prominent and one of the few visible remains.[1] Following the transition of Istanbul from Byzantine to Ottoman rulership in 1453, the Genovese held their rights but were forced by the sultan to decrease the height of their fortifications. Following the settlement of the Ottoman rulership in Istanbul, non-Muslims were increasingly attracted to the Galata area. Eldem provides a beautiful description of the impressions of Dominique Fornetty, second dragoman to the French Embassy in Constantinople at the end of the seventeenth century, who he describes to 'be at a loss when he tried to explain that variety [of people in Galata and among those defined as "Levantines"] to foreigners'.[2] He points out that the travellers coming to Istanbul were eager to find 'the Orient' and were often underwhelmed by Galata, which reminded them of other port cities along the Mediterranean, yet were at the same time amazed by what appeared to be a Christian enclave and to them was surprisingly diverse for such an oriental place.[3] Eldem argues that for them it was not the most spectacular place in the city, since it may have resembled Venice, Genoa or Marseille. Paolo Girardelli nuances this, however, and points out that the district in historiography has been compared by some to a 'typical, fortified North Italian town' before 1453 and several centuries afterwards, which he argues is rather exaggerated.[4] Eldem suggests that it might be possible to call the Galata district in the seventeenth (and eighteenth) century a city in itself, within Constantinople, as it was walled until the late nineteenth century. The 'otherness' of this district, however, is a representation, or, one might suggest, even a representational culture, that has been – and continues to be – actively cultivated. The cultural and religious otherness of Galata, Eldem argues, neglects the gradual integration of the district into the city with a growing community of Muslims moving towards the district, reflected, for instance, in the presence of twelve mosques against six churches following a major city fire in 1696.[5] This pushed the non-Muslim communities to expand the district further beyond the walls, towards the Pera hill and Taksim cemeteries.[6]

The appearance of the Galata/Pera area, its architecture more specifically, poses a highly revealing example of how the area's cultural hybridity was expressed in physical form. As Girardelli indicates, the newcomers that would populate Istanbul would integrate elements distinct to the architectural traditions of their native regions, which resulted in a fairly homogeneous typology of residential architecture, based on community traditions of constructing in timber. Maurice Cerasi indicates that broadly speaking what became known as the 'Ottoman house' was a constant in the Ottoman urban landscape, in Istanbul and beyond during the eighteenth century.[7] Timber constructions, despite their vulnerability to the all too common city fires, were common in much of Istanbul without bearing reference to any particular identity in the architectural language.[8] This would hold true for both districts on the shores of the Golden Horn, Stamboul and Galata/Pera. Girardelli indicates that apart from the higher density of buildings in Galata and despite the emphasis that is typically put on the alleged difference between the two quarters, they in fact were strikingly similar. Even many of the buildings occupied by the foreign representations appeared in various cases to be decisively more 'local' than 'foreign' until the first half of the nineteenth century.[9]

Monumental architecture, on the other hand, reveals a breach with the typological boundaries of the 'classical period' in Ottoman architecture and a new phase in the cultural hybridity of Ottoman monumental architecture. Hamadeh points out that the eighteenth century added a broader lexicon to the monumental elements in the urban landscape, with old and new as well as local and foreign elements. She attributes the change to a disintegration of stable power elements and a diffusion of artistic patronage, from the traditional elite to, among others, a growing urban middle class.[10] A new social order invoked a response of the imperial elite to press its stamp on Istanbul's public spaces, claiming its presence. This imperial elite expressed its presence and power through the public space, which had previously been the privilege of the sultan and grand vizier, with their own tastes and preferences for self-representation.[11] Representation and display of power, moreover, moved from Stamboul to the shores of the Bosporus. Hamadeh argues that eighteenth-century monumental Ottoman architecture is wrongly considered to have suddenly shifted towards Western vocabularies, similar to the construction of 'Ottoman houses', which were essentially also architectural testimonies of cultural hybridity. This, she explains, on the one hand, poses a reductionist view of the preceding centuries during which there had been continuous (political, economic, diplomatic and cultural) interaction with European powers, while, on the other hand, the novelties in architectural style were equally appreciative of Western and Eastern traditions of building.[12] Rather than 'Westernization' it thus seems that 'novelty' was the key word in the changing architectural vocabularies of the Ottoman urban context, with attention to a variety of local and foreign styles. This architectural bricolage had been a reality before; it became even more visible in the urban landscape since the imperial elite could lay claim to it as well.[13]

As strong as the impact of the eighteenth century may have been on Istanbul's urban landscape, the events that unfolded in the Ottoman Empire during the final years of the eighteenth century and, most significantly, the first half of the nineteenth century would have a decisive effect on the physical integrity and appearance of the imperial capital again. This time, however, the impact would be particularly large in Galata/Pera. The Ottoman rulership had become aware of the limits of the imperial army's power, particularly in contrast with the modernizing armies of the dominant European powers. The successive failures of the Ottoman army against the revolting Ottoman governor of Egypt, Mehmed Ali Pasha, and the war against the Greek independence movement, which resulted in the reluctant acknowledgement of an independent Greek state by the Ottoman government, made Sultan Mahmud II aware of the need for an extensive reform program. Before him, earlier attempts at reform and modernization had already been initiated. As Erik-Jan Zürcher points out Mahmud II followed in the footsteps of his predecessor Selim III as well as his rival in Egypt Mehmed Ali, by identifying the need for a modern army which was backed by a modern state structure, with an extensive bureaucracy, taxation system, as well as Western-style education and legislation.[14] Though it would not be right to pinpoint Mahmud II as the sole initiator of this process, it was ultimately his decision-making that would set the agenda for an extensive wave of reforms in the Ottoman Empire. Zürcher argues that Mahmud II's push to set up a new army entirely under his control in 1826 would incite a response from the traditional military core in the Ottoman Empire – the Janissaries – which was quite rapidly suppressed and the old corps were disbanded, effectively ending their military and social influence in the Empire.[15] Prussian army officers were invited to guide the Ottoman leadership in building a modern army virtually from scratch. Eventually the new army and the infrastructure it required would initiate a period which is often described as the *Tanzimat-i Hayriye* (Beneficial Reforms), formally starting with the Edict of Gülhane focusing on the introduction of new legislation on equality of Ottoman citizens, taxation and military conscription.[16] Even before, however, the term *Tanzimat* had been used and reforms affecting the Ottoman state structure had obviously already been set in motion by Mahmud II, who died a few months before the realization of the Edict.

As the *Tanzimat* both explicitly and implicitly aimed to bring the Ottoman Empire up to speed with its European allies and rivals, the influence of the Western powers, intellectually, financially, culturally and politically over the Ottoman Empire grew tremendously.[17] Lorans Baruh points out how this also had rather immediate effects on the planning of Istanbul's urban environment. She refers to a letter by one of the leading figures behind the Gülhane Edict, Ottoman statesman Mustafa Reshid Pasha, who wrote to the sultan in 1836 that the dominance of timber architecture in Istanbul's urban landscape was criticized in European newspapers as they would pose a recurring problem in the destructive city fires that Istanbul was continuously faced with in its history.[18] Mustafa Reshid Pasha, who admired the urban landscapes of Paris, Vienna and London during his diplomatic missions, therefore suggested to the sultan to have buildings constructed in stone or brick rather than wood. The Ottoman government then tried to regularize the urban landscape and in the second quarter of the nineteenth century several regulations were drawn up which stipulated, among other things, that apart from the lower classes, no one was allowed to construct in timber any longer and that timber structures moreover were not allowed to be constructed across from masonry buildings, have significant distance from mason buildings and should be separated from other construction with a masonry wall reaching to the height of the roof.[19] Girardelli points out that it would take until the second half of the nineteenth century before a noticeable difference in terms of architectural design became apparent between Muslim and non-Muslim communities. The great city fire of 1831 did, however, have an impact on the properties of the foreign embassies and upper-class families. The embassies chose styles and sizes that would reflect grandeur and a 'European' identity, opting in most cases for neoclassical or neo-renaissance designs.[20] Meanwhile the urban government was subjected to a program of reform as well. Zeynep Çelik points how the 'classical' Ottoman city had been organized along principles and theories adhering to Islamic modes of government, which did not recognize religious corporations (the individual and communities were recognized) and would leave administration in the urban setting to professional, ethnic and religious communities.[21] Islamic judges, the *kadıs*, should according to Çelik be identified as the principal power bearers in the city as they were entitled to supervise all matters of a juridical nature, in the case of the city also notably that of the city's real estate. Four juridical boroughs, the *kadılıks*, divided the city: Eyüp, Galata, Istanbul and Üsküdar, which further separated into smaller neighbourhoods (*mahalle*) and larger districts (*semt*).[22] Municipal administration took a much more decentralized and, to a certain degree, informal character – based on traditions, jurisprudence and various written and unwritten sources, including imperial orders (*ferman*).[23]

This would change during the *Tanzimat*. In line with the desire of the Ottoman state for full control of the governmental system, the administration of the capital also was brought under the control of a centralized bureaucracy, bringing the power of the *kadı* and local councils to ministries instead.[24] The government aimed to bring Istanbul's urban landscape's 'quality' to the standard of its European counterparts, regularizing, beautifying, lighting and widening streets, and improving construction methods. To that end the Commission for the Order of the City (*İntizam-ı Şehir Komisyonu*), set up by the Ottoman government in 1855, proposed to reorder the city in four *arrondissements*, after the French model, making Galata/Pera and Tophane the Sixth District – arguably with reference to the upscale *sixième arrondissement* in Paris.[25] This Sixth District would become a pilot area for urban modernization, which was expected to be more broadly implemented in other parts of the city at a later stage.[26] By then the status of the district had already been growing considerably while the social composition and existing architecture of the area made that the Ottoman government considered it particularly suitable for further modernization. Çelik quotes from the *Takvim-i Vekayi* (Calendar of Facts, the Ottoman official gazette), which makes this point particularly clear: 'Since to begin all things in the above-mentioned districts [meaning the thirteen districts except Galata] would be sophistry and unworthy, and since the Sixth District contains much valuable real estate and many fine buildings, and since the majority of those owning property or residing there have seen such things in other countries and understand their value, the reform program will be inaugurated in the Sixth District.'[27]

As much as the reform program may have implemented significant and highly apparent reforms, Istanbul's urban landscape would retain the hybridity and mixing of styles beyond the thresholds of community lines. As Girardelli indicates architectural typologies in Istanbul/Constantinople's urban landscape have been a testimony to the cultural intricacies of Istanbul's hybrid society since Byzantine times.[28] The nineteenth-century Ottoman capital is no exception: a reflection of the complex sociocultural realities faced by Constantinople's urban dwellers. As pointed out earlier in the context of the eighteenth century, Girardelli stresses in his work that the architectural languages used by the various communities in the city should not be considered as representations of nationality, religion or 'lineage' to a different geographic area, political or religious institution. This holds true for the attempts to reform the city's urban landscape of the nineteenth century as well, which had by no means the effect of the urban planning strategies implemented in Paris and Vienna. Moreover, the urban redevelopment did also not resemble the increasing spatial segregation of 'local' and 'foreign' communities in semi-colonial urban settings such as Alexandria, Cairo, Tunis or Algiers where sharp divides were cultivated by European communities.[29] In Galata, the typologies remained much more mixed, while at the same time an overhaul of building styles towards a 'Western' model was not observable. Girardelli argues that instead the model of the Ottoman house was further developed, using less timber and more masonry. Entering the second half of the nineteenth century, however, Galata/Pera's growing significance as the centre in the city – in part due to the growing economic, cultural and political influence of foreign powers – gradually found spatial expression with a growing conglomeration of monumental buildings.[30]

Giradelli suggests, however, that the idea of a top-down imposition of urban reform in Galata/Pera underplays earlier attempts at introducing novel modes of construction.[31] Considering this also means retracing greater continuity in the changing urban landscape. Much of the radical shifts in Galata/Pera, moreover, were not incited by planning ideals, but by the need to rebuild or reconstruct after city fires such as the ones in 1831 and 1870, as will also become clear in following chapters. The urban form and architecture of the area that constitutes Galata/Pera, or Beyoğlu nowadays, should nonetheless be considered as an evolution in which 'local' methods and styles were mixed with 'Western' ones. The fragmentary change and combination of styles in the district counters ideas that the Sixth District became a regularized space with clear demarcations imposed from the top.[32] Girardelli describes this as the 'Levantine environment', in which rigid models either 'Ottoman' or 'Western' are very much the exception and in the latter case limited to the embassy buildings. The categories here are hyphenated, as Girardelli indicates that the Levantine practice of construction and architectural design can simply not be limited to either of these categories. He explains furthermore that this hybridity was also recognized, or rather criticized and dismissed, by various local and foreign observers: for Young Turks and Republican architects it was too cosmopolitan, for foreign observers it was not quite exotic enough.[33]

Representing diversity in Beyoğlu

It is this hybridity that has been represented by artists, public administrations, NGOs, novelists, journalists, politicians and citizens, particularly since the 1980s, as a cosmopolitanism in which there was a seemingly colourful and nearly idyllic coexistence of various communities and classes in this urban centre. This representation has been extensively criticized by Eldem over the past decades.[34] He questions the validity of using the term in the context of the communities in Galata/Pera which, rather than *with* each other, more often appeared to have lived *alongside* each other. Superficial observation from an outsider would not reveal the relative lack of intermingling between members of the various communities. Eldem typifies cosmopolitanism as a community which is constituted by the diversity of its members while simultaneously changing the members of such a community by the milieu as well. A form of cosmopolitanism that he identifies would flourish only in an institutional context such as the Ottoman Bank and was more than anything a concept defined by boundaries of class, shaped by education, linguistic proficiencies. This way of life was thus limited to a particular segment of society in the district, by people who were able to navigate between their various identities that they were required to perform in the different settings that they navigated through.[35]

With regard to the district's demographic and cultural diversity, Stanford Shaw notes that the Ottoman census in the 1880s registered a heterogeneous urban population, in the case of Istanbul, but even more so in the case of Galata/Pera. For the year 1885 he presents the following segmentation of the urban society, in a total population of 873,565: 44.06 per cent Muslim, 17.48 per cent Greek Orthodox, 17.12 per cent Armenian Gregorian, 1.74 per cent Catholic, 5.08 per cent Jewish 0.09 per cent Protestant, 0.5 per cent Bulgarian, 0.12 per cent Latin and 14.79 per cent foreigner. For the Sixth District of Pera and Dolmabahçe there was a total population of 237,293 with 18.9 per cent Muslim, 7.4 per cent Greek Orthodox, 12 per cent Armenian Gregorian, 1.3 per cent Catholic, 9.6 per cent Jewish, 0.001 per cent Protestant, 0.04 per cent Bulgarian, 0.03 per cent Latin and 47 per cent foreigner. Shaw notes that the large amount of foreigners overall, and in the Sixth District in particular, is not (exclusively) an effect of a sudden rise in the number of foreigners in the second half of the nineteenth century, but rather an effect of the decision of local Ottoman citizens to adopt foreign citizenship. One of the main instigators was the capitulations that the Ottoman Empire had granted to foreign powers. Particularly the right of foreigners to own property was important in the decision of various members of the millets to adopt foreign citizenship.[36] Will Hanley provides a thorough discussion of how the Ottoman government in fact tried to counter the naturalization of Ottomans into foreign citizenship through successive rounds of legislation, notably the Ottoman nationality law of 1869.[37]

The rising influence of foreigners in the Sixth District was nonetheless notable, through the popularity of Western architectural patterns and typologies in the Ottoman vernacular architecture or the capitulations towards European powers. Significantly also, through the course of the second half of the nineteenth-century numerous schools and clubs catering to either a particular or several communities within the city were founded, establishing new secular or semi-secular places of encounter. These clubs, societies and schools would create important links among members of a linguistic, ethnic or (later) national community. At the same time, in several cases, links between members of heterogeneous communities were built in these institutions. Clear examples are the Germanophone Teutonia, French *Union Française* and Italian *Società Operaia di Mutuo Soccorso*. The aims of these clubs could go from building ties with the 'motherland', to assisting members of the community or building social ties within community in the Ottoman capital. This can be said to a certain extent of some masonic lodges as well, who, could in particular cases, cater to brethren who were also nationals of the country where the Grand Lodge was located or at least function in the language of the respective country. In other cases, however, the lodges would be internationalist and specifically aim for initiating men from a diverse range of communities, not in the least case to build networks between foreigners and local Ottoman nationals.[38] This was also, from the onset, the goal of the gentleman's club Cercle d'Orient, founded in 1882.[39] The cultural diversity was one of the most remarkable features of the latter categories. The foreign schools as well, with their highly mixed communities, also present a condition of considerable diversity. What is more is that this condition of diversity in the case of particular schools endured until well into the twentieth century.[40] This mostly re-emphasizes that processes of cultural exchange and the cultivation of culture existed within the boundaries of a particular institution and limited space rather than within the urban community, the district or even the city in its entirety. As will be shown in the following chapters, these clubs and schools can be interpreted as 'embodied communities', nodes in transnational networks for what Joep Leerssen has defined as the cultivation of culture and its articulation as national.[41]

Others, however, have attributed a somewhat broader interpretation of diversity in the area. Ulrike Tischler speaks of the 'Pera society', with 'Perotes' being the representatives of an ambivalent cross-cutting identity in which ethno-denominational criteria separated them from other communities, while at the same time relying on interculturalism or 'cosmopolitanism'.[42] Interestingly, she notes how in the interviews with the oldest group (born 1900–1927, speaking mostly Greek or French and little Turkish) among her informants, there was a recurring shifting between the times of childhood and the present. The intermittent periods in which the transformation of their lives and that of Beyoğlu occurred were largely exempted or mentioned only in passing. They speak of the *milieu de mémoire* or, in Tischler's words, 'the authentic Pera' that they witnessed, but appear to exclude the shifts in their livelihoods caused by 'the authentic Pera's' displacement or erasure to the fringes of their recollection.[43] The younger generations typically reproduce the idyllic memories of the district that they have heard from the oldest generations, while adding experiences of rupture, such as the 6–7 September 1955 pogrom, the Cyprus crisis and 'targets of animosity', establishing a dichotomy between themselves and anything or anyone Turkish or 'other'.[44]

For the most part the surroundings of that 'authentic Pera' would be shaped during the second half of the nineteenth century. Çelik indicates that the Ottoman government considered beauty to be causally associated with regularity, taking obvious inspiration from contemporary European cities. She argues furthermore that many of the most crucial reforms took place in the Sixth District. She adds, however, that many of the plans could be executed only after fires had destroyed parts of the district and city at large. Quite to the contrary of European cities or some European districts in colonial cities, the street plans of Galata/Pera would remain patch-like, with grid planning implemented in places where fire had created empty lots. The Grande Rue de Pera (current İstiklal Caddesi) is a notable example from that perspective, since its enlargement was incited by the 1870 fire which blazed from the Taksim area westwards, destroying much of Tarlabaşı, Taksim, the Grande Rue de Pera itself and the area around the *Mekteb-i Sultanî* at Galatasaray.[45] At first planners had imagined to build a second monumental artery through Tarlabaşı, but by that time such a high degree of monumental buildings had amassed around the Grande Rue de Pera that, as Çelik indicates, it was no longer feasible to follow such a plan through. Instead the Grande Rue was significantly widened, which meant that remaining buildings were at times also required to be demolished. Girardelli refers to the case of the Saint Anthony Church, directly adjacent to the Grande Rue de Pera. The municipality forced the Franciscan friars to demolish part of their prayer hall or choose a new site. The first alternative was not considered an option by the friars as their prayer hall could already not meet the high demand of believers, whereas the French Embassy, under whose protectorate the Saint Anthony Church lay, was not willing to support the second option. Eventually in 1895 the friars asked for help from the newly founded Italian state, which considered it an excellent opportunity to stake Italian belonging in Constantinople and 'the Orient'. Harking back to the long-standing Genoese and Venetian presence this cooperation between the friars and the Italian state resulted in the current neo-Gothic Saint Anthony Church with numerous references to the Venetian past.[46]

The many improvements in the district – sewage works, street lighting, road improvement and embellishment, tram lines, electricity – were of particular benefit to the higher classes concentrated around the Grande Rue de Pera, both the Ottoman bourgeoisie and Europeans.[47] The neighbourhoods of Kasımpaşa, parts of Taksim and Pangaltı, predominantly inhabited by the poorer Armenian, Greek and Turkish classes, would experience little benefit from the new facilities.[48] This is a notable issue to emphasize as it renders clearly how Pera was a mixed place beyond the limits of ethnicity. The economic divisions that ran through the district segmented various communities not only in terms of ethnicity or religiosity but also in terms of class.[49] It appears that these then were further emphasized by the authorities' decision to provide the new municipal services only to the neighbourhoods inhabited by the communities who could be considered to be in the upper echelons of the socio-economic strata. Çelik, following Steven Rosenthal, argues that the services were mostly directed to benefit the Europeans in the district. This, however, disregards the significant economic divides within the 'European' communities. As the case of the German community shows – and this would likely be applicable in part to the larger European communities of Italian, French or English origin as well – several Germanophone residents of Pera in fact belonged to the working classes or lower middle classes, and it seems unlikely that they would be able to afford living in the upscale areas around the Grande Rue de Pera.[50] Taking into consideration the large share of residents that the Sixth District held in comparison to the rest of Istanbul – 237,293 for the Sixth District and 389,545 for Istanbul in total – makes it fair to assume that a variety of income groups from foreign origin would live in the poorer neighbourhoods.[51]

Architecturally, the district also retained much of its hybridity, with the Levantine influences still visible in the architecture constructed between the 1930s and the 1960s, notably in Cihangir, Teşvikiye, Şişli and other parts of the older districts on the city's European and Asian shores. This image would in fact continue to influence the urban landscape until the 1950s Girardelli argues. He also stresses that the top-down impositions that architects and urban planners had imagined were therefore often disregarded.[52] A notable example is the 'National Architecture Renaissance'. Sibel Bozdoğan describes how the 'National Architecture Renaissance' took shape around 1908, which, not coincidentally, coincided with the Constitutional Revolution of the Young Turks which brought their Committee of Union and Progress (*İttihat ve Terakki Cemiyeti*) to power and effectively ended the autocratic regime of Sultan Abdülhamid II. The national style that took shape, in various cities of what would soon be the Turkish Republic, was based on the combination of novel elements from modern architecture, reinforced concrete, steel, iron, beaux-arts principles and decorative elements that took inspiration from what Bozdoğan refers to as classical Ottoman architecture, with semispherical domes, roof overhangs, tile decoration and pointed arches. This new national style also found limited expression in Beyoğlu, as the style was widely used for various public buildings, such as banks, offices, cinemas and ferry stations. In that sense it was strikingly similar to the way public buildings with neo-Gothic and neoclassical building-style elements were imagined and constructed in Europe and North America.[53] The effects of this 'National Style' on Beyoğlu's landscape were relatively limited, with notable exceptions such as the building of İş Bankası and Tütün Han (Union Han) at Bankalar Caddesi in Karaköy.[54] Girardelli argues that in contrast to the Levantine image, which was visible throughout the urban landscape, the examples of the National Style remained isolated icons within the landscape, rather than becoming integrated environments.[55] Ironically, moreover, Bozdoğan argues that the architects responsible for the National Architecture Renaissance, most notably Kemalettin Bey and Vedat Bey, were also trained and cultured by the eclectic typologies of the nineteenth century against which they reacted.[56] Kemalettin Bey was educated in Germany and Vedat Bey in France, while both were Muslim architects in an industry which for a considerable time had been largely dominated by non-Muslims and Europeans. They were, however, contemporaries, colleagues or students of other influential architects such as Vallaury and Giulio Mongeri and should therefore also be considered as elements within a larger professional community, simultaneously influencing and being influenced by this community.[57]

The hybridity that was strikingly visible in the built environment also remained a social reality in Beyoğlu's demography. The so-called minorities (in terms of their numbers it would be in fact wrong to frame them as such in the context of Beyoğlu's population) were part of Ottoman society across all social classes and a significant factor in the Ottoman economy.[58] Alexis Alexandris indicates that 50 per cent of capital investments in 1914 were made by the Greek community, followed by the Armenians with 20 per cent, the Turks with 15 per cent, foreigners with 10 per cent and Jews with 5 per cent. He argues that this asymmetry in wealth distribution over different ethnic groups in the empire paved the way for hostility and animosity against the Ottoman multi-ethnic constellation.[59] As will be made clear in the following chapters, apart from capital, education was an important factor in the advantages that the middle and upper classes of the non-Muslim communities had over the Muslim communities. Alexandris points out that in the case of the Greek *millet*, efforts to educate the community had been highly successful through its advanced school system. By 1912 the community had 112 schools, complemented by a large number of private high schools.[60] These institutions also would turn out to be efficient vessels for disseminating Greek nationalism, although Vangelis Kechriotis has shown effectively that what exactly is 'Greek nationalism' in the context of the late Ottoman Empire is a complex issue that cannot be reduced to an identification of a nation with a state.[61] Alexandris argues that in the rapidly nationalizing Ottoman capital, the Greek community would remain the second most important around the turn of the century and puts forward an interpretation of the city's cosmopolitanism typified by two groups which co-existed: 'each perfectly distinct and each perfectly at home, there was remarkably little assimilation of one element by the other.'[62]

Beyoğlu and Istanbul in transition from imperial to post-imperial spaces

Animosity and tension had been growing between communities nonetheless. The distance between different communities became apparent, for instance, with the constitutional regulations calling all young male Ottoman citizens for obligatory military service, which prompted many young men of the minorities, particularly Greek, to leave the country or take on a different citizenship.[63] The Ottoman leadership was confronted first with the Balkan Wars in 1912–13, in which large parts of its territory in South-eastern Europe were lost to the countries of the Balkan League. This caused mass immigration to the Ottoman capital, with Murat Gül suggesting that the city's population rose to 1.6 million. Without further reference to this number it is hard to check its veracity. Shaw provides the census data from

1906 and 1914, which are 782,231 and 909,978 respectively. A sharp rise in the number of Muslims in the city is noticeable in any case, with the community's numbers rising from 370,343 in 1906 to 560,434 in 1914.[64] Ayhan Aktar moreover indicates that the influx of 250,000 Turkish/Muslim refugees led to a special law, the Law for the Settlement of Immigrants, which installed a special directorate for the settlement of these refugees.[65] Meanwhile the CUP tried to modernize the city, with a new bridge between Galata and Eminönü and introduce street lighting and a power station, the latter being built in 1914. Telephone services were set up by a consortium of British, French and American companies in 1911 and an electric tramway was put into service in 1912 between Karaköy and Ortaköy. More large-scale modernization was cut short, although Mayor Cemil Pasha managed to push forward significant improvements between 1912 and 1914.[66]

Following the Ottoman Empire's unsuccessful attempts to form an alliance with France, tension in Europe was rapidly rising. Finally the CUP settled in making an alliance with the Central Powers. Zürcher argues that the CUP knowingly brought itself in an alliance that would lead to war, as the German Empire had accepted to treat the Ottoman Empire as an equal partner; a significant gain for the CUP which tried to break with its semi-colonial status in Europe.[67] The war situation, however, incited a further escalation of domestic tension and brutality between factions, which resulted in the mass expulsions and fleeing of non-Muslim communities from the Ottoman Empire and of Muslim communities from the surrounding countries towards the Ottoman Empire. It, moreover, led the CUP to aggressively take on the issue of a possible foundation by Armenian nationalists of an independent state in Eastern Anatolia, while siding with Russia. Uğur Üngör argues that the nationalist elements in the CUP welcomed the prospect of war as a way to deal with the elements in Ottoman society which were considered to have undermined the state as well as cut short the humiliating capitulations. Driven by paranoia and panic the CUP became increasingly aggressive towards the non-Muslim populations and set up numerous initiatives to eradicate the presence of Armenians from public life. Armenians were fired from public offices at first, while Armenian conscripts were disarmed and treated as traitors. Gradually, the CUP government, under the direct control of members of the CUP triumvirate leadership, fronted in this case by Talaat Pasha, set up a vast campaign to exterminate the Armenian population, carefully micromanaged by Talaat Pasha and brutally executed by CUP officials such as Mehmed Reshid, governor of the Diyarbekir Province. At a local level the persecutions targeted oftentimes indiscriminately Orthodox Armenians, Catholic Armenians, non-Ottoman Armenians and numerous other Christian communities. Hundreds of thousands of people were murdered, raped, enslaved, while those who resisted to comply with the vigorous campaign of pillage and destruction were dismissed, prosecuted or murdered.[68] These tragic events have now widely been acknowledged in international historiography as the Armenian Genocide.[69] The genocide would be a significant step in an ensuing project of social engineering, including mass deportations and massacres against various ethnic or religious communities, that would continue during the Turkish Republic. Üngör points out that the campaigns of resettlement and deportation, particularly of the

Kurdish communities in the 1920s, were supported up to the highest ranks of the Kemalist regime, with pivotal figures as İsmet İnönü claiming that it was solely the Turkish nation who had the right to make any claims to ethnic and racial rights.[70]

Following the defeat of the Central Powers at the conclusion of the First World War, Istanbul was occupied by Allied forces. The Allied forces set up their headquarters in the Pera district. Istanbul's minorities had not been affected as devastatingly as their counterparts in Anatolia by the mass persecutions of the CUP and the multi-ethnic demography of the city therefore remained largely intact. New complexities started to materialize, however, as Alexandris indicates that the Greek community decided to no longer acknowledge the sovereignty of the Ottoman government and released itself from its civic duties. Greek representatives and sailors visiting Istanbul were welcomed as liberators by Istanbulite Ottoman Christians, symptomatic of the cooperation between Armenian and Greek Ottomans. The communities were enthusiastic in expressing their hopes that the Allied forces would protect them.[71] Alexandris cites the Turkish-language press, which complained about 'the recent ostentatious display of the city's Greek character'.[72]

A turning point would arrive when the Greek army landed at Anatolia and occupied Smyrna. This would in part incite a Turkish national resistance to come together, putting the position of the Istanbulite minorities in a more precarious position. Greek flags were taken down at various places in Istanbul and Turkish pamphlets were spread throughout the Muslim parts of the city, further contributing to the resentment against Christians in the city. The Treaty of Sèvres imposed harsh conditions on the Ottoman side and further provoked revolt among the Turkish National Movement (*Türk Ulusal Hareketi*).[73] Parallel governments were formed in Istanbul and Ankara, and ensuing clashes between the resistance army and the Greek army eventually led to the Greeks being pushed out of Anatolia. A new treaty was negotiated on the initiative of the Entente Forces in Lausanne. Representatives from both the Ottoman and national Turkish government were invited, after which Grand Vizier Ahmed Tevfik Pasha suggested that a joint delegation should be sent to Lausanne. This caused the National Assembly in Ankara to adopt a motion to abolish the sultanate, after which Tevfik Pasha resigned his office to the Istanbul representative of the Ankara government who ordered the termination of the Ottoman ministries. Sultan Mehmed VI fled to Malta, while his cousin Abdülmecid became the new caliph.[74] The Turkish delegation, instructed by Ankara and under the leadership of İsmet İnönü, took a rigid stance against the opposing side which on its part treated the Turks with considerable contempt. Eventually, however, they were forced to give in to the Turkish demands and accepted the full sovereignty of Turkish territory and the new state. During the First World War and right afterwards hundreds of thousands Greeks and Armenians had left Anatolia, but following the stipulations of the Lausanne Treaty 900,000 of Greeks (among others Turkish-speaking Greek Orthodox communities) were 'exchanged' for 400,000 Turks, which finalized the dramatic demographic change of Anatolia which had turned from 80 per cent Muslim to 98 per cent Muslim between 1913 and 1923.[75]

The non-Muslim communities in Istanbul would retain their position as a significant minority in the city, in part secured by the major share they held in the urban economy. Charles King cites numbers of Greeks owning 1,169 of 1,413 restaurants in the city, compared to 97 owned by Turks, 57 by Armenians and 44 by Russians.[76] Yet the city had lost significant parts of its population and no longer held the privileged position of the capital of a vast empire. Gül argues that near to no public buildings were built in Istanbul until 1940.[77] The new regime under the leadership of Mustafa Kemal in Ankara was heavily invested in making the new capital a spatial showcase of the new republic. Based on the model of the Istanbul municipality, the Ankara municipality was established and started expropriating and developing an area which was called Yenişehir (New City). International competitions were launched to attract urban planners and architects to design the plan for the new capital. Following the German urban planner Hermann Jansen's winning of the first prize, the Ankara urban planning office was set up and from 1932 onwards the plans of Jansen were implemented, setting up infrastructure, government buildings and other public facilities.[78] Sinem Türkoğlu Önge argues that the buildings in particular would in fact aim to communicate the power of the new regime.[79] The German architects who were invited to design these new public buildings would have a vast impact on a new modernist architectural paradigm for early republican Ankara.[80]

It would be fair to say that the Kemalists and the one-party government of the CHP (*Cumhuriyet Halk Partisi/Fırkası* – Republican People's Party) gave priority to Ankara and even Izmir over Istanbul's urban development after the foundation of the republic. Yet to say that the city was entirely disregarded would be a false assessment and neglect the significant bottom-up efforts to develop the city on the micro- or meso-level. İpek Akpınar argues that the discourse on Istanbul's post-1923 neglect is in fact a result of the manner in which revisionist historians have criticized the one-party regime since the 1990s.[81] On the other hand, she points out that much less attention was paid to developments in Istanbul by the Kemalist regime than those in Ankara, for which the Kemalists were at pains to indicate how much progress they made in the new national space. Akpınar furthermore explains that the 1920s were in fact a significant period for Istanbul as these were the years when new cadastral city maps were drawn up by Jacques Pervitich between 1926 and 1928. He would cover three areas: the historic peninsula, Beyoğlu and Üsküdar.[82] Rather than neglect, what appeared to have happened to Istanbul was that it had lost its privileged status as the capital, which until then, as Eldem indicates, had a decisive impact on the city.[83] Cânâ Bilsel points out that the first international competition for preparing a masterplan for Istanbul was organised by the Istanbul Municipality in 1932, only a few years after the reconstruction plans for Izmir and the first plans for Ankara. Henri Prost declined the invitation, and the award went to a German planner, Herman Elgötz. His plans were never implemented, and in 1936, the Istanbul governor-mayor invited Prost again, after which he was requested to prepare a master plan for the city.[84]

Shedding further light on the former capital's appeal as a place of social gathering and culture, Charles King points to the flourishing night life in Istanbul during the 1920s. Beyoğlu would remain a centre of entertainment, with jazz bands performing at the Pera Palace, Tokatlıyan and Park Hotels and the Garden Bar, near the Pera Palace. Carole Woodall in addition describes how the jazz scene had entered the city with the arrival of US soldiers and black musicians. The attitude of the Kemalist regime was not surprisingly ambivalent: Woodall cites articles from *The New York Times* in which Mustafa Kemal alternatingly supports jazz and denounces it in favour of 'local' dances such as the Zeybek.[85] After the First World War, as an effect of the Allied occupation and the inflow of foreign refugees, journalists and travellers, Beyoğlu attained an even stronger reality and reputation as a zone of contact. As such, it also initiated an increasingly transnational offering of entertainment. Jazz in particular was considered with a mix of appreciation and concern, described by an author at the time as a 'monster'. Establishments such as the Garden Bar were criticized to be a *sefahathane* (house of debauchery) and non-Turkish.[86] The typification of jazz as something to be afraid of or consider as a by-product of US imperialism, an audible expression of the dichotomy between 'machine-age America' and 'old Europe', is described, for instance, in the context of France by Jeremy Lane.[87] References to Beyoğlu as a place of perversion, a historically recurring theme, became increasingly pervasive since the nineteenth century. Arus Yumul quotes Osman Yüksel Serdengeçti, an influential nationalist columnist and politician who described the district in the second half of the twentieth century as 'a prostitute lodging in the bosom of Turkishness'.[88] Habil Adam narrated how Turkish is hardly heard in this polyglot environment and noted that he could hardly see any Turks between the Beyoğlu crowd. Woodall indicates that in 1934 cultural critic Ercüment Behzat Lav would argue that other countries 'where the musical culture is not as weak as our own' did not allow their people's taste in music to be perverted by jazz and simply forbade it, probably hinting at the Nazi regime's banning of jazz as *Entartete Musik*.[89]

As the demography of the city had only been relatively mildly affected compared to Anatolia, Istanbul was still a testimony to the Ottoman multicultural reality. Sossie Kasbarian notes that by 1927, 28 per cent of Istanbul's population did not speak Turkish as their native tongue.[90] Nevertheless, existing tensions worsened and the Turkish state's rhetoric and attitude towards foreigners and non-Muslim Turks became increasingly hostile. In Turkey's Republican Archives numerous police reports can be found with the charge 'Person who has insulted Turkishness' (*Türklüğe hakaret eden*). This was in fact a recurring charge in Beyoğlu, but hundreds of reports (1032 in total) can be found from the years between 1926 and 1938 all over Turkey.[91] The list becomes substantially longer if charges also include insulting the government, president, the army or a combination of these. In its 17 September 1943 issue, *The New York Times* reports in an article titled 'The Turkish Minorities' on 'the extremely cosmopolitan nature of Turkish business enterprise' and how particular groups within it have been targeted in the preceding months. They cite figures by the Foreign Chamber of Commerce which state that a wealth tax instated by a secret commission in November 1942 was effectively making it impossible for minorities or particular groups of foreigners to sustain their businesses. Greek Orthodox, Jewish and Armenian citizens received excessively higher amounts of income taxation as opposed to their Turkish Muslim counterparts. The enterprises of particular groups of foreigners – Greeks, Italians and Yugoslavs – were much more heavily taxed than those owned by French, Germans and Bulgarians, while taxes for American- and British-owned businesses were even lower.[92] In line with the nationalization policies of the 1920s and 1930s the Kemalist regime aimed to reduce the heterogeneity of Turkey's population. To that end, elaborate and racist language policies, notably the 'Citizen, Speak Turkish!'-campaign was launched, aiming to enforce speaking Turkish in the country's multiglot environments, of which Beyoğlu can well be considered one of the prime examples. Other initiatives included the 1934 Surname Law, which imposed surnames on individuals, which were required to be composed of elements from Turkish.[93] These and other policies resulted in economic discriminatory measures, aiming at the development of an ethnically Turkish bourgeoisie and making it significantly harder for other communities to sustain their socio-economic standing.[94] One of the most notorious instruments that the regime used was the previously cited wealth tax. Prior to that, particular professions were already blocked for non-Turks with legislation, such as civil service positions. Additionally, Aysun Akan indicates that religious trust properties of various non-Muslim communities were confiscated by the state. With the pretext of finally taxing the people who had taken advantage of Turkey's hospitality without paying their fair share, the government decided to instate the Wealth Tax in 1942. There was some economic rationale behind the policies, which was to put an end to the large share of non-Muslim business owners in the Turkish economy. Akan argues that this created a class of 'war-rich', with policies primarily driven by a racist ideology of the ruling elite, industrial bourgeoisie and the bureaucracy, stretching in particular cases towards a degree of sympathy towards Italian Fascism and German Nazism.[95]

Reimagining the old city

These examples show how also in Istanbul the Kemalists walked down their ambivalent and paradoxical path between nationalist and xenophobic resentment for anything foreign – that is, not Turkish and Muslim – and a historical admiration directed towards 'the West'. The second part of the paradox also becomes clear in the plans for urban planning at the time at large and the plans of Prost for Istanbul. What Prost envisioned for Istanbul was modernization, in line with the expectations of the regime in Ankara.[96] Open public spaces and modern, clean residential areas would contribute to this goal. Bilsel explains that Prost's plan essentially aimed for the enhancement of transportation, making better connections between the historical peninsula and the new residential districts developing to the north of Beyoğlu. What would prove to have a particularly destructive impact on the city's urban landscape were the streets and avenues that were necessary to facilitate traffic circulation. Prost himself, however, did not consider his plans harmful, but rather 'a chirurgical operation of the most delicate nature', which would 'protect the incomparable landscape' with its 'glorious edifices'.[97] His plans would highlight imposing monuments from Byzantine and Ottoman times, emphasizing these landmarks while destroying significant parts of the late Ottoman urban landscape.

Sibel Bozdoğan and Esra Akcan argue that the Cumhuriyet Caddesi connecting Beyoğlu with the newer neighbourhoods of Nişantaşı, Teşvikiye and Şişli was planned by Prost as the new, modernist face of Istanbul. At the lowest point of the hill, the Dolmabahçe Stadium was constructed in 1946, leaving the green space in between unaffected according to the plans of Prost. The further development of residential architecture that Istanbul witnessed, on the other hand, did not affect Beyoğlu at first. The upsurge in construction concentrated on the newer districts on the developing axis north of Taksim Square towards Levent on the one hand and in districts closer to the Marmara Sea, such as Yeşilköy and Ataköy, on the other. Mass housing projects could in certain cases take the shape of planned and high-quality dwellings. Bozdoğan and Akcan indicate, however, that the layout of these spacious houses – 140 square metres, with four bedrooms, maid rooms – countered the concept of social housing as it would in no way meet the financial possibilities and lifestyles of the people in need of social housing. What would have a much larger impact on the urban landscape of Istanbul, including that of Beyoğlu, which lost nearly all of its wooden residential architecture to concrete apartment buildings, is the so-called yap-sat (build-sell) construction that would start from approximately the late 1950s onwards. Referring to Rem Koolhaas' concept of 'Junkspace', Bozdoğan and Akcan explain that cheap and anonymous (designer unknown) architecture became a trend in which contracts between landowners, contractors and buyers were made to develop individual slots of land with a building. Helped by an import-substitutive construction industry through which Turkey started to mass-produce inexpensive building materials, the small contractors played a major role in the housing boom of Turkey, being responsible for 40 to 45 per cent of the total development in the country's main urban centres.[98] New regulations regarding the maximum number of a building's stories moreover gave property owners the possibility to have their house demolished and redeveloped into taller buildings – a trend which continues up to the present day.[99]

In the 1940s the first efforts toward redevelopment were made by the Kemalists. Although the areas around the İstiklal Caddesi remained largely unaffected by the urban transformation the projects had a profound impact on the area surrounding Taksim Square. An important landmark from the late Ottoman era were the Halil Pasha Artillery Barracks, which flanked the square and had been in use as the Taksim Stadium since 1921 and used by the three major Istanbul football clubs: Beşiktaş JK, Fenerbahçe SK and Galatasaray SK. The barracks were demolished in 1940 and replaced by a large public park, with terraces, flower beds, trees and the new *Taksim Belediye Gazinosu* at its northernmost point.[100] Yet it would be particularly during the 1950s, when the Democratic Party (*Demokrat Parti*) won a landslide victory during the national elections of 1950, that the most dramatic parts of Prost's plans would be executed. The DP heavily criticized Prost's plan, but would follow through with these by and large nonetheless. Bozdoğan and Akcan indicate that the DP would, however, interpret the plans of Prost in a more pragmatic fashion as they decided to build one of the most iconic examples of 1950s modernism in Turkey in a green space that Prost had planned to be left unaffected, the Hilton Hotel.[101] The hotel may be considered to be significant for a variety of reasons; the most noteworthy is that it may have marked a shift in the representation of nationalist ideology through space and architecture. The successful purges against and expulsions of non-Muslim communities, as well as the growing confidence of Turkish nationalism were exemplified by a shift in the national approach towards architecture, Bozdoğan and Akcan argue. Architecture was no longer the showcase for Kemalist modernity that it had been in the 1930s and early 1940s. Instead a more internationalist modernism was considered more befitting for private and public projects in Turkey. Bozdoğan and Akcan present the Hilton Hotel, designed by Gordon Bunshaft as the principal architect and the renowned Turkish architect Sedad Hakkı Eldem as the local co-operator, as a first step in a process of reorientation. Significantly, they also present it as a successful example of American Cold War cultural foreign policy. The United States invested considerably in the project through the Bank of America and the Economic Cooperation Administration, flowing to the Turkish *Emekli Sandığı* (Pension Fund) as the local public investor.[102] The authors argue that buildings like this were strong visual representations of the US influence in their partner countries as well as providing the DP with a symbol of American modernity and capitalism, to which it had so heavily subscribed.[103] As Sara Fregonese and Adam Ramadan point out, Conrad Hilton's hotel chain may well be considered to be an example of US soft power 'designed to reproduce American values at the furthermost boundaries of the Western sphere of influence such as Cairo, Athens and Istanbul'.[104] This is in the context of Istanbul hard to overstress; Begüm Adalet shows how the commitment of local and national governments to the Hilton were presented as an example of Turkey's commitment to transatlantic and European treaty organizations.[105] She discusses how Conrad Hilton himself stressed his commitment to combating communism through his hotels, symbols of American imperialism. His hotels thus would assist the foreign policy of the US secretary of state, adding to conventional aid programs.[106]

İpek Türeli indicates that the urban reforms had a devastating impact on the old residential architecture, which was, considering the fashionable ideas on urban planning, praised in Europe and the United States as a successful example of modernization. To such an extent even that the Council of Europe awarded Istanbul with the 'Europe's Prize' in 1959 for its achievements in the urban reform of Istanbul.[107] The reforms had made the city 'more European' and the president of the Council of Europe remarked to the occasion: 'We all know the courage and determination of Istanbul, the guard of the Straits, in the spectacular rebuilding effort it has undertaken without damaging any of its historical treasures that are the living witness to its bright past.'[108] The quote signifies the rather limited understanding of architectural heritage in Turkey and some European institutions alike, equating historical or monumental value with size and historical canons rather than the integrity of a historical urban landscape. One reason may have been that, as pointed out by Sven Grabow, the framework for European heritagization had only recently started to develop, since the Council of Europe's European Cultural Convention in 1954.[109]

Beyoğlu, however, still presented the new government with a complicated situation. The district was a living and physical testimony to the history of ethnic and cultural diversity during the Ottoman Empire. It had been one of the primary objectives of the Kemalists to found an ethnocentric nation state around a Muslim-Turkish population and the DP replicated the racist and xenophobic elements from Kemalist national discourse. During the years of the one-party regime, nationalist sentiments had maintained the awkward attitude towards the district's cosmopolitan image and built on the discursive alienation of its 'foreignness' similar to their Ottoman predecessors of the CUP. In that sense the attitude of nationalists during the years of the DP may well be considered as a continuation, albeit possibly even more aggressively. What Pera or Beyoğlu was or wasn't had been an ongoing discussion in history. A particularly strong motive of representation was, especially since the foundation of the Turkish Republic, that the district's identity deviated from national Turkish values. Yumul provides two noteworthy examples. Writer and public official Yahya Kemal Beyatlı (1884–1958) wrote on how the Turkish children raised in Pera *alafranga* became estranged from Islam because they were not used to hearing the call to prayer, framing the district as alienated from Islam. The second example dates from 1948, when an author in the journal *Haftalık Çınaraltı* claimed that students on opposing sides of the Galata Bridge, connecting Beyoğlu with the historic peninsula, had mentalities so vastly different that it seemed as if the distance between Beyoğlu and Paris or Hollywood was closer than the distance between Beyoğlu and Beyazıt, Aksaray or Kocamustafapaşa, all quarters on the historic peninsula.[110] Ali Çoruk points out that such districts in the historical peninsula, notably Aksaray and Fatih, were often portrayed as the opposite of Beyoğlu, and as the authentic, Turkish Istanbul. Beyoğlu is represented as a paradoxical mix of (unlawfully appropriated) wealth, luxury and moral decay. The brothels of Beyoğlu were also a popular theme for novelists. Çoruk indicates that Beyoğlu is represented as a place that housed a 'whirlwind of lust', for instance, in Ethem İzzet Benice's *Beş Hasta Var* (There are Five Patients, 1931).[111] Frequently in these novels, the brothels are associated with the minorities. In several books the protagonist will end up in a brothel or lodging (often used as a euphemism) with an Armenian or Greek woman, while the female brothel-keepers are often portrayed as Armenians or Greeks as well. Mustafa Hakkı Akansel also subscribed to this perspective and stated that Beyoğlu was considered as the symbol of alcohol, prostitution and debauchery.[112] In fact, prostitution was certainly not limited to this district, and Mark Wyers explains that non-Muslim prostitutes dominated the brothels on the European side, while Muslim prostitutes dominated those on the Anatolian side. Before 1914, Muslim women engaged in prostitution, although they were not allowed to be registered as sex workers, whereas the Ottoman Muslim authorities did not really engage with Jewish and Christian women in the profession. That changed in 1915 when legislation was amended.[113] The CUP government appeared to have no interest in forbidding the existence of brothels, but made efforts to segregate

Muslim and non-Muslim prostitutes. Health checks on the two groups were, for instance, to be performed in different hospitals.[114] Hospital records, however, show that a significant group of Muslim women resisted the segregation and worked clandestinely – without registration – on the European side. When the Turkish Republic was founded, foreign prostitutes were no longer allowed to work in the city and many were deported.

In any case, Beyoğlu and the brothel sector were represented as a venture that was alien to the Turkish nation, further playing into the existing dichotomies that involved Beyoğlu as a place of bad, foreign habits that did not belong in Turkey.[115] In the novel *Zâniyeler* (Adulteresses, 1924) by Selahattin Enis, the dichotomy between the place and people of Beyoğlu as a place of perversion is further extrapolated vis-à-vis the people of Fatih and Aksaray, where one finds the good moral of the Turkish nation. The latter are portrayed as forced to eat dry bread after the First World War while the 'debauchery' in fact increased in districts like Beyoğlu and Şişli where there was no a shortage of anything.[116] Çoruk also points to a later quote from Samiha Ayverdi, a prominent nationalist author, who wrote in her *İstanbul Geceleri* (Istanbul Nights – 1952) about the otherness of Beyoğlu, which can be indeed considered to be a symptomatic example of the antipathy towards Beyoğlu and what it supposedly represented.[117] She considers the area essentially as a void in Turkey, a place that should not be, as it embodies everything foreign, repeating a trope from Turkish nationalism that everything foreign should be considered with suspicion:

It wasn't ours in the past and it isn't ours now. It has viewed this land, whose air it breathes and water it drinks, with contempt in the past and it does so now. It didn't resemble us in the past with its customs, appearances, and views [. . .] and it doesn't now. Leaning on its capitulations, bankers, Masons, Levantines, various languages, bars, taverns, public houses, in a word – on all sorts of Western mimicry, it looked at us from above with contempt in the past, as it does so now.[118]

Violence, loss and contested transformations

In part it were sentiments like these that can be considered symptomatic of the hate campaigns and animosity that were stimulated by the state, satellite organizations and the media. Dilek Güven considers the 1955 pogroms as an organic outcome of the national politics that had dominated the 1930s and 1940s, in which ethnic homogenization played a crucial role.[119] More significantly, however, she points out that the events should be considered as a performance organized by the state. Menderes' DP was confronted with growing domestic tensions as an effect of the Cyprus crisis and sought for means to control the public opinion. The September pogroms then provided the government with an opportunity to declare the state of emergency which enabled them to exert greater control over public life, politics and the media. The event revolved around a newsflash on 6 September 1955, which reported that the birth house of Atatürk at Thessaloniki had been bombed by Greek nationalists. The event received further attention in an Istanbul-based newspaper in the afternoon and soon after student organizations as well as the *Kıbrıs Türktür Cemiyeti* (Cyprus is Turkish Association) called for a protest on the Taksim Square. This would provoke a number of groups to proceed down towards Tünel over the İstiklal Caddesi and throw stones at the properties of non-Muslim shop owners. The second wave, however, had an even more devastating effect, with large masses swarming through the district and vandalizing shops, apartments, schools, churches and cemeteries with materials and tools they brought along.[120] They would proceed into the adjacent districts like Kurtuluş, Nişantaşı and Şişli, but Güven points out that the violence even spread to the Asian side and Princes' Islands as well as other cities in Turkey.[121] Police forces at the Taksim Square did not act upon the violence and even expressed their sympathy: a police inspector who refused to help his Albanian neighbour stated that on that day he was not a police officer, but a Turk.[122] Güven describes how the event facilitated directed targeting to particular communities: the Hilton Hotel was protected by the police, as well as the premises of the Orthodox Patriarchate and the Greek Consulate. Particularly insightful is also the account regarding a French shop in Tünel which was guarded by a police officer who told off the mob that vandalized stores of the local non-Muslim communities. He warned them that they were not allowed to damage the shop since it was owned by a Frenchman.[123] Güven goes on to explain that a lack of police force was also certainly not a reason for the lack of intervention, since in the wake of the events policemen from the provinces close to Istanbul had been called to the city. A police officer explained the passivity by indicating that they had explicit orders on that day not to act, except for cases of theft or arson.[124] Although all groups were affected in the district, the Greeks were hit hardest in relative and absolute numbers. The violence ended when the army was deployed in the late evening of 6 September, but Güven indicates that unrest would smoulder for the days and weeks after the events.[125] Damages amounted to 150 million Turkish lira (54 million in US dollar value at the time). Alexandris indicates that the Greek communal properties were hit particularly hard with damage and destruction to seventy-three churches, twenty-six schools, five athletics clubs and two cemeteries. Menderes refused to acknowledge responsibility and hinted at a communist conspiracy instead. Any form of transparent or objective reporting on the events and its aftermath was banned by the government, going as far as to seize telegrams of foreign correspondents reporting on the event.[126] Alexandris points out that the Turkish press framed the events as a conflict of class rather than of ethnicity or nationality. Most of the rioters came from the villages in Thrace and Anatolia that were close to Istanbul. They allegedly revolted against the wealth accumulation of the Istanbulite bourgeoisie, not discriminating between Turks and Armenians, Greeks or Jews. The resentment, however, particularly targeted the properties of non-Muslims, damages to Turkish businesses or private property were limited (due to involvement of the Turkish police), further pointing to an orchestrated hate campaign. He argues that at the time inflation was increasing with 30 per cent annually and it was hard for the many young, single men in the city to establish a livelihood. Those who had some capital – and by 1955 there still seems to be a relatively high degree of capital accumulation among non-Muslims – were able to get by, despite economic difficulties. The non-Muslim well-to-do were the target for a mob which was, according to Alexandris, the instrument of a group of racist fanatics.[127]

Güven concludes that the major consequence of the events was a growing estrangement of non-Muslims from the Turkish state and their gradual exodus from Turkey or from the quarters where their communities had resided historically to different parts of the city. This had surprised them because the relations between the minorities and the DP government had at first been positive and relatively beneficial for them, with the lifting of restrictions for minority schools for instance.[128] Economic and political problems that the DP was faced with, however, called for measures to overshadow and suppress these issues with a different agenda of violence. Güven argues that next to this, the events were a continuation of the expulsion of non-Muslim Turks from Anatolia during the Kemalist regime. Finally, the connection between the events and the Cyprus conflict became even more direct due to British involvement. The British wanted the Greeks to continue their appeasement of British control over the island, by pointing out that the alternative would be Turkish claims to the sovereignty over the island. A diplomat noted that violence against the Greek minority in Turkey could be beneficial for Britain, as it would help them to make their argument towards the Greeks. They reasoned that the Greeks might well risk losing all claims to the island if they would not continue to support British rulership over Cyprus.[129]

The escalation of the crisis over the political future of Cyprus ensued, leading to a continuation of popular grievance and contempt towards the Greek and, arguably, other non-Muslim communities. Alexandris notes that the 'Citizen, speak Turkish!'-signs began to reappear on the windows of Armenian and Greek shops in Beyoğlu in the second half of the 1950s.[130] By 1960, the number of Greeks with Greek nationality had dropped to nearly a third of the population in 1927, from 26,431 to 10,488. This comprised less than a third of the total Greek community in Turkey. Alexandris explains that the difference between the Greeks of Greek nationality and those of Turkish nationality was negligible and that they de facto constituted a single community, their nationality merely based on the origins of their ancestors. In addition, İlay Örs has shown that the diversity among the community was substantial and that many members of the group considered themselves neither Turkish nor Greek. In her research she has shed light on the paradoxical nature of the nationalist framework that was not able to accommodate the Greek community of Istanbul. She explains that within the community there was and is a strong sense of relating to locality or geography, rather than nationality, feeling attached to Istanbul and its past environment marked by diversity and cultural hybridity.[131]

During the 1960s the numbers of Greek Istanbulites would be even further reduced as a result of geopolitical strife. When violence flared up in Cyprus in the winter of 1963, the Turkish government decided to pressurize Greece by unilaterally ending the 1930 Convention of Establishment, Commerce and Navigation on 16 March 1964, in which the rights of the Greek nationals in Turkey were secured. Ending the treaty directly affected these nationals and a deportation campaign was started, leading to a registered amount of 1,073 deportations by August 1964. Greece turned to the UN Security Council, which effectively did nothing but denounce the Turkish actions, which Turkey stated was only directed at people involved in criminal activities.[132] A year later, however, more than 6,000 Greek nationals had been deported and by the late 1960s a mere few hundreds were left in Istanbul.[133] The Turkish state effectively confiscated their properties and obstructed liquidation of businesses or real estate. It would also have a severe effect on Greeks with Turkish nationality, who were closely tied to the Greeks with Greek nationality. The effects on other communities were detrimental as well, and Kasbarian notes that the non-Turkish nationals were forced to leave the country with nothing but some cash. In the increasingly Turkified environment differences were sometimes abruptly rendered visible and as an exemplary anecdote of this trauma, Kasbarian cites the story of an Armenian girl who one day could no longer play with her Turkish friend as the Turkish grandmother forbade it due to the Armenian girl's ethnicity. She went home in tears and asked, 'what does being Armenian mean'?[134] Alexandris notes that 30,000 Greeks with Turkish nationality had left the country by the fall of 1964.[135] Restrictive legislation regarding the Greek schools in Turkey also caused the collapse of the schools' educational standing and its student numbers. The numbers dropped from 15,000 in 1923 to 5,000 in 1964 and 816 in 1980.[136] Estimates from 1978 indicated that some 7,822 Greeks were left in Istanbul, following a further drop in the aftermath of the Cyprus division in 1974. Çağlar Keyder remarks that the numbers in Istanbul by the 1980s had further dropped to less than 2,000, while the Istanbulite Armenian community was around 50,000 and the Jewish community at 25,000.[137]

Whereas Beyoğlu and the city at large were gradually left by the minorities entirely, Bensiyon Pinto, former president of the Turkish-Jewish community, recounts how many of the Jews of Istanbul from the Kuledibi neighbourhood in Galata moved to Şişli, to the north of Beyoğlu. At the same time many working migrants from Anatolia were attracted by the prospects of jobs in Istanbul from the 1950s onwards. Keyder and Öncü point out that the housing of these labour migrants concentrated on the outskirts of the city in slums (*gecekondu*) on the one hand and in the city centre, which had considerable capacity – not in the last part due to the gradual exodus of minorities and foreigners. The rapid and uncontrolled growth of Istanbul would lead to the deterioration of its infrastructure and real estate, insufficiently addressed by the governments at the local and national levels.[138] Zürcher adds that 80 per cent of the Anatolian population consisted of small farmers by the mid-1940s, with vastly different standards of living between the city and countryside. When the DP came to power in 1950 they started investing heavily in the position of small farmers, providing them with cheap credit, subsidizing equipment and upholding the prices of crops artificially through the *Toprak Mahsulleri Ofisi* (Agricultural Product Office). Despite this, more than one million people had left the countryside for the city by the end of the 1950s in search of jobs. Zürcher indicates that the major cities were growing by no less than 10 per cent a year by the end of the decade. Keyder and Öncü indicate that growth rates from 1950 escalated from a growth of around 100,000 per five years between 1935 and 1950 to around 400,000 per five years until 1965, after which the rates further increased to 1,000,000 every five years until 1985.[139] State tariffs and quotas protected new enterprises from the global market, which centred around Istanbul. Zürcher argues that the workers who came to Istanbul could not find enough vacancies in the growing industry and were often forced towards more informal modes of labour, as street vendors or casual labourers.[140]

In the 1950s and 1960s Beyoğlu had still been the city's heart in terms of business and culture, although that position would change in the coming decade. As substantial parts of the non-Muslim communities were forced to leave the country, many properties were abandoned as had been the case for the past decades. Several of these properties were squatted, claimed or 'guarded' by newcomers to the city. Vedia Dökmeci explains that in 1960 Beyoğlu was the core business district, with the largest concentration of businesses and banks, but as an effect of industrialization, urban development following the DP's urban restructuring and investments in infrastructure, particularly motorways, new centres started to develop to the north of Beyoğlu. This gradually dwarfed the significance of the old city centre. Between 1960 and 1990 the number of firms in Beyoğlu was reduced from 30.4 per cent to 15.5 per cent of the total in Istanbul.[141] The district had become a conservation area, following the instalment of the High Council for Historical Real Estate and Monuments (*Gayrimenkul Eski Eserler ve Anıtlar Yüksek Kurulu*) in 1951, although much of the real estate rapidly dilapidated in the following years.[142] İpek Türeli points out that the efforts of the council primarily focused on registering monumental buildings and possibly restoring them, with little regard for the urban context at large. In 1973, new legislation was introduced which would also consider the spatial context of the preserved architectural object. Türeli argues that during the 1940s and 1950s considerable parts of Istanbul's landscape had been destroyed to make way for urban development, which triggered a strong debate on heritagization, eventually leading to efforts to restoration.[143] As previously mentioned, old businesses had in part left the Beyoğlu district, due to the nationalist policies towards the minorities, while new businesses refrained from opening offices due to the limited available space in the district and the restrictions on the height of buildings.[144] Nevertheless, this did not hinder the construction of probably the first example that drastically affected the urban landscape of the İstiklal Caddesi, the Odakule building of the Turkish Chamber of Industry. In the 1960s and 1970s, moreover, several large upscale hotels and a cultural centre (the Atatürk Cultural Centre) were constructed in Beyoğlu. In combination with the many significant schools, social institutions, consulates and foreign research and cultural institutions that were based in Beyoğlu which could or would not move from the district, it would be an exaggeration to argue that Beyoğlu lost its significance. In the tourist guides of Hachette, the *Guides Bleus*, on Turkey and Istanbul, the district is still marked as the *quartier moderne d'Istanbul* and *le quartier résidentiel par excellence* – although Harbiye, Maçka and Şişli are conveniently summed up as the suburbs of the area, which in the case of Şişli might already be somewhat of a stretch by 1969 due to the increasing impact of the Şişli district in Istanbul's economy.[145] The guide moreover recommends this area as the place with the most comfortable hotels which are frequented most commonly by foreign tourists:

> Beyoğlu, formerly Pera, the modern district of Istanbul is, with its new suburbs Harbiye, Şişli, Maçka, etc., the residential district par excellence. It is here where the most comfortable hotels can be found, which are generally frequented by foreign tourists. It is therefore the radiating centre from which one can make various trips that will allow to visit Istanbul and its surroundings.[146]

As has been indicated previously, however, the demographics of the district had changed dramatically, with direct effects on its sociocultural profile. This phenomenon has often been associated with the alleged ruralisation of the district, due to the inflow of Anatolian migrants. Quoting Reşat Ekrem Koçu, author of the *İstanbul Ensiklopedisi* (1961), and Özdemir Arkan's *Beyoğlu* (1988), Çoruk and Ayfer Bartu both refer to how various writers describe the change as perceptible through the change of smells, from lavender and sesame to *lahmacun* and *çiğ köfte*, while 'decent' patisseries were replaced by bars and nightclubs.[147] Interestingly, the perceived 'change' of Beyoğlu is, like in the 1930s, associated with a rise in the number of places of late night entertainment. Çoruk states that this increase was also a consequence of the growing numbers of Anatolian migrants who thought of the entertainment industry in Beyoğlu as a business opportunity.[148] On the other hand, the quote signifies a rise of 'low culture' to the detriment of different cultural lexicons, often framed as 'high culture', observable through the smells of the bourgeoisie versus the smells of rural villagers. Ayşe Öncü argues that what is instrumental in this context is the concept of '*arabesk* culture'. With the arrival of migrants from Anatolia alternative modes of entertainment also entered the city. An entire scene of artists and aspiring artists flooded the nightclubs and bars of Beyoğlu with a style of music that was inspired by popular Western, Arabic and Turkish music. The topics of the lyrics often referred to the situation of the migrant from Anatolia who left his hometown for the big city and faced hardship and a tough life over there. The music was banned from state radio and was considered to be a corruption of the 'authentic' character of Turkish folk and classical music. This music, however, had great appeal to the newcomers and soon would expand to an entire genre that included film as well. The genre was, in a derogative fashion, referred to as *arabesk*. Öncü explains that these representations were the outcome of a novel dimension in local identity politics, based on a class dichotomy. Öncü argues that the adherents of this 'arabesk culture' were framed to be neither really urban nor peasant.[149] The way in which the newcomers were regarded reveals contempt and their consideration as a nuisance that was in no position to make claims to place-making. The newcomers would, however, prove to have a lasting presence in Istanbul and a considerable impact on the imagining of Istanbul during the 1960s and 1970s as will be shown in Chapter 3.

Dökmeci and Berköz point out that the decrease in the significance of Beyoğlu as the central business district was in part an effect of the incompatibility of dominant modes of transportation from the 1960s onwards, that is, car traffic. The decrease of businesses should, however, not exclusively be considered as an absolute decrease, but rather as a relative decrease to the newly developing central business district around Şişli and Mecidiyeköy on the one hand and the development of sub-centres on the other. At first the process at hand thus was one of internal expansion instead of displacement.[150] Vedia Dökmeci and Hale Çiraci indicate that processes of suburbanization and the unappealing prospects for transportation and construction meant that major developers started to ignore the district, which had a negative impact on the overall image of the district and the prices of properties.[151] Overall, Istanbul had by the 1970s reaffirmed its position as Turkey's economic catalyst and centre. The city accounted for 51 per cent of total employment in the Turkish private sector by 1973.[152] Keyder indicates that the Turkish government had reluctantly accepted Istanbul's dominant position in Turkey's economy, but failed to further invest in its infrastructure. The areas around Istanbul's old centres were quickly surrounded by shanty towns inhabited by more and more working migrants and their families.[153]

In the meantime, Turkey's politics in the 1970s had become increasingly tumultuous, following two coups (1960 and 1971, the latter technically being a military memorandum), and paralyzed coalition governments, which were unable to execute serious social and political reforms. Heavily affected also by the polarization of Cold War geopolitics, anti-Americanism, anti-communism and international backlash for Turkey's military presence in North Cyprus, violence between left- and right-wing extremists was ever-increasing.[154] Zürcher points out that the leftists were particularly vulnerable and found themselves to be at the disadvantage since the fascist party MHP (*Milliyetçi Hareket Partisi* – Nationalist Action Party) held a strong influence over the police and security forces. The groups fought their battles on the streets and university campuses and were guaranteed new 'recruits' due to the disastrous prospects for jobs in the country and the extreme undercapacity of higher education (only 20 per cent of 200,000 eligible high school graduates would be admitted to university).[155] An episode that as a consequence has been engrained in Turkish collective memory, particularly in the contexts of Taksim and Beyoğlu as a public space, were the 1976 and 1977 1 May Labour Day celebrations. The Revolutionary Confederation of Labour Unions (*Devrimci İşçi Sendikaları Konfederasyonu* – DİSK) organized a 1 May Day Celebration in 1976. The event was organized again by DİSK the year after, but managed to mobilize a much larger crowd this time. The plan was to approach the square from the North and Southwest. A highly heterogeneous crowd gathered at the square and allegedly amounted to a few million protestors on Taksim and other places in the city. Ayşegül Baykan and Tali Hatuka indicate that the organizers had, in collaboration with the police, appointed volunteers to maintain order in the crowds. After the speech of DİSK president Kemal Türkler around 6 pm, gunshots were heard around the Tarlabaşı quarter. When more shots followed, police vehicles approached the crowds from two sides and fired sound bombs, which caused mass panic and resulted in thirty-four casualties, with numerous people being trampled or hit by police vehicles.[156]

The seemingly irresolvable violence and the perceived 'soft attitude' of Prime Minister Bülent Ecevit in the end led to the most violent coups Turkey would witness in its entire history. Kerem Öktem describes the situation of Turkey months before the 12 September 1980 coup as a country which was at war with itself. He argues that the social and political impasse that Turkey had reached brought daily life to halt and made the military elite and their henchmen in civil society realize that the decades following the breach with the one-party state had yielded insufficient results. The military 'saved the day' onstage, but used the opportunity to push the country in the desired direction backstage.[157] Apart from the military elite and their sympathizers in the judiciary, politics, bureaucracy, business and media securing their position, the years following the coup were marked by a turn towards Islam as a binding element in society, violence against the Kurds, political suppression, affirmation of the guardian state and reactionary Kemalism as well as a turn towards neoliberal market reforms.[158]

The effect of these neoliberal market reforms was felt particularly strong in Istanbul. The electoral success of the *Anavatan Partisi* (Motherland Party), which came to national power under the leadership of Turgut Özal in 1983, was followed by the party's success during the first elections for the metropolitan mayorship in Istanbul, which brought Bedrettin Dalan to power. Dalan set himself the goal to transform Istanbul into a 'world city' with drastic interventions in the urban landscape. Dalan had little regard for the historical value of the residential architecture in historical districts and had a considerable part of the Tarlabaşı quarter in Beyoğlu destroyed in order to construct a six-way car lane. Many properties were not claimed, giving the metropolitan government a carte blanche for urban destruction.[159] This would create a spatial and social segregation in Beyoğlu which has an effect on the district up to this date.[160] On the side of İstiklal Caddesi, however, local actors started to consider the potential of the historical Beyoğlu district. By then Beyoğlu's significance in the rapidly growing business sector was crippled to the benefit of the Şişli, Mecidiyeköy, Levent and Maslak districts. Dökmeci et al. point out that city officials and speculators started to become aware of what Beyoğlu could become in a new aspiring global city. The arrival of hotels and bottom-up gentrification also gradually increased the economic value of the dilapidated district. Interestingly, Dökmeci et al. note that despite the gradual disappearance of the middle- and upper-middle classes from the residential areas in the district as well as the subordination of its commercial share to the new districts, the area had remained a significant area for local and foreign tourists.[161] This is not surprising considering the relatively large amount of historical and new hotels in the area. The authors consider this as one of the principal catalysts of the district's revival.

One of the most significant actors in the process of Beyoğlu's regeneration was the *Beyoğlu Güzelleştirme Derneği* (BGD – Beyoğlu Beautification Association), a cooperation of major business owners in the district and the local municipality.[162] As the area gradually started to be claimed by the intelligentsia, architects, journalists and artists, often attracted by a combination of the district's historical appeal and cheap rental options, the BGD would start initiatives to renovate the district's fabric, primarily İstiklal Caddesi and its direct surroundings. Later on, initiatives from civil society, like the Cihangir Beautification Association (*Cihangir Güzelleştirme Derneği*) in Beyoğlu's Cihangir quarter, were set up in order to upgrade the quality of living. As an effect the quarter's demography changed radically and the area became one of the most upscale places in Istanbul.[163] Edhem Eldem furthermore notes that the 1980s brought an industry of cosmopolitan nostalgia in popular literature, city and tourism branding, which revolved around the claim to multiculturalism and cosmopolitanism in a period between the 1980s and 1990s during which most of the 'celebrated' non-Muslim communities had left the area.[164] As indicated previously, this is in fact a phenomenon that can be observed around the same time in other cities around the Mediterranean, Türeli has, for instance, noted similar dynamics in Damascus in the 1990s.[165] In the case of Istanbul, Eldem points to the popularity of the translations of Said Duhani's 1940s and 1950s nostalgic narrations of Beyoğlu into Turkish in the early 1980s, which had a particularly strong impact on the intelligentsia at the time. Orhan Pamuk in his debut *Cevdet Bey ve Oğulları* (Cevdet Bey and his Sons, 1982) took a long passage directly from Duhani's translated work and used it as an introduction.[166] Another contributing element in the way this 'reinvented cosmopolitanism' became so pervasive was certainly Turkey's turn towards neoliberal politics.

The instrumentalization of Pera or Beyoğlu's past is problematic as it celebrates and romanticizes a selective historical and imagined representation of the district in which the historical social texture – those who were absent at the time of writing – were gone.[167] In the wake of this rise of interest the gentrification of Beyoğlu skyrocketed. Eldem argues that coinciding with this, nostalgia for an imagined multiculturalism and high culture started to be exploited by the 'stakeholders in the area', meaning the municipality, real estate owners and local businesses. Adjoining this, museums and cultural centres started to be named with references to the district's 'former social and topographic nomenclature'.[168] Eldem as well as Asu Aksoy and Kevin Robins point out that the reinvention of cosmopolitanism was in large part a consequence of the desire to stimulate the urban economy and tourism sector.[169] Gradually, the district would lose its character as a business and residential district, ridding itself also partly of its image as a seedy place at night, and gradually becoming remarketed as a place of entertainment and consumption.[170]

Chapter 2

GALATA/CLUB TEUTONIA AND THE BOSPORUS GERMANS

National societies in Istanbul and the Germanophone communities

In Galata, along the Galip Dede Caddesi, the former Grande Rue de Pera or Cadde-i Kebir together with the present-day İstiklal Caddesi, lies the building of the German Teutonia club. A modest building with neoclassical details and in restoration for several years now. Since its construction the building has been, with ups and downs, a place of social gathering for German speakers, students, migrants, expats and tourists. In the popular imagination of historical Istanbul and Beyoğlu the German-speaking communities appear to play a lesser role when compared to their counterparts of French, Italian and even English origin. Although the presence of communities from Italian city states and France predates that of German-speaking communities, the heritage of the latter communities remains physically omnipresent in Istanbul and Beyoğlu. Istanbul had held a German-speaking community since before the 1800s. Prominent examples of tangible heritage are, for instance, the Sankt Georg High School, Church and Hospital, the German School, the former Prussian Embassy (in place of which is an apartment building known as Doğan Apartmanı since the 1890s), the Teutonia club building and the former German Embassy, currently housing the German Consulate and German Archaeological Institute.[1]

A great variety of national and multinational societies in Istanbul emerged in the nineteenth century, from the French Union Française (1894), the Italian *Società Operaia Italiana di Mutuo Soccorso a Istanbul* (1863), the multinational Cercle d'Orient (1882) to a variety of Masonic Lodges which adhered to various national European Grand Lodges.[2] These societies can be usefully examined by adopting the framework on the dissemination and cultivation of national culture developed by Joep Leerssen. These societies fit the 'bottom-up' category of Leerssen's social ambiences – associations, societies, clubs and others – in which national culture could blossom through its active cultivation.[3] As will be pointed out in this chapter, these societies are also excellent examples of 'embodied communities', having a significant role in the dissemination of national culture through the performance of imagined traditions as lived experiences.[4]

In the context of Istanbul, the German community was extremely diverse in terms of both geographical provenance, hailing from various German principalities,

Austria and Switzerland, and class. The community started to expand from the nineteenth century onwards, particularly after the trade liberalizations that were initiated in the 1830s.[5] As Erik-Jan Zürcher points out, the Ottoman government during the reign of Mahmud II (1808–39), aware of its falling behind the major imperial powers of Europe, sought to recruit instructors in Europe to build an officer corps for the new Ottoman army.[6] Due to the Ottoman Empire's troubled relations with the British, French and Russians, the government decided to invite instructors from the Prussian army. Zürcher argues, however, that the Prussians were nonetheless confronted with strong reservations by the Ottomans due to their non-Muslim background.[7]

Yet the base for a long-lasting Prussian and later German cooperation with the Ottoman Empire was laid. A small community of traders and diplomats, mostly from Prussia and the Hanseatic states, also resided in Istanbul. Malte Fuhrmann discusses that engineers from German and Habsburg lands tried to compete with the British in the construction of railway networks and harbour facilities. Only after the unification of Germany in the German Empire and after the French and British pushed their policies towards the Ottoman Empire into an increasingly wary and hostile direction, the Germans would gain significant influence in the Ottoman Empire. The German influence on the Ottoman reforms – that took off after Sultan Abdülmecid's announcement of the *Tanzimat* reforms in 1839 – would rise after 1876 and German officers from Prussia began to acquire an increasingly larger role in the modernization of the Ottoman army.[8] İlber Ortaylı points out that especially from the 1880s onwards the Ottoman army's organization increasingly resembled one that was based on the German system, strongly connected to the strategies of the German military command, the German arms industry and dependent on the officers that were designated to the Ottoman Empire by the German command.[9]

It was also from this period onwards that the German Empire started to gain influence in the Ottoman Empire and consequently the German community in Turkey and Istanbul in particular started to grow. Around 1880 mostly Ottoman officers were sent off for training to the German Empire, though from 1890 onwards also students of medicine started to head to Germany for training, followed by students of related professions. Selçuk Akşin Somel explains that though German was hardly known in the Ottoman Empire before 1870, it became one of the foreign languages taught at Ottoman schools in 1900. The numbers of German speakers show a drastic increase between 1800 and 1900. Accordingly, the ambiguous question of who counted as 'German' in the nineteenth-century Ottoman Empire became, as argued by Erald Pauw, Sabine Böhme and Ulrich Münch, reflected in the diversifying landscape of Germanophone societies or clubs. Although according to these authors the Teutonia club, established in 1847, held a pivotal role in the German-speaking social life of Istanbul until the 1970s, there were also other societies with a more substantial Austrian or Swiss member profile. The predecessor of the German School, the 'German and Swiss Civic School' (*Deutschen und Schweizer Bürgerschule*), reveals how these identity demarcations were rather vague in a gradually expanding German-speaking community. Nonetheless, the issue of what and who was 'German' and who was not appeared to have been an intensely debated topic among German speakers living in mid-nineteenth-century Istanbul.[10]

Somel indicates that Teutonia was founded by a socio-economically heterogeneous community including tradesmen and craftsmen. Anne Dietrich shows that the Munich-based humoristic weekly *Fliegende Blättern* suggested in 1850 that the German-speaking community of Constantinople comprised approximately 1,000 individuals: 320 from the German states and all others from the Austrian Empire. Most were said to be craftsmen; only fifty or so at most were bureaucrats or tradesmen.[11] Franz von Caucig, member of the Teutonia board in the 1950s and author of a historical overview of Teutonia's early history, cites Dr Säuslein, the chairman and organizer of Teutonia theatre plays around the 1870s, who argues that the origins of Teutonia lay in a group of about ten to twelve German glass traders who would gather in a Greek restaurant every day to chat and sing in 1846.[12] This alleged history of origins is in fact in line with the dissemination of national culture through choral societies. Leerssen describes how these forms of gathering as embodied communities could facilitate a fertile breeding ground for the promotion of national loyalty.[13] He argues that these and other forms of embodied communities, for instance, gymnastic societies (another significant element in the German community of Istanbul as well), made crucial contributions to the making of cultural nationalisms in this era. The development of Teutonia in fact holds significant parallels with the broad definition that Leerssen provides regarding the increase in the number of choral (and other musical) societies in Europe and chronologically emerges around the mid-nineteenth century, a period of a few decades that Leerssen acknowledges as foundational for the dissemination of choral societies in the German states.[14] Teutonia's association with music would resonate in the decades after its foundation in the many concerts and prominent musical guests that were invited to Istanbul, among others, the '*Wiener Chor*' (presumably the *Wiener Singverein*, the concert choir of the *Wiener Musikverein*) in 1891. Moreover, notable German artists were celebrated with festivities and other 'national' holidays were celebrated regularly as the club developed beyond its roots as a group of singing and drinking men.[15]

Von Caucig argues that Säuslein, a medical practitioner, composed a history of Teutonia's first fifty years based on oral narrations of older members.[16] According to these, the idea arose to formalize their gatherings in an institution and thus Teutonia was born, with *die Hebung des geselligen Lebens durch die Pflege deutschen Gesanges* (the improvement of the social life through the practice of German singing) as the main aim of the club.[17] Dietrich points out that despite uncertainties about the early years of the club – such as the supposed founding date: 1 June 1847 – the club gradually developed from a drinking club for men into a 'respectable' association where festivities were celebrated in the presence of families.[18] The 1850s proved to be fruitful years for the new club, bringing together members who played in Teutonia's theatre company; attended plays, concerts and parties; or used the club's first library facilities, skittle alley or billiard.[19]

According to Von Caucig and Säuslein, the club settled in various rented locations during the 1850s and 1860s. The many changes were required due to the

many fires in the city, as well as the dilapidated state of buildings, the unsafe nature
of the area and the desire to have a building in the centre.[20] All locations which are
described by Säuslein, however, were in the Pera district and the direct vicinity of
the Grande Rue de Pera.[21] Around the early 1870s, the club's chairman at the time,
a Mr Köhler, rented a 'somewhat dilapidated timber house' next to the Dervish
Tekke on the current Galip Dede Caddesi. Säuslein describes the disappointing
state of the house as follows:

> When I was introduced there as a guest by the bookseller Mr Christian Roth on
> 6 October 1870, I felt like the boy in the fairytale, who was promised a shining,
> rich mirror hall. Yet suddenly [I] found [myself] in a little barn and curiously
> looking around in anxious anticipation of the magical spell and metamorphosis.
> The mirror hall did not appear and I had to make do with a large room with a
> pool table and reading table, which looked very primitive.[22]

The owner of this house, who is described by Von Caucig as a rich and high official
at the Sublime Porte, was requested to have a new timber house constructed which
Teutonia would rent for five years.[23] After a mere twenty-one days the building
was destroyed by a fire, caused by a gas leak in the building. In the night after the
fire, chairman Säuslein and the accountant sat together to draw up an invitation
for a member meeting the day after. During this meeting it was decided that a new
house should be built in stone.[24] The faulty gas pipes, which according to Säuslein
had caused the accident, were dug out and brought to the German Embassy at the
instruction of the German ambassador. The purpose was to safeguard evidence
for a lawsuit against the gas company, which eventually Teutonia would lose in
1878. The club did manage, however, to reclaim the advance in the rent paid to the
owner of the burned down building.

Crucial beginnings: Towards a new building

The architect who already designed the German embassy in Gümüşsuyu, Hubert
Göbels, was commissioned to design a new building on the Grande Rue de Pera,
the parcel of which had been bought for the amount of 4048 Turkish Pounds.[25]
The Grande Rue de Pera at the time consisted of what is nowadays İstiklal Caddesi
and Galip Dede Caddesi. Currently there is a sharp demarcation between the
landscape of the former as opposed to the latter – where the Teutonia building
is situated. The building process was supervised by Giovanni Battista Barborini.[26]
Teutonia member Barbara Radt argues that by 1874 the club had turned into a
respectable and frequented meeting place, with a gymnastics and choir singing
club. This is confirmed by Von Caucig, who states that when Säuslein retired as
chairman, the position would be held by the Ottoman imperial inspector of mines,
Mr Ernst Weiss, and Wilhelm Albert, director of the Metropolitan Railway.[27] This
prominent manifestation of a German presence in the development of Ottoman
public infrastructure and state building is strikingly similar to other regions in

the world where the German Empire started to make its presence felt, notably in Japan. Hoi-eun Kim argues that in the context of Meiji Japan the German teachers and advisers that were sent to Japan should be considered as an attempt of the German Empire to gain a foothold in Asia, which was otherwise predominantly under the influence of Great Britain.[28] Likening them to the Japanese in Korea, Kim suggests the term 'brokers of empire' for these Germans in Japan, who provided, similar to the Germans in the Ottoman Empire, knowledge and expertise while communicating an image of the German Empire as a collaborative power and an alternative to other European powers, notably France and Great Britain.

Säuslein in the meantime profiled himself as a productive producer and director of theatre plays, operas, operettes, comedies and other stage cooperative plays.[29] Von Caucig argues that the fact that Teutonia had its own building was of crucial importance for the flourishing of its club life and that of other German clubs, such as the *Deutsche Turnverein*, an Austrian charitable society and the Swiss Helvetia club. A recurring problem in these years of Teutonia, however, appears to have been finding suitable board members. Teutonia's building was turned into a restaurant annex bar around the turn of the century. This process was further stimulated by the growing amount of activities that are organized in the other German clubs, such as the *Deutsche Handwerker Verein* (Alemannia from 1912 onwards), the *Deutscher Turnverein*, the *Deutsche Frauenverein*, the *Deutsche Hilfsverein*, and Helvetia.[30] Around 1892 a large number of members left the club and Dr Schwatlo, director of the German School between 1893 and 1907, argues that a lack of decisive and energetic young men was a cause for Teutonia's decline. Another cause mentioned by Schwatlo and Von Caucig was the abusive behaviour of Teutonia's innkeeper towards his wife (who apparently beat his wife before the eyes of their guests).[31] His qualities as innkeeper are also contested by Von Caucig, who mentions the innkeeper was accused of 'bad food and dirtiness'. The new building would, moreover, again be burnt down to the ground floor walls in 1895 during another one of Pera's fires. Von Caucig indicates that the fire this time spread from the timber houses in Ester Çıkmazı (Currently Yörük Çıkmazı) and hit the back part of the Teutonia building. Two-third of the library, some furniture and a few paintings were all that could be saved.[32]

Von Caucig is of the opinion that this incident helped create a further sense of solidarity within the German community. The club had been in tough waters prior to the fire due to an apparent lack of commitment, but thanks to the fire and the new chairman, a German engineer, Otto Kapp von Gültstein, chief of construction at the Anatolian Railways, Teutonia was brought back to life. Kapp led the reconstruction of the club on the same site as the former building.[33] A temporary reading room was set up in the German School, the board meetings would take place in the Janni Brasserie, while large meetings or events were organized in the newly constructed Pera Palace Hotel, the Tokatlıyan Hotel or the building of the *Società Operaia Italiana* in the Rue Ezadji (currently Deva Çıkmazı). By 1896, the remains of the old walls were torn down, foundations were laid and the construction was supervised by an architect mentioned by Von Caucig as Semprini (Guglielmo Semprini, architect of the Istanbul Research Institute's building, and memorialized with an inscription in the present-day building). On 16 January 1897 the new building was inaugurated.[34]

With Kapp's building a new period would begin. Von Caucig mentions that member numbers would increase from 130 in 1896 to 249 in 1912. Radt points out that in the following twenty years the club's esteem started rising and it became referred to as the *Deutscher Club*, a meeting place for embassy staff, bank directors, influential businessmen, German officers and members of the evangelical Church community.[35] Von Caucig explicitly points to the presence of non-German nationals, high-ranking Ottoman officials and officers as well as other 'reputable' German-speaking individuals from 'Turkish' and other communities.[36] It seems thus that at least until the Balkan Wars in 1912 Teutonia indeed housed a lively club life. Mr Scheuermann, director of the German School between 1929 and 1944, however, argues that after nationalist tensions started to rise, the club's visitors profile started to change notably. As the Ottoman Empire's military ties grew closer with the German Empire, the number of military men in the Ottoman Empire increased as well.[37] As a consequence, Teutonia turned into a *Deutsches Haus* rather than a club house, when officers from the German Empire and its allies started frequenting the club.[38] The accommodation, and possibly its surroundings, appear to not have lived up to the desires of this *Deutsches Haus*, however, since already in 1913, when the building of the Swedish Consulate was for sale a discussion on its acquisition by the club started. Insufficient funding was available and the club resorted to taking an option on a building across the Saint Antoine Church on the Grande Rue de Pera instead. The building was for sale for 27,000 liras, but Teutonia would never acquire it.

When the First World War broke out and the Ottoman Empire sided with the Central Powers, Teutonia tried to move to a different building one more time. The German-Turkish Association wanted to have a *Freundschaftshaus* (Friendship house) built, for which a first stone was laid in 1917 on the historical peninsula near the Cisterns of Philoxenos (Binbirdirek Sarnıcı) to bring – in the words of Teutonia's board – Germanness in Istanbul to 'a new and worthy stature' and in the direct proximity of the historical Ottoman dynastic centre.[39] According to Radt, the plan was then to sell the property that was used since 1897 for an amount of 40,000 liras. That, however, would never happen. Following the armistice signed on 31 October 1918 at Moudros, Greece, between the British and the Ottomans, the Triple Entente stipulated an armistice treaty that effectively legalized military interventions by the Entente wherever and whenever it saw fit.[40] This culminated in the British occupation of Istanbul in March 1920. Dietrich indicates that at the end of the year the Germans and Austrians were deported from the Ottoman Empire, with the exception of elderly, sick and women married to men of other nationalities. They were put under the protection of the Swedish Embassy.[41] The German properties were seized by the English and French occupation forces. Teutonia came into the hands of the English; the building was handed over to the occupying forces of the Triple Entente on 3 December 1918. The club was disbanded and its building was used as an officers' club by the British, a barrack for non-commissioned officers, a shelter for Russian refugees and finally as the building of the British YMCA.[42]

On 12 September 1923 the property would be transferred to the Swedish envoy Holstein, who represented the German interests during the occupation. On the same day the envoy sent an invitation to the Teutonia members that he was acquainted with and asked them to discuss the restitution of the seized property.[43] A new board was elected on 2 November 1923, with the approval of the Swedish envoy. The statutes of Teutonia had to be adjusted to the new situation, and the club had to be registered with the new Turkish authorities. Money for a restoration was particularly hard to find, according to Radt, but in the end emergency loans were provided by German banks and companies. Compensation from the British was never received. The social position of the club, which also becomes clear from the desire to build new property befit to the stature of the German Empire during the war, was a top priority before 1918. Radt writes that while previously it was considered an honour to be a member of Teutonia, the exclusivity was lost after the war.[44]

Nazism and Turkey's German community in the 1930s and 1940s

The club was still reserved for Germans and German speakers, but of all socio-economic levels. Adolf Hitler's ascent to power in 1933, however, would have a strong impact on Teutonia. Interestingly, Von Caucig argues that Teutonia risked to become a political forum as well, but the leaders of the club at the time managed to prevent this and thus managed to prevent the closure of the club preceding and during the war. He also states that Teutonia was a place where all Germans in Istanbul could meet and speak freely, 'without anyone judging them'.[45] Dietrich, however, comments to this that Teutonia in fact was a political forum, where Nazi holidays, festivities and Hitler were celebrated, where the local *Hitlerjugend* was gathered and indoctrinated. Since the Turkish educational law forbade public antisemitism and classes on Nazi racial theory in the German School, racial theory was taught to German children in Teutonia's building. The so-called *Heimabende*, for the ideological indoctrination of the children in the *Hitlerjugend*, took place in Teutonia. Dietrich quotes a phrase from the activities of the Istanbul *Jungmädel* during which the leader of the *Hitlerjugend*, a man named Walter, discussed with the children what they should be cautious of, with Jews mentioned explicitly: 'Comrade Walter spoke of the Jews, how we should behave towards them and several other issues that we should take into account here.'[46] Meanwhile the role of Jewish members was rapidly marginalized. It should also be pointed out that Von Caucig himself was a representative of the *Völkischer Beobachter*, the newspaper of the National Socialist German Worker's Party.[47] His post-war comments should thus in part be understood in that context. Dietrich suggests that Teutonia would not lose its reputation as a 'Braunes Haus' until the 1980s and that it was only able to reclaim its reputation as a house for all Germans for a short period of time after the war.[48]

Radt additionally argues that despite the drastic increase in numbers of German residents in Turkey since the 1920s, the activities of Teutonia remained at a relatively modest level. One of the reasons seems to be that many newcomers opted for one of the other Germanophone clubs and charity associations, whose more politically neutral environment had a particular attraction especially after 1933. Teutonia acquired a strong national-socialist profile, and, if not the club, certainly the building itself became an important place for local Nazi representatives, a place from which Jews, socialists, liberals and refugees from Germany preferred to stay away.[49] An example of the marked levels this political orientation reached is the proposal to expel a Jewish female member of Teutonia from the club because of the opinions she expressed on the situation in Nazi Germany, particularly with regard to the poor state of the country's industry.[50]

In the context of Turkey this is particularly interesting since a significant number of political refugees from Germany (and later Austria as well) fled to Turkey in those very years. Fritz Neumark, himself a German refugee and academic, indicates that though these numbers did not equal the numbers of refugees who headed to the United States, the impact of particularly German academics was nowhere felt more strongly than in Turkey. The reason was that most of the refugees who were academics came together with their families and assistants. Azade Seyhan notes, however, that despite the relatively large intake of German and Austrian refugees by Turkey, many were also refused access. It was not necessarily a humanitarian incentive that led the Turkish state to grant refugees access, but the need for intellectual capital.[51] Atatürk and his circle wished to modernize the Ottoman *Dar-ül Fünun* (House of Multiple Sciences a proto-university that was founded in 1845) and reform it into an institute of higher education comparable to universities in Europe.[52] This desire would be the basis for the closure of the *Dar-ül Fünun* on 31 July 1933 and its reopening as Istanbul University on 1 August 1933. The exact numbers that were recruited among German refugees to replace and expand the academic staff of the newly founded university vary, but the most conservative estimate seems to be ninety-six. Regine Erichsen estimates that around 1,000 people from Germany came as political refugees to Turkey from 1933 onwards, though this number includes a far larger group than the German academics alone.

One of the chief reasons for academics to leave Germany for Turkey – apart from those who were forced out of their profession and country due to issues of an ideological or social nature – was their Jewishness. With the 'Law for the Restoration of the Professional Civil Service' that was instated in Germany on 7 April 1933, a few months after the National Socialist German Workers' Party came to power. This law stipulated the dismissal of all civil servants who were of 'non-Aryan' descent. The Nazis further specified what this meant: 'A person is to be regarded as non-Aryan if he is descended from non-Aryan, especially Jewish, parents or grandparents. It is enough for one parent or grandparent to be non-Aryan. This is to be assumed especially if one parent or one grandparent was of Jewish faith.'[53] This meant the end of the careers of Jewish civil servants and thus academics in Germany. Stephan Conermann indicates that around 3,000 academics in total fled Nazi Germany to various destinations, which was approximately 30 per cent of the total German academic community at the time.[54]

The acceptance of some of these Jewish refugees by the Republic of Turkey is all the more remarkable considering the cultivation of antipathy and hatred towards non-Turks and non-Muslims in the 1930s. As Konuk and others indicate, the formation of the new Republic's national identity was strongly based on ethnicity and religion. The Muslim citizens of the Republic of Turkey were forcibly homogenized into the category of 'Turkishness'. Christians and Jews were subjected to aggressive assimilation, forcing them to abandon their mother tongues and communicate in Turkish and many adopted Turkish rather than more typical Jewish, Greek or Armenian names. Konuk argues that to the Turkish hosts, the Jewish Germans on the other hand – as well as a smaller group who had other reasons to be forced into exile – were perceived as 'Europeans'. The chief reason for the Kemalist regime to invite these scholars was their 'Europeanness', rather than their 'Jewishness'.[55] He refers to Turkish minister of education Reşit Galip who stated the academics' arrival compensated for the Byzantine scholars who had fled Istanbul in 1453.[56]

Turkish authorities chose not to stress the reasons as to why these academics were no longer welcome in Germany, one viable reason for it being the parallels that may have been drawn between the Turkish strategies of exclusion and assimilation and the attitude of Nazi Germany towards dissident voices.[57] Interestingly, Bahar indicates that the German scholars themselves were in fact hardly, if at all, performing their Jewish identity while in Turkey. Both representatives of the native Istanbul and Ankara Jewish communities noted that on the rare occasions that they interacted with some of the German Jewish scholars, they did not show in any way that they were practising Jews. Aykut Kazancigil, Uğur Tanyeli and İlber Ortaylı argue that no records of Jewish marriages, birth, *brit mila* or *bar mitzvah* from these scholars were registered in Istanbul's Ashkenazic community registers.[58] Those who died in Istanbul were buried in Muslim rather than Jewish graveyards. Bahar argues the German Jewish intellectuals were 'aloof' to their religion, relying more strongly on *Bildung* ideals – a humanistic ideal of self-development. Despite their disassociation with religion, however, exiled scholars such as Fritz Neumark, Karl Hellmann and Felix Haurowitz indicate that it was also not uncommon – as an insurance against rising antisemitism in Turkey – for German Jews to have their children baptized.[59]

In July 1933 the *Dar-ül Fünun* (House of Multiple Sciences) was closed and Istanbul University was opened, based on a German model of university education.[60] Some of the exiled academics, like Ernst Hirsch, even became Turkish citizens when Nazi Germany took away their citizenship. Yet the Turkish authorities' attitude towards Nazi Germany (and Fascist Italy) remained ambivalent due to its desire to remain neutral. As Sibel Bozdoğan and Esra Akcan indicate this ambivalent attitude is, for instance, reflected in the diverse array of political preferences of German architects working in Turkey. Bruno Taut poses one of the most prominent examples of an architect and refugee from Germany in Turkey, designing various university buildings in Ankara.[61] Margarete Schütte-Lihotzky, Wilhelm Schütte and Ernst Reuter were active in movements against Nazism. Yet other architects such as Hermann Jansen, who designed the master plan for Ankara, and Paul Bonatz had and maintained their ties with the regime in Berlin.[62] The indebtedness to the Nazi and Italian Fascist architectural styles is in any case visible up to this day, particularly in Ankara.

When the Second World War broke out, Turkey decided to stay neutral. Only at the very last moment it decided to join the Allied forces, in order to avoid not being able to become a member of the United Nations in 1945. After the war, all residents with German passports were 'repatriated'.[63] Those who refused were put into camps, able to return after sixteen months of internment in December 1945. Those who did return to Germany were not able to return until 1951. The members of Teutonia that were able to remain in Istanbul were the Swiss, German Hungarians, German Czechs and those who had taken up Turkish citizenship.[64] The club was closed, while the building was watched over by a caretaker and the Swiss consulate posed as a trustee for German properties.

Post-war Teutonia and the changing relation with Istanbul's German community

It would take until 1954 before the club's building was transferred to the club once again. Teutonia's post-war constellation may well be considered as a reflection of what Jörn Rüsen has described as the first phase of Germany's dealing with its past: the initial externalization and suppressing of the memory of the Holocaust and Nazism in general. With the presumption that it was a 'devilish Nazi seduction' that made 'ordinary Germans' victims of a totalitarian rulership.[65] In the context of Teutonia, a letter from Teutonia's archive to a lawyer named Murad Ferid cited by Dietrich is significant to comprehend how this first phase was echoed in Istanbul. In the letter Ferid is asked for his advice in reacquiring the building. Interestingly, in the letter Teutonia's connection with the NSDAP (*Nationalsozialistische Deutsche Arbeiterpartei* – National Socialist German Workers' Party) and Nazi ideology is portrayed as an imposed one. The author claims that Teutonia was forced by the local *Landesgruppenleiter* (national group leader) of the NSDAP to have their building made available for party activities. It was thus not the club itself, the writer states, but its building which was subjected to Nazism.

Many members of Teutonia decided to stay away from the building, according to the letter Dietrich cites. Dietrich points out that no one appeared to take responsibility, as it were always 'others' who were responsible for complicity.[66] She, however, also points to the first chairman of the new board, Rudolf Belling, a sculptor who had been forced to move to Turkey after his art had been denounced as *entartet* (degenerate) by the Nazi authorities during the 1930s. Belling's case provides insight into the complexity of Teutonia's post-war appreciation by the Germanophone community. Belling became the head of the sculpting department at the later Mimar Sinan University for the Fine Arts upon arrival and later a professor at the department of architecture of Istanbul Technical University. Dietrich suggests that Belling's nationalist sympathies for Germany allowed for a rehabilitation in Istanbul by the local NSDAP authorities, particularly due to the sympathy that NS-*Landesgrüppenführer* Martin Bethke felt for him. It is perhaps more interesting even that despite his difficulties with the Nazi regime that after the war he became the chairman of Teutonia, an institution which until recently had been so closely connected to local representatives of the Nazi regime.[67]

Despite Belling being a victim of the Nazi regime, he did not choose to denounce an institution that had become embedded in Nazi organizational structures. Dietrich also points to the fact that Belling would become chairman after the war yet claims that he would not stay on as chairman for long, vacating his position several months after. She provides neither dates nor references to these claims. The minutes from Teutonia's archives in fact show that one of the earliest dates in which he is mentioned as president are the minutes from 13 November 1952 and he would not resign as the club's chairman until March 1957 when he was succeeded by Sylvio Raymund.[68] This may well show that the attitude of some members and board members towards the post-war Teutonia, despite continuities in the club's leadership, may have been more complex than Dietrich suggests. Belling's attitude in that sense may be considered to be in line again with Rüsen's definition of first phase of coming to terms with Nazism in the post-war period: by suppression and denial rather than by displaying outright aversion.[69]

The club in any case tried to push forward its mission of regaining the status of a centre point for the German community in Istanbul. That did not occur without problems. In a document from 27 November 1956, it is indicated that although Teutonia had always had serious financial difficulties, the successive boards had managed to keep the club alive. It is indicated that this was not in the least thanks to a support fund from Germany, and only through this was it possible to 'endow the club with the regard that granted it with considerable recognition from both the German and Turkish side'.[70] The report also recounts how several old members took the initiative in 1952 to bring Teutonia back to life and the building was, through the intervention of the German Embassy in Ankara, returned to the club in 1953. The writers indicate that great financial misfortune hit the club subsequently since the building had been badly damaged during its confiscation.[71] They go on by indicating that other German institutions, such as the German Hospital, the German Archaeological Institute and the Evangelical Church had all received contributions from the state in Bonn to repair the damage of the preceding years. Teutonia, however, was treated 'like a stepchild' (*stiefmütterlich*) by the government. The board asks the German ambassador to mediate between the club and the government and requested an amount of 190,000 Deutsche Marken in order to 'arrange the German prestige in Turkey of our society in as good a manner as it used to be in the past decades'.[72] To underline the appeal to the ambassador and the Federal Republic of Germany's government they closed with a quote from Goethe's Faust: 'what you inherit from your father must first be earned before it's yours!' ('*Was du ererbt von deinen Vätern hast, erwirb es, um es zu besitzen!*').

The club held a first meeting with its members, a group of approximately forty with their partners, on 27 February 1954. The club appears to have been quickly revived by this group, since a reflection on the first years of the club after the reopening claims that the cultural programme of the years 1954 and 1955 consisted of fifty activities.[73] Exactly a month after its first gathering in the old club house, the club welcomed Chancellor Konrad Adenauer in its building during his visit to Turkey.[74] The poor state of the building was pointed out in the same document as well. The club's statutes meanwhile had retained their validity after they were last updated in 1939, though in 1960 new statutes were introduced. In the first issue of the Teutonia bulletin – *Teutonia Mitteilungsblatt* – from May 1956 the editors of the Teutonia Bulletin memorize how the club was reopened in September 1951 and how until 1954 meetings would be held in various locations in Beyoğlu: the Park Hotel, Lido, Liman Lokantası, Taxim Kasino and the Municipal Marriage House (*Belediye Evlenme Dairesi*). With the cooperation of the German consul, Dr Seelos, the club got its building back and after a number of repairs the building was reopened on 27 February 1954. The board appeared to be also pleased that in the same year the club's private beach and sports fields on the Anatolian side in Moda was acquired anew.[75] By April 1957, however, the Teutonia bulletin reports that in a general meeting of the club, the chairman had announced that the club was forced to let go of its private beach and sport fields, after the decision of an Ankara court of appeal.[76] In 1958 a new beach and sport field was found in Fenerbahçe, Kalamış.[77] Meanwhile the library had been reopened on 17 May 1956.[78]

The board reports to its members in 1959 that in line with the club's desire to become a meeting point for Germans in Istanbul once again, its member base has increased to approximately 220. They proudly announced that many new members who recently settled in Istanbul had joined Teutonia and that the member base comprised over 50 per cent of the total German community in Istanbul.[79] Nevertheless, the club appears to have experienced some problems in motivating its members to participate in the organization of the club's activities. On the opening page of the Teutonia bulletin's second issue, the editorial board considers it necessary to remind its readers of the lexical definition of a society or club: 'a society is a network of people with the purpose of fostering common interests.'[80] The authors ask their readers to contemplate on this definition. What follows is a slightly disgruntled appeal to the members to contribute to organizing activities, rather than paying their contribution and simply enjoying the programme. They ask if it is still possible to find a common cause for over 200 members, from Germany, Austria, Switzerland and Turkey. Interestingly, however, the authors wish to stress that it is not only the wide variety of interests – sports, concerts, film screenings, theatre plays and socializing (*geselligkeit*) – that they wish to cater to but to be the centre point of Germanness in Istanbul and to help deepen the ties between club members and Turkey.[81]

In 1957 to the occasion of the club's 110th anniversary, the bulletin's board argues there is no older club in Istanbul and that the club's member base has never been as big. Later that year at a general assembly 212 registered members are cited.[82] It seems that the initial problems were somewhat resolved as the report from the 1958 general assembly cites a table tennis group, a theatre group, a library with volunteers, as well as numerous events; theatre plays, concerts, carnival and anniversary celebrations.[83] Another major development was the opening of a seamen's home in 1957, which aimed to replace the one that was lost in 1918 (presumably following the disownment of German properties in Istanbul after the First World War).[84] It should be noted that elsewhere the opening of the seamen's home is cited to have taken place a few years earlier, in 1954.[85] The club was indeed an important meeting point for members in those years, frequented, according to the Teutonia bulletin in 1961, even during the low-season in the summer. The restaurant was a meeting place for members, despite a lack of activities in the summer season. The club's restaurant had been reopened again in 1953 and, according to Radt, held a significant position in the German colony. Men would gather here for their lunches and women, many of whom would not become members, came here after afternoon shopping in Beyoğlu. It turned out to be difficult to retain a reliable innkeeper and after successive German, Greek and Turkish innkeepers the restaurant was finally closed in 1970.[86]

'Der alte Teutonia': A 'new' Teutonia for a new German community

In the meantime, Teutonia's building at Galip Dede Caddesi appeared to continuously provide problems despite renovations in the past years. In 1963 the Teutonia bulletin reports a lunch meeting of club members and their wives. The authors of the bulletin argue here that the renewal and enlivenment of the club are dependent not only on the building's deplorable condition but also on the spirit which ought to govern the house and the requirement of members to get to know each other more closely.[87] Yet, problems became of such nature that in the summer of 1964 the bulletin announces that, after many years of talking and false promises, the building would finally be renovated. The chair of Teutonia's board Sylvio Raymund meanwhile was supervising this makeover 'from roof to basement'.[88] Contrary to renovations after the First and Second World Wars, which aimed for continuation and small repairs, the author states that according to the chairman everything was being renewed. In the old kitchen, a new club and play room was introduced, with a skittle alley, pool tables and table tennis, aimed at becoming 'the midpoint of club life in the future'.[89] The chairman hoped for a reopening of the building in November 1964. In the same year, a report from the Teutonia board states that for the past two years the club held a member base of 240, yet mentions this fact in a point titled 'take up the struggle against the indifference of members'.[90] The club gradually grew towards a role as caretaker and landlord of its building, with the rents of various institutions using its facilities becoming increasingly important for the continuing existence of club and building.

It is important to note that Teutonia had acquired new functions in Beyoğlu from 1954 onwards. On 26 April 1954 the seamen's home was opened with the cooperation of the local German church community.[91] As indicated earlier, the opening (although the *Mitteilungsblatt* suggests the opening actually took place in 1957) of a home for German seamen aimed to fill a 'cultural void' (*eine kulturelle Lücke*) following the disownment of the home in 1918. The Teutonia bulletin described it as a particular meeting point for seamen from German ships docking in the harbours of Istanbul.[92] Despite its conflicted history, Teutonia once again aimed to be a cultural and social meeting point for Germans. Interestingly in that context is also the diverse range of people the seamen's home would cater to. It seems that essentially all German institutions in Istanbul had become connected to the Federal Republic of Germany (FRG, or *Bundesrepublik Deutschland*) rather than the German Democratic Republic (GDR, or *Deutsche Demokratische Republik*). Teutonia would occasionally also feel the geopolitical impact of the homeland's separation into West and East part. As options for East Germans to flee the GDR grew more and more limited, they would become more resourceful and desperate in finding ways to cross over to 'the West'. One of the dangerous passageways was jumping into the Bosporus while GDR ships passed from the Mediterranean to the Black Sea. The second floor of the Teutonia building, reserved for the seamen's home, would therefore also shelter other travellers, working migrants and notably refugees from the GDR. Radt writes that the seamen's home came under the supervision of a pastor named Bott. Ingeborg Çelik, a former kindergarten teacher at Teutonia, recounts how this pastor would ready small rowing boats whenever the East German passenger ship *Völkerfreundschaft* travelled through the Bosporus, often successfully saving refugees who jumped from the ship into the sea. That this appeared to be common practice is recounted by a traveller on a ship called the *Völkerfreundschaft*, Hartmut Ehbets, who planned to leave the ship together with his wife while sailing through the Bosporus. Ehbets recounts, however, how many young people were very disappointed to see that sails would be used to cover the safety rails, while men with bats in front of the rails would keep an eye on the passengers.[93]

Following the decreasing amount of ships with the ports of Tophane and Karaköy as their destination, due to the introduction of container freight facilities in Kadıköy and an increase in passenger air travel, the importance of the seamen's home decreased through the course of the 1960s.[94] New renovations of the Teutonia building and the seamen's home were nonetheless announced in the bulletin in 1966, as well as the construction of a consular school in the garden of the Teutonia building.[95] Interestingly, another example of the enduring usage of the Teutonia building by the German community was the kindergarten. The aforementioned pastor Bott and four German mothers took the initiative to open a kindergarten for the German community in Beyoğlu around 1961 as the community's numbers were increasing. Marcel Geser points out how historically there had been a German kindergarten in Istanbul since the 1850s, yet in 1944 – following Turkey's decision to join the Allied forces and the closure of German institutions – all German nationals were ordered to return to Germany or deported to camps in Anatolia. In December 1945, those in the camps were allowed to return to their residences. Despite the intention of the German School's new rector, Karl Steuerwald, to reopen the kindergarten and a promise from the German Ministry of Education, the kindergarten was not reopened. The official reason was that the demand was too low and that many of the parents who were entitled to bring their children to a kindergarten lived too far away.[96] Many parents therefore entrusted their children to au pairs or private kindergartens, but Geser explains that in 1961 the aim to teach children German at an early age led the mothers and Bott to set up the Teutonia kindergarten. A lady named Helga Blanke was hired as the first teacher and the kindergarten received children from teachers of the German School, business people and employees of the German Consulate. Thirty-four small children were under the supervision of a kindergarten teacher in the afternoons, the Teutonia bulletin reports in 1965, though Geser argues that the number generally did not exceed twenty-five.[97] A report from Teutonia's general assembly in the early spring of 1965 indeed reports that until 1965 twenty-five children would be admitted, but since an additional supervisor could be hired thirty-four children were admitted.[98] As time progressed, Dutch children were admitted to the kindergarten as well, while the kindergarten's supervision remained with Teutonia.[99]

Meanwhile, the German-Turkish Cultural Institute – supported by the Goethe Institut from 1957 onwards and the official Goethe Institut since 1991 – was also housed in Teutonia as the German Library. Yet, Istanbul's urban development during the 1970s started to have an impact on the usage of the Teutonia building as well. More generally speaking, rising migration, the construction of new suburbs and the construction of new commercial buildings particularly meant that Beyoğlu's older buildings lost some of their historical occupants. Construction of commercial properties in the old centre of Beyoğlu was relatively limited, possibly in part due to the complexity of opening Beyoğlu to mass car traffic, with the notable exception of the Odakule Building along the İstiklal Caddesi. It was there that the Goethe Institut would move to in 1980.[100]

Radt claims that as of 1968 the evolving social and spatial structure of Istanbul also had strong implications for the city's, and particularly Beyoğlu's, social life. The Beyoğlu district became less and less desirable for most German speakers. The urban middle classes withdrew entirely from Beyoğlu and moved to Topkapı, Etiler and districts that started to be industrialized.[101] Unfortunately, this could not be confirmed with member lists from the 1960s or 1970s. Member lists from the 1980s, however, do indeed show that the majority of members had moved to Bosporus districts like Tarabya, Etiler, Emirgan, Bebek and Rümelihisarı or Levent and Yeniköy. Only a few were registered as living in Tophane or Cihangir, including Barbara Radt and her husband.[102]

From this perspective it is important to realize nonetheless that it was only in 1959 when Beyoğlu was still described as the 'residential district par excellence' in the Istanbul edition of Hachette's Guides Bleus. The guide goes on by stating: 'It is here where you will find the most comfortable hotels frequented, in general, by the foreign tourists.'[103] What follows is a description of İstiklal Caddesi's institutional richness, which hardly gives the impression of a waning district. This certainly holds true for the German institutions in the area as well. In fact even after the late 1960s, the German School, research institutes, consulate and German-Turkish Cultural Institute remained. Different reasons may have been at play here. It may have been tough to get a good price for the properties, institutions may have attributed a certain attachment to their real estate, yet as shown in the case of the English School for Girls and German School, it was also complicated for foreign institutions to acquire or construct new properties elsewhere in Istanbul. The case of Teutonia, however, shows an increasing detachment from the club as an institution. That being said, members, other German speakers and German institutions in Istanbul were interested in using Teutonia's facilities.[104] The building was used daily as a kindergarten and primary school, was intensively used by the German School and housed the German Library. Newly added parts for the schools were still constructed in the name of the club, though this appeared to have become a growing problem for the Turkish authorities. The club had been nearly inactive in the second half of the 1960s and the last general meeting had taken place on 5 June 1968, though Turkish legislation called for annual meetings.[105] The club in the end came to a standstill in 1971.[106] The decline in the club's activity during this period is reflected in the relative scarcity of source material in Teutonia's archives; whereas there is an abundance of material – correspondences, notes, minutes, invitations, reports – from the 1950s, 1960s, 1980s and 1990s, the material from the 1970s is limited to some communication and reports on the problematic situation in which the club found itself.

The changing social life in Beyoğlu runs parallel to the decline in the periodical announcements of Teutonia's activities in the *Cumhuriyet* newspaper. Numerous classical music concerts and lectures are organized and announced in *Cumhuriyet* since 1954, approximately two to three times a year, but in 1968 the announcements disappeared, not reappearing until 1986.[107] The general meeting of the club on 5 June in the club building was announced by the board on 1 June 1968 in the *Cumhuriyet* daily. In the minutes from a meeting at the German Consulate General on 6 May 1970, it is decided that the club's beach in Kalamış would be closed. A period of relative abandonment was followed by the removal of the club from the Turkish registry in 1972, because no activities or required general meetings had taken place. A variety of factors may have been at issue here and the archives of Teutonia did not provide a single conclusion. Dietrich has pointed to the stigma of Teutonia, although this seems to have been less of an issue during the 1950s and 1960s, and Radt, more plausibly, has mentioned how German residents of Istanbul moved away from Beyoğlu and towards the new districts of the city or the areas around the Bosporus.[108] In earlier times, moreover, the lack of engagement of Teutonia's members with its administration has also been quoted as a persistent problem.[109] These, in addition to Beyoğlu's changing demography and sociocultural composition at large, may all have been elements that contributed to the status quo that Teutonia reached in the early 1970s. It could have had severe consequences, however, for Teutonia. The club did not meet the bureaucratic requirements of the Turkish state, which, among other things, meant that registered clubs and associations needed to organize regular member meetings.

The club was thus at risk of losing its building to the Turkish state. A new club under a new name needed to be founded in 1974, but this new club was not entitled to the ownership of the building. Arthur Kapps, the manager of the old club and building as well as the initiator of the new club, had been appointed to ensure that daily affairs in the building would be able to continue. He pointed out in a letter from 1979 that there had been a risk that the building would have been confiscated by the Turkish state.[110] As this did not happen, the new club made efforts to claim ownership of the building, of which the plot of land in itself represented a value of

60 million Turkish lira (approximately 1.7 million US dollar at the time).[111] In 1978, through the involvement of the German Consul General, the old club managed to absolve itself in a special general meeting and transfer its assets to the new club. Radt describes how it was, nevertheless, near to impossible to sustain a community that would build a flourishing club life. She argues that it would have been one thing to become part of a flourishing community, but another thing to become a participant in the preservation of a 'national' institution. What she means by this is that the incentive to preserve German heritage in Istanbul was not felt significantly enough throughout the community of German speakers in Istanbul. One reason may have been, as indicated by Dietrich, the fact that Teutonia's reputation still was overshadowed by its pre-war past.[112]

The question remains what the objective of Arthur Kapps and the other founders of this 'new' Teutonia was. Uncertainty about the building's future had started to arise since the 1960s. In 1972 Teutonia was even removed from the club register, but this did not have a direct consequence for the building. The Teutonia building was never sold to a third party, possibly because the building's condition made it a tough sell. The German Federal Building Authority (*Bundesbaudirektion*) came to check the building to ensure its suitability for a Goethe Institut in Turkey, but argued against it in the end. In the annual report of 1964, the board indicates three options for the future of the club house, namely selling it and constructing a new house elsewhere, renting the ground floor for commercial purposes (making it an *iş hanı* or office building with *Teutonia Pasajı* as the suggested name) or acquiring funds to renovate the building. The board decided to choose the third option, but indicated that the first option, that is, selling the building and constructing a new one elsewhere, would have been the ideal option. The reasons not to sell were that the board could not be sure whether the club could acquire a plot of land and construct a new building. It was, moreover, unsure whether the sale of the old building would yield the necessary funds for such a move, which appears to have been a concern for other foreign parties in Beyoğlu. They had also considered around these years selling their monumental buildings: the British Consulate at Galatasaray had unsuccessfully been on the market.[113] In the 1970s, however, Teutonia's building had been at risk of being lost as a *Treffpunkt der Deutschen in Istanbul* forever. The decision of Kapps and others to prevent this could not have been an entirely economic one, and it seems very likely that motivations of a more 'sentimental' nature instigated the decision to save Teutonia from being permanently expropriated by the Turkish state.

At the start of the 1970s, Radt describes the building to be in a poor condition despite several renovations in the 1950s and 1960s. This is reflected also in the notes that Kapps makes in his letters, explaining that the roof of the building had been fixed with funding from the German Consulate.[114] The financial situation of Teutonia also was such that its daily costs could be barely met. The only income the club had came from the rooms that were rented to the embassy school and the cultural institute, since the members at the time were not willing to make any financial contributions. The dire situation that the club found itself in did not mean it was no longer recognized as a 'German landmark' in Istanbul. This is exemplified by an unfortunate outcome when it became linked to Germany's geopolitical vicissitudes as well. In 1977 a bomb was thrown into the building by a group of fifteen to twenty people while they supposedly screamed 'German murderers'.[115] Not entirely clear about the ideological orientations of the perpetrators, the *Milliyet* daily reported on 26 October 1977 that some individuals called the news desks of newspapers stating that the attack was a response to the termination of the Lufthansa 181 hijacking on 18 October 1977 by a German anti-terror unit in Mogadishu.[116] The children from the primary school who were in the building at the time were quickly evacuated and apart from significant damage to the façade and the site inside the building where the bomb exploded and three wounded passers-by, the consequences of the attack were limited.[117] In spite of these difficulties, the usage of the club's building fared rather well. In addition to the cultural institute, the embassy school and the kindergarten, an initiative was started in 1979 to teach German courses to Turkish teachers in several of the rooms of the Teutonia building by instructors from the German High School.[118] It is interesting to note that, unlike the German School, Teutonia appears to have built few connections with Turkish citizens who had temporarily lived in Germany but returned to Turkey. The chapter on the German High School contains, indeed, further discussion on the effects of the return to Istanbul of large numbers of Turkish guestworkers from Europe during the 1970s had on the school.

From the perspective of the club's building it should be mentioned that the condition of the building was far from unique in Beyoğlu. Just like Teutonia, many monumental buildings in Beyoğlu had suffered from severe neglect throughout the second half of the twentieth century. The disrepair of such previously important sites drew the attention of resident Europeans, and two Dutch consul generals wrote in respectively 1979 and as late as 1995 about the condition of buildings in Beyoğlu. In 1979 Consul D. H. M. Speyaert wrote about how the church community of the Union Church of Pera had gotten used to being relieved by the view of the flowery consulate general's garden after strolling through the neglected streets of Istanbul. In 1995 Consul Bloembergen complained about the desolate condition of the consulate general's building itself to his superiors in The Hague. He writes: 'even Turkish guests, who are definitely used to the sight of shabby buildings, have started noticing the sorry state of the Palais de Hollande.'[119] Beyoğlu was losing ground to the modern districts of the rapidly expanding city. Earlier, Çelik Gülersoy, one of the key actors in Istanbul's controversial restoration and preservation initiatives and chairman of TURING Club, writes about Beyoğlu in a travel guide, published in 1969:

> This is Istiklal Câddesi. It was the main meeting place for Europeans 70 or 80 years ago. Since the modern part of the city has been greatly enlarged, Istiklâl Caddesi has not kept its monopoly. Moreover, the fact that it is a one-way street has caused it to lose a great deal of importance. But all the same, old or new, there are 10 cinemas, 7 theatres, 4 exhibition galleries, a large number of snack-bars and restaurants on this stre[e]t, which leads to Taksim.[120]

The building would turn out to remain a cause of worry for the board of Teutonia as well. The chairman in the mid-1980s, Stephan Kroll, argues that according to the strict Turkish club regulations the club was barely eligible to conform to regulations which could have consequences for its ownership of the property. To avoid the risk of losing the building altogether, the club decided to provide the German Consulate General with a leasing agreement for the duration of ninety-nine years, during which the club would be able to use the building together with other parties, among others the embassy school, kindergarten, German High School and the Turkish state television channel TRT, that had been using the building up until then.[121] The board even considered to disband the club altogether and transfer their assets to the Consulate General, but in the notes from 20 October 1987 the board states that this had proven to be 'politically impossible'. If the club were to be disbanded in the future, however, the immoveable assets would be transferred to the General Consulate.[122] The club that had fifty-seven members on 17 March, thereby, had been able to safeguard one of its main rationales of existence, whatever would happen to the club itself.[123]

The Beyoğlu area meanwhile is described in a building report by two engineers, Adolf Hoffmann and Klaus Nohlen, from 1984 as 'somewhat neglected'. Only four years earlier the social and political turmoil at the national and local levels had been brought to a halt by Kenan Evren's military coup. A year before Turgut Özal had managed to bring his Motherland Party to power, with Bedrettin Dalan as his representative in the metropolitan government. In the years to follow politicians would not let an opportunity go by to stress how they would change the face of Istanbul and 'clean up' Beyoğlu in particular. A telling example is a publication from the Beyoğlu municipality, *Beyoğlu İçin* (For Beyoğlu – 1984), with articles titled 'Famous Beyoğlu is returning to its old beauty' (*Ünlü Beyoğlu eski güzelliğine dönüyor*) and quotes from the Beyoğlu mayor Haluk Öztürkatalay that indicate the discovery of the district's marketing potential: 'Istanbul is famous for Beyoğlu' (İstanbul Beyoğlu'yla bilinir).[124] The report by Hoffmann and Nohlen also indicates that the area will soon be restored by the Beyoğlu municipality, with the prospective pedestrianization of the İstiklal Caddesi contributing to the reinvigoration of the district's profile as well. The building's location is described as 'favorable' due to the adjacency of the Tünel funicular. Access with private cars is, on the other hand, complicated, though this is – according to the report – a general problem in Istanbul.[125] It does not appear from any document that the Teutonia board expressed the desire to sell its building, and its decision to connect its future in the case of Teutonia's dissolution to the Consulate General indicates that it was felt to be important that the building would be preserved for the German community even if there was no future for its namesake. That, in fact, was an implicit expression of the de facto situation for over two decades; despite recurrent calls to recruit members among the local German and Germanophone community, the reality was that a large part of the building's users had no formal connection to the club. Compared to the celebrated mid-1950s its member base dropped by a factor of four, while the majority of its users were non-members and other institutions.[126]

As such it is fair to conclude that Teutonia has continuously played a significant role in the German and Germanophone community, though since the mid-1960s less as a club and more as the caretaker of a building that catered to the different needs of the community. The crisis of the early 1970s, during which the club risked losing its building to the Turkish state, rendered visible the changed relationship between club and building: whereas the building served the club at first, it became clear during the 1970s that the reality was that the club was serving its building. Since so many had become dependent, for practical reasons primarily, on sustaining the occupation of the Teutonia building, it was in their interest that the club would remain, at least in a somewhat artificial manner, active. Both Radt and Geser hint at this when they respectively mention the involvement of the German School's teachers in Teutonia in the 1980s and the overlap between the board members of the kindergarten and Teutonia's board.[127] It should therefore be considered what the meaning of this place in Istanbul as a locus for a variety of institutions with a German connection was not limited in its purpose to the historical club. Though it may have become increasingly difficult for the club to live up to the aims indicated in its statutes, its caretakership of the building ensured that one of its important goals – being a centre point for Germans in Istanbul – was indirectly met for a long time after the club itself failed to be a relevant contributor to the social life of the German community.[128] The building's adjacency to the German School – more or less around the corner – its relatively close proximity to the German Consulate in Gümüşsuyu, and its housing of various German institutions ensured the continued existence and link with Istanbul's German-speakers. In that sense the building may be seen as a place-marker that bears witness to the continuing presence of German communities in Istanbul.

Within Teutonia's long history, the composition of the German community had grown and shrunk several times before. Although its member base had different proportions relative to the German community, the 'crisis' that Radt and Von Caucig described around the turn of the nineteenth century, during which the club house had become something that resembled a members-only restaurant rather than a club, also shows that what made Teutonia was very much connected to the interests and motivation of Istanbul's Germans at the time rather than a static and stable entity. On the other hand the enforced or voluntary involvement of Teutonia with the NSDAP in the 1930s and 1940s, and the differing historical representation of how events would unfold, can possibly show the intricate connection of the building and the institution. The absence of discussion regarding the club's Nazi associations, referred to in the Teutonia archives in euphemistic terms (war years or *Kriegszeit*), mirrors the general attitude to the (lack of) memorialization in Germany in the immediate years following the Second World War. The stigma of the building's involvement and the club's integration in the infrastructure of the Third Reich abroad, may have had an impact on the club's appeal, although this hardly showed after its reopening in the immediate war years. It seems more likely that local factors, the moving away of German speakers from the old city centre and the gradual change of Istanbul's and the Beyoğlu district's sociocultural, demographic and services profile had a more considerable impact on Teutonia's post-war history. Even then, the building was used by various German actors, which – as will be shown in the chapter on the German High School – were unable to move to different areas. Today, the club's activities are quite limited while its building is being renovated, with the aim that in the future it will host new institutions, including the Orient Institut, a research institute.

Chapter 3

YEŞILÇAM STREET/CINEMA IN BEYOĞLU
AND URBAN RESISTANCE

In between Galatasaray Square and Taksim a building is situated that may well be considered to have one of the most imposing and monumental façades on İstiklal Caddesi (see figure 1). The building historically known as Cercle d'Orient, after the club that occupied one of the floors in the building since its opening in 1882 until at least the late 1970s, was built by one of the most prominent Istanbulite architects of the second half of the nineteenth century, Alexandre Vallaury.[1] The architect made his name in Istanbul designing the Pera Palace Hotel, the Imperial Museum, the Imperial Ottoman Bank buildings, the building of the Ottoman Public Debt Administration and several other prominent monumental buildings in Beyoğlu, the historical peninsula and along the Bosporus. The main building stands out in the eclectic mosaic that constitutes the architectural landscape of İstikal Caddesi: the size of the parcel is reflected by the colossal symmetric façade which for a long time stretched beyond any other building along the street. In its most recent incarnation, the Cercle d'Orient building has become a shopping mall and a cinema centre as well as housing a number of cafés, restaurants and a branch of the *Madame Tussaud* wax doll museum. The newly constructed annex to the historical building is hardly visible due to the density of buildings in the area. This is where the rear part of the historical Cercle d'Orient parcel was before its demolition, particularly known for housing the iconic Emek Cinema.

Originally the building was constructed for the club, which started as a meeting place for Ottoman and foreign dignitaries, founded by Alfred Sandison, the British Levantine chief dragoman to the Ottoman Empire in 1882. The building was commissioned and owned by an Ottoman Armenian bureaucrat and diplomat Abraham Pasha, one of the wealthiest men in Istanbul at the time. Following his bankruptcy as a result of unfortunate bourse speculation and gambling the Ottoman Bank seized his properties, including the Cercle d'Orient building. The properties then came into the possession of an Ottoman Armenian stockbroker in 1919, who is mentioned in the archives of the Ottoman Bank as Manuk Manukyan.[2] The Cercle d'Orient building is listed, as a first-grade historical building, initially becoming protected in 1971 in an order by the High Council for Historical Real Estate and Monuments to protect a large number of buildings along the Istiklal Caddesi.[3] Its categorization as a first-grade historical building does not allow for

Figure 1 Enno Maessen (2018) – Exterior view of the Cercle d'Orient, seen from İstiklal Caddesi.

any changes to be made to both the building's interior and exterior. The building has been restored with remarkable detail between 2012 and 2016, particularly considering the fact that the surrounding buildings, also listed buildings, have been entirely destroyed. Despite ongoing protests by civil society organizations since the 1990s, the buildings behind the Cercle d'Orient, including the Emek Cinema, were destroyed as part of the parcel's redevelopment.[4] The Emek Cinema building on the same parcel as the Cercle d'Orient building was marked as a second-grade historical building, which theoretically should have made it impossible to make any changes to the building's exterior.[5] New legislation that was introduced in the early 2000s, however, made it possible to overrule the safeguards of the building's protected status.[6]

Parallel to the destruction of the Emek Cinema, the main building of the Cercle d'Orient building facing the İstiklal Caddesi was carefully restored. Despite its restoration, including original interior and exterior details, references to its previous functions or occupants have been erased. To a certain degree the Cercle d'Orient building as it is today has been 'whitewashed', in order to re-fashion it as a monumental entrée to a shopping mall complex. The concept of whitewashing is defined by Michael Herzfeld and is marked by process of radical redefinition of a place's meaning. Such reimaginings of urban landscapes have been the focus of an extensive body of scholarship in history, geography and anthropology, including Herzfeld's own work that examines the varied processes through which urban boundaries are redefined on both a symbolic and a physical level and former residents framed as intruders.[7] In particular, the obsession with 'cleanliness' that Herzfeld notes in the context of Thailand and Greece is, in fact, strikingly similar to the Cercle d'Orient case: here, an idealized image crafted by real estate developers has taken precedence over the messiness and informality of small shops and old cinemas. Although to compare this to what Herzfeld notes to be a 'quasi-colonial nervousness about making a good impression on foreigners' seems unwarranted, the case of the Cercle d'Orient's renovation does mark an obsession with idle references to value, quality and reviving the former glory of Beyoğlu.[8] On the website of the shopping complex Grand Pera a return to the alleged glory of the Cercle d'Orient is promised, without further defining what this glory consists of. A similar process is observed by Andreas Huyssen of banners displayed all over Berlin in 1996: 'BERLIN WIRD, BERLIN BECOMES', leaving open what Berlin was becoming and ironically (and possibly unwittingly) referring to the building pit that made Berlin in the 1990s.[9]

Since no changes were allowed to be made and – apparently – were made to the Cercle d'Orient building, a lucrative exploitation of the building's bulk by the concessionaire appears to be complicated. Currently, the Cercle d'Orient building houses a café in a newly constructed annex, the entrée to a Madame Tussaud wax museum, some temporary exhibitions or displays by prominent local and international brands, as well as the entrance to the shopping mall, which will have to account for the majority of the project's income.[10] The process of 'whitewashing' could be seen as the final step in a longer sequence of growing disconnection between the building and its namesake: the elite club Cercle d'Orient known since 23 April 1944 as the *Büyük Kulüp* (Grand Club). The Cercle d'Orient club used the first floor of the building for its activities, whereas the ground floor facing İstiklal Caddesi was used by shops and cinemas. The building was formally connected with the elite club Cercle d'Orient club until the early 1980s. The original Cercle d'Orient club held a heterogeneous audience, with businessmen, diplomats, state and military officials from various nationalities and ethnicities until the Second World War. The club is mentioned in numerous British newspapers as the most elite club in Pera.[11] Elsewhere it is described in *The Times* as 'the well known diplomatic club'.[12] In recollections from foreign diplomats it was presented as a focal point of power. In 1938 Sir George Clerk, a diplomat in Istanbul/Constantinople before the First World War, for instance, recounts a few memories about the club. He describes it as an elite meeting point for the crème de la crème in Istanbul/Constantinople: 'You could lunch at the Cercle d'Orient and incidentally eat some of the best food and drink some of the best wine in Europe, and see Talaat [Pasha] embracing the Armenian deputy whom he was to send to his death or watch Enver [Pasha] saluting Nazim Pasha, the Minister of War, whom he shot in the Sublime Porte.'[13] It would also feature in foreign reporting on Istanbul with regard to more trivial matters: in 1926 *The Daily Telegraph Diplomatic* reported how the Turkish Liquor Control Board, in control of the liquor monopoly in the newly established republic, confiscated 7,000 bottles of French champagne, other wines and nine 300-litre barrels of wine.[14] As Istanbul's political significance at the national level decreased, following the installation of Ankara as the Turkish capital in 1923, the significance of Beyoğlu and its international clubs would also gradually decline.

Orhan Koloğlu claims that the differentiated membership changed significantly, after the Second World War, with a drastic decrease of foreign members.[15] In the 1940s, French was entirely abandoned as an official club language and on 23 April 1944 *Büyük Kulüp* (Grand Club) would become its official name and thus effectively Turkified.[16]

One of the few local observers who made some remarks on the club and its building is Said Naum Duhani (1892–1970), who writes briefly on the Cercle d'Orient in one of his books. A note on Duhani is required here. Born in a renowned Christian Arab family and part of the Pera community, he was, as Edhem Eldem notes, the first to start a trend of nostalgic reflections on Beyoğlu. Contrary to the many publications of the 1980s and 1990s, which followed the translations of Duhani's work from French into Turkish, Duhani's work is different since he wrote his two books about Pera/Beyoğlu at a time when the described communities were still present in the city. In addition, the books were in French and thus for 'internal consumption' within the Pera community. Eldem is right to note that Duhani's work is imbued with melancholia and nostalgia, and much of the information in his essayistic writings is hard to check for its 'historical veracity'. This holds true for many other (later) sources of a similar nature.[17] Yet the fact that Duhani's remarks were also included in the files on the Emek Cinema and Cercle d'Orient composed by the Istanbul branch of the Chamber of Architects (*Türk Mühendis ve Mimar Odaları Birliği* – TMMOB, Union of Turkish Engineers and Architects Chambers) gives an impression of how this source – translated to Turkish – is considered by experts of law and architecture in Turkey. Duhani recounts how all the shops in the building of Abraham Pasha (Cercle d'Orient) were very upscale and luxurious, whereas at the time of his writing there were only small shops 'which could never compete with the esteem of the gentlemen that had left'.[18] To enter the club one would require a password. He cites a chairman of the club who was an ambassador and stated that diplomats or high officials would become members. From among the 'Turks' only vezirs could enter the club.

The club itself also occupied a summer residency in Caddebostan, on the Asian side of Istanbul since the early 1950s.[19] When the club's administrative board decided that the summer residency would be bought in the fall of 1976, the dominance of the summer residency increased and the club became further estranged from the Beyoğlu building. Despite this, Koloğlu indicates that the 1977 programme of the building in Beyoğlu was still quite rich. That would change when in 1978 the decision was made to only organize activities in the Beyoğlu building in December.[20] A group within the club wanted to push towards increasing the activities and participation of members at the Beyoğlu building nonetheless. The board in the end decided that the Beyoğlu building was no longer suitable to keep up with the changing desires of the club members. The decisive reason to entirely leave the building, however, seems to have come from external factors. When a fire in the winter of 1983 severely damaged parts of the building and the club refused to pay the rent until the damage was repaired, the owner decided to serve an eviction notice to *Büyük Kulüp*, definitively severing the ties between club and building.[21]

Nights at the movies: The other Cercle d'Orient parcel

Rather than focusing on the *Büyük Kulüp* itself, this chapter will focus on the lively history of the Cercle d'Orient parcel, which stretches far beyond the club's history and imaginary. As will be shown in this chapter, the Cercle d'Orient parcel would acquire a prominent position in the cultural and social memory of Istanbul and Turkey, exceeding that of the history of the former gentleman's club. The building and its surroundings had acquired new meanings, particularly during the second half of the twentieth century. As this corner of the city became both the virtual and actual heart of a local cinema industry, Yeşilçam – named after the street that runs next to the Cercle d'Orient building – the block's identity would be renegotiated; it became a place in the imagining of a new generation during the 1960s and 1970s. In fact the area around Yeşilçam had been the locus of Turkey's film industry since the late nineteenth century. That is noteworthy in a Turkish context since cinema would become a commodity from the 1960s onwards, for women living in cities (the most important group of viewers initially) and middle-class families but also subsequently young male working migrants.[22] Dönmez-Colin argues that the case of Yeşilçam cinema is even more important since cinema did not simply function as a neutral medium in negotiating or contesting various intersectional identities. The process of finding new identities in the complex sociocultural and political landscape of the young republic was also reflected in cinema itself. Turkish cinema struggled to find an identity of its own, mirroring processes in the country of its origin.[23] One of the more interesting studies on Yeşilçam's landscape has been executed by Özlem Öz and Kaya Özkaracalar. They argue that the film industry by the late 1930s had concentrated in Beyoğlu. They add that Istanbul had been the cultural and financial centre of Turkey (and the Ottoman Empire) and present this as the main reason why the concentration of a film industry occurred in Istanbul. Pera/Beyoğlu constituted itself as the quintessential centre for movie screening and production, despite the arrival of cinemas to various parts of the city. Öz and Özkaracalar explain that the reason for this was that in the early days of film screening in the Ottoman Empire, the industry was mostly import-based. The importers came predominantly from the non-Muslim millets and Levantine subjects, with some notable exceptions, whose companies were based in the Pera and Galata quarters. They use the example of a Turkish Muslim entrepreneur who started his film venture in Sirkeci, adjacent to Beyoğlu, but on the other side of the Golden Horn and thus in the former traditional 'Muslim' quarters. He moved his offices to Beyoğlu soon after the establishment of his company, which brings into focus the significance that the area had gained for the film industry by the early 1920s.[24] Kaya Mutlu notes that by that time cinemagoing was still a luxury of the urban elites, limiting its scope. The audience, moreover, would prefer foreign cinema over local productions, as the latter was framed as 'bad taste'.[25] Cinema consumption was thus largely class-based, as the number of cinemas in smaller cities and towns in Anatolia was limited. During the 1950s, however, the impact of cinema on Turkish society at large and that of Istanbul in particular would change significantly.

Kaya Mutlu's work also shows that Beyoğlu had been the quintessential centre of cinema production and screening since its onset. She refers to the memoires of Ekrem Talu, who as a boy witnessed the first public screening of a thirty-minute film in a venue called the Sponeck restaurant or pub in Beyoğlu in 1896 or 1897, across Galatasaray, by the local representative of the Pathé Brothers, Sigmund Weinberg, a Polish Jew of Romanian descent. Talu recounts how people were terrified by the footage of a crashing train, while the room was filled with the smell of the petrol used to drive the projector.[26] Further on Kaya Mutlu refers to an advertisement in the cinema journal *Sinema ve Tiyatro Heveskârı Mecmuası* from 1934 in which Beyoğlu is used as a benchmark of 'urban quality'. The advertisement claims Beyoğlu is 'the location of the most distinguished and cultured families of İstanbul'.[27] An implicit link between cinema as an art form befitting to Beyoğlu as a 'wealthy area' is established.

Öz and Özkaracalar note that most of the major film companies, as well as several minor ones, have their origins in the mid-1940s. These companies set up their offices in the Yeşilçam Sokak, its parallel street Sakızağacı Sokak and the street across on the other side of the İstiklal Caddesi, Alyon Sokak. A number of large cinemas had opened their doors in the vicinity of the Cercle d'Orient parcel since the 1910s. Several older establishments in the parcel's direct surroundings, such as the horse circus *Cirque de Pera*, a variety theatre, the Odeon Theatre as well as several large apartment blocks, contributed to the attractiveness of the area for cinema entrepreneurs, they argue. This resulted in the situation in which, by the 1940s, six cinemas had flanked the Yeşilçam Sokak, most with capacities of over 1,000 seats, making it the de facto centre of Istanbul's cinema screening. By then two of the cinemas were owned by the İpekçi Brothers, who had their offices in the building of one of the cinema halls.[28] This had a clustering effect on the area, attracting more and more entrepreneurs in the movie industry, that gradually became less import-dependent and more oriented towards domestic film production.

Kaya Mutlu argues that the material screened by the cinemas in Beyoğlu and elsewhere in Istanbul and Turkey was dominated by imported movies from Europe and the United States until the end of the 1940s. Until the Second World War forty-three movies were locally produced, which was probably due to the high profit taxes charged by the state. Until 1938 producers would be charged with 32.5 per cent, after which Atatürk reduced the rate to 10 per cent. Due to the demanding years of the war period, this steeped to 75 per cent at the end of the 1940s, while ticket prices were not increased accordingly. In 1948 taxes for screenings of films that were produced in Turkey were decreased to 25 per cent while those for foreign movies were brought back with just 5 per cent to 70 per cent. This development, which went hand in hand with the liberalization of raw film import, facilitated a favourable climate for Turkish cinema production and screening.[29]

Different socio-economic groups started using the building for recreation and employment as cinemas and movie production houses started to cater to the working and middle classes, for whom these movies were an attractive and affordable mode of entertainment. Kaya Mutlu explains that from the 1950s onwards the local cinema industry gained traction as it spread to Anatolia and became a more popular medium for entertainment.[30] She notes, however, that film critics still looked down on local productions, distinguishing 'art' from 'entertainment' and framing the audience of popular Turkish productions as 'passive', 'irresponsible' or 'mindless', essentially imagining a class rift between local low culture and foreign high culture.[31] Whereas Yeşilçam was a popular form of entertainment for women and families at first, producers played into a new market of young men coming to the major cities, particularly Istanbul, in search of jobs. This would fit into a category of films that became particularly popular from the 1970s onwards and fitted a wider trend of so-called *arabesk* culture, previously discussed in Chapter 1. Ayşe Öncü describes the term as a derogatory framing of music that is characterized by contestants by it 'impurity, hybridity and bricolage and designates a special kind of kitsch'.[32] She argues it is a mix of popular Turkish, Western and Egyptian music, disregarding established musical canons and taking hold of large shares of the 1970s cassette market. In broad terms the people enjoying *arabesk* culture were framed as the binary opposites of the 'cosmopolitan', educated and accultured Istanbulite. It is interesting that Öncü notes that the perceived danger of *arabesk* culture was particularly in its hybridity; it did not adhere to existing categories of music or film. Its audience, moreover, lost its rural authenticity and nativity, yet was due to its ignorance also unable to embrace the 'urbanity of cosmopolitan life'.[33] Meanwhile, she argues, in the discourse of Turkey's 1980s (and as we will see later on the 1970s as well) *arabesk* culture's hybridity essentialized the 'purity of Istanbulite's culture and endanger[ed it].[34] Coming back to the context of the Cercle d'Orient, Orhan Koloğlu argues that the increase in popularity of the club building's direct surroundings to a more socio-economically and culturally diverse crowd would around the 1970s in fact be much to the dismay of those belonging to the building's namesake, the Cercle d'Orient, and may also in part explain why the elite club left the building for a different one on the Anatolian side.[35] Despite its separation with the club, the building would be known as the Cercle d'Orient or *Serkldoryan*, until the building's recent renovation by Kamer İnşaat.

The purpose of the Cercle d'Orient buildings has been an ongoing discussion since at least the 1950s. In a short news message from 1 December 1951, the *Cumhuriyet* daily announces that the municipality had decided to sell the building that it had acquired during the 'war years' for one million liras.[36] In a publication of the municipality titled '*Güzelleşen İstanbul*' (Beautifying Istanbul), it is stated that all of the Serkldoryan buildings were bought for a total amount of 1.1 million Turkish liras, while the land estate was acquired for an additional 71,500 Turkish liras. The total plot of land that was acquired comprised 410.350 m², consisting of three adjacent plots, including the Cercle d'Orient building, as well as the Melek (which would later become Emek Cinema), İpek and Sümer cinemas.[37] The Cercle d'Orient building gave access to the club, while the ground floor facing İstiklal Caddesi housed eight stores and gave access to two of the cinemas. On the side street, Yeşilçam Sokak, there was another shop, a printing house, the five-storeyed

Melek and Sümer apartment blocks as well as two houses. The entresol floor was used as a beer brewery and sewing studio. The club used nine salons and an annex building, while the top floor housed two flats.[38] The total revenue from rental agreements is estimated as close to 100,000 Turkish liras annually. It seems possible that the municipality acquired the block from the previous owners, who are in news items indicated as H. Arditi and Saltiel, during the 1942 Wealth Tax (*Varlık Vergisi*) campaign which particularly targeted the properties of Turkey's non-Muslim communities.

After these tumultuous years another episode in the building's history as a contested place begins. It is important to note that the struggle over this particular place from the 1990s onwards should be considered in the light of contested beginnings as well. The very name of the cinema, Emek Cinema, carries a troubled history that reflects local and national policies geared towards changing the sociocultural profile of the area, city and nation. After acquiring the block, the *Cumhuriyet* daily announces that the municipality had unsuccessfully tried to evict the tenants from the building. The newspaper on 7 December 1951 reported that the municipal council, moreover, blocked the decision to sell the building. On 6 January 1957, the *Milliyet* daily reported that the building block was finally sold off to *Emekli Sandığı* (Pension Fund), the only participant in the public bidding, for 16.5 million liras, despite the municipality's aim to sell it for at least 25 million liras.[39] In accordance with their newly acquired ownership, the *Emekli Sandığı* decided that the biggest of the cinemas in the block, the Melek Cinema should from then onwards be known as Emek Cinema, setting the scene for an 'urban legend'. The problematic acquisition of the Cercle d'Orient parcel thus entered a new phase, turning hands from the local government to a national governmental institution. The name change from Melek Cinema to Emek Cinema may also be interpreted as an attempt to turn to another page in its history.

It is unclear whether exploitation until the 1960s was successful, but the fact that a change of hands was discussed at length in national newspapers in 1968 is significant. On 17 September 1968 the *Cumhuriyet* reports that the Emek Cinema will be turned into a variety theatre by director and scenarist Turgut Demirağ, who according to the newspaper had previously rented the Rüya Cinema, next to the Cercle d'Orient building. The Emek Cinema building was planned to be used for film screenings during daytime and operettas, musicals, variety theatre and concerts of foreign artists in the evening.[40] The repertoire does not yet appear to cater to an audience of working-class men, so strongly associated with the area in the 1970s. An investment of 100,000 Turkish Lira was made by Demirağ to make the necessary changes to the building. Less than two months later, on 4 November 1968, an announcement is made for the opening of the cinema season of the year 1968–9 in 'Istanbul's most luxurious cinema'. The movie *Dear Brigitte* (*Tatlı Hayal* in Turkish) is announced, featuring Brigitte Bardot and James Stewart, and will be screened in colour five times a day.[41] According to the advertisement, the operators of the cinema appear to pride themselves in being able to screen movies from MGM, Fox, Paramount, Walt Disney as well as the most popular European films. Apart from notes on the prospective screenings, the advertisement announces that visitors will also be able to watch international revue shows on a new stage of twenty-five meters.[42] Atilla Dorsay recounts that Yeşilçam Sokak had not witnessed such a crowd in years and tickets had to be booked days or even weeks in advance. For the first time 70 mm and six-channel audio was used in Turkey.[43]

The cinema on the same block, Rüya Cinema was also owned by *Emekli Sandığı* and had for a short period been known as *Küçük Emek*, until its name was reversed to Rüya again after 1963. This cinema acquired a particular reputation after it started screening adult movies from the mid-1970s onwards. Dorsay states that most of the material shown in the cinema was local production, shot in the backstreets of Yeşilçam. According to him it would never be the same again from those years onwards, leading it 'as an unavoidable development' into becoming a meeting place for gay men.[44] It seems thus that by the mid-1970s the area around the Cercle d'Orient had at least in part turned from an elite space for social gatherings and entertainment into a refuge for those who were forced to live their sexual identity, quite literally, in the dark.

Cinema production in Turkey had by then already reached its extraordinary peak, with film production tripling between the early 1960s and the early 1970s to approximately 300 movies a year.[45] By 1962 the number of people working in Yeşilçam – as the industry and thus the street with its direct surroundings – had come to 1,185. Yeşilçam appears to have created a transgression between reality and fiction, with the place and the people that acquired a sense of belonging from it, from everyday life into fiction and vice versa. The audiences that the bulk of the cinema production catered to identified with the protagonists in the stories. Another example noted by Kaya Mutlu is that in films and magazines people all over Turkey were able to witness the dynamic life associated with Yeşilçam and thus Beyoğlu, further establishing the ties between the place in the movies and in reality throughout Turkey. Additionally, she argues that the exceptional popularity of Yeşilçam cinema was expressed through the desire of audiences in letters published in cinema journals to have their favourite stars cross from other artistic industries to Yeşilçam.[46]

The number of movie theatres in Turkey meanwhile had increased from 170 in 1960 to 281 in 1966, with visitor numbers increasing from 25,161,000 in 1960 to 41,606,506 in 1965 (no data was available for 1966).[47] Since the coup of 1960 and the relatively liberal constitution that was instated consequentially in 1961, the film industry had flourished in what was probably the most liberal political climate ever witnessed until then in the Turkish Republic.[48] Erik-Jan Zürcher indicates that it was mostly liberal in the sense that it gave greater freedom to the political left and right and, towards 1970, Islamism.[49] Savaş Arslan argues that the Yeşilçam industry moved in consonance with the political developments of the time, even 'echoing the hegemonic power relations of the state, filmmakers, and its audience'.[50] As indicated in the first part of the book, these years were marked by mass migration to Turkey's urban centres, particularly Istanbul.[51] Arslan states that this led to cinema going to become one of the most prominent modes of family entertainment.[52] The spatial node of these vibrant years in Turkey's cinema production was the area around Yeşilçam Sokak, bringing a considerable and crucial part of Turkey's popular cultural production to Beyoğlu. In sync with the sociopolitical developments of the 1960s, Kaya Mutlu indicates that the 1960s would become the 'golden age' of theorizing and thinking on Turkish cinema. Terminology aiming to define or perhaps also claim certain branches of cinema, such as people's cinema (*halk sineması*), social realism (*toplumsal gerçekçilik*), national cinema (*ulusal sinema*) and revolutionary cinema (*devrimci sinema*), emanated from this period in which Turkish politics and Turkish civil society was reinventing itself.[53]

The direction of cinema was also determined to some extent by tough censorship in Turkey. Dönmez-Colin argues that most cinema production during the golden years of Yeşilçam would evade sensitive issues.[54] Since 1939 censorship laws had been in order, executed by a censorship board under the auspices of the Ministry of Interior. Dilek Kaya Mutlu and Zeynep Koçer indicate that until 1932 movies were screened to two police officers who would report to city governors. They would subsequently have the authority to censor movies, until film censorship was centralized in 1932. The 1939 Regulations on the Control of Films and Film Screenplays were inspired by Fascist Italy's *Codice di censura* according to Gönül Dönmez-Colin, while Mutlu and Koçer remark that it was inspired by the 1934 Police Duty and Authorization Law. This law would be sustained practically unchanged until 1977. Mutlu and Koçer indicate that the Commission's approval was based on ten criteria, ironically referred to as Turkey's 'Ten Commandments' of film censorship. They rightfully argue that these motivations are not only nationalist (and militaristic) but also vague to such a degree that virtually any movie could be banned based on this.[55] Motivations for banning films or scenes reveal a state in deep conflict, excruciatingly paranoid about anything that might reflect remotely negative on its reputation or incite undesirable criticism. Dönmez-Colin refers to the example of Metin Erksan's film *Aşık Veysel'in Hayatı* (1953) about the life of the famous minstrel and poet Veysel. Scenes showing crops in the minstrel's hometown were banned for showing crops in Anatolia undersized. Considering the harsh repression during Adnan Menderes's governments and his Democrat Party' populist efforts to acquire a voter base among the Anatolian rural population such a move does not seem surprising.[56] Another instance that she quotes is Erksan's *Susuz Yaz* (1963), which was awarded with the Golden Bear at the Berlin Film Festival. A scene in which a woman marries the brother of her dead husband was banned since the authorities were worried this would negatively reflect on Turkey's image abroad.[57] Though somewhat speculative, in light of Turkey's efforts to become further integrated in 'the West' – with the 1963 Association Agreement (Ankara Agreement) with the European Economic Community as an obvious benchmark – it once again seems logical that the Turkish state would make efforts to control its desired image to populations abroad, particularly in the context of a high-profile cultural platform.

Mutlu and Koçer show that the reality of the censoring deviated from the commission's 'Ten Commandments', since it was impossible for them to make sure that the copy that would be screened to representatives of the committee was the same as the one that would be screened. They refer to a quote by a representative of the commission in the 1960s, Feriha Sanerk, who features in the 1993 documentary *Siyah Perde: Türk Sinemasında Sansürün Tarihi (The Black Curtain: the History of Censorship in Turkish cinema)* by Behiç Ak:

> I knew that my work was in vain. I did my job but it was rather a joke. They [filmmakers] were adding scenes later, so you were unable to control them. They were omitting some scenes before submitting. So you do not see those scenes and you cannot cut something you cannot see . . . Therefore, in my view, it [censorship] was totally unnecessary.[58]

The greater ideological freedom of the 1961 constitution in combination with a paranoid, but also ineffective censorship, would encourage producers and directors to experiment with social realism. Dönmez-Colin points out that in this period film-makers experimented from both a thematic and cinematographic point of view: through Marxism and cultural avant-gardism. The experiments between 1960 and 1965, were, however, met with financial constraints and a return to harsh censorship. So harsh in fact that it led Yılmaz Güney, the most prominent director in Turkish social realism, to compare it to the persecutions by Senator Joseph McCarthy in the United States, a decade before. The smallest detail could lead the authorities to define it as inciting separatism and banning the production altogether.[59]

Dönmez-Colin describes the Yeşilçam genre nonetheless as one dominated by Hollywood-like heterosexual relationship narratives, conflict between good and bad and issues of tradition versus modernity.[60] She argues that the attitude towards the 'West' was ambivalent: an object of desire and corruption at the same time embodied. She goes on to explain that the audience identified with the melodrama of the movies, in part explaining their popularity and the reason why so many productions revolved around more or less the same narrative of a young (male) protagonist who heads for the city. This inclination towards melodrama coincided or perhaps culminated in the previously discussed *arabesk* genre. Emanating from the music industry, *arabesk* in this context propagates a deep nostalgia for the hometown in Anatolia and the impossibility to return. Several successful musicians in the genre, such as Orhan Gencebay and İbrahim Tatlıses, along with many of their less fortunate peers, started to appear on the film screen. Whether or not identification explains the full picture of this booming film industry is questionable, as will be explained further on.

The reality of the industry shows that the quality of the product in terms of its cinematography, screenplay and acting was largely subordinate to the potential profit that the movie could make. Arslan explains that many Yeşilçam films were used with handhelds cameras, without making use of any of the technological innovations. Innovations that became commonplace, like zoom on cameras, was often used in an amateurish fashion. Actors often did not receive formal education, as the examples previously cited also indicate, and were required to bring props and costumes themselves. Most interesting in terms of the places of Yeşilçam is that there were hardly any studios. Production companies rather rented houses from the upper classes in and around Istanbul or would use actual sites instead.[61] The genres of Yeşilçam were highly diverse, from comedy to melodrama, action, 'spaghetti (or kebab) Westerns' to horror and pornography. With reference to spaghetti westerns and other 'genre films' in Italy, Christopher Wagstaff makes an interesting observation that may in fact be fitting to that of much of the Yeşilçam production and reception as well. These movies specialized in providing so-called 'quantitative gratifications', for instance, a lot of shoot-outs or splatter. Wagstaff compares it to Coca Cola: it will not nourish you, but you do want to consume more.[62] Wagstaff posits this against the idea that movies should resonate with the 'needs' of 'the people' for the movies to be profitable, that is, the audience needs to be able identify ideologically with some of the characters to become popular. He argues that this in fact conflates the concerns and the gratifications of the people: one can enjoy a blockbuster without their private concerns being addressed.[63] Given the steep increase in Yeşilçam production it seems unlikely that addressing private and ideological concerns was a genuine motivation for most producers. This lets us reconsider the argument posed by Dönmez-Colin regarding the cinematic trope of the young male from the countryside who moves to the city. Was it solely the young men's nostalgia for their hometowns that drove them to the cinemas, or rather a mixture of nostalgia and an urge to be entertained and to be able to forget?

Though identification with protagonists may have been one reason to explain the success of the film, it would seem that Wagstaff's more mundane explanation for the success of Italian genre cinema is convincing in the context of Yeşilçam as well. Another indicator of this is that audiences would have an impact on the appearance of particular individuals on the screen. For the artists that had already built a reputation for themselves the film industry may have been a lucrative source of income or of advertisement at least. People like Gencebay and Tatlıses were able to make their fortune in music and, to a lesser extent, film industry, yet many young men and women faced a tougher reality in the Beyoğlu *gazinolar* (nightclubs) and bars. Asu Aksoy and Kevin Robins tell the story of Adil Tekirdağ, who used the stage name Adil Tokses during his years as a musician in the Beyoğlu nightlife in the short documentary *Improvised City: Adil Kebap Dürüm*, which was part of an exhibition during 2012's Istanbul Design Biennial.[64] Adil, a native of South-eastern Turkey's city of Urfa, came to Istanbul as a young man around the 1970s to pursue his dream of becoming a professional musician. He settled on the southwestern slope of Beyoğlu, in the old working-class district of Kasımpaşa, where he worked in a restaurant and took singing and saz lessons. He claims to know between 1,500 and 2,000 songs, calling Beyoğlu his 'world conservatory', where he catered to the customers from all corners of Turkey, playing the songs and local styles they would request. Sustaining himself and his family later on with music and a small kebap shack, he quite possibly exemplifies the tough life of many young men and women in the Beyoğlu nightlife of the 1970s and 1980s. He explains:

Nowadays it is hard to earn bread from music. In early days there was no television, so you have to personally go to see the performer. (. . .) After the

TV stations were opened and cinemas were closed. The nightclub scene ended. (. . .) So I have many friends in this business. They all suffered a lot from this business like I did. We were being dragged around between restaurants and night clubs. Couldn't play at upscale locations. I was being sent to film sets as a guest artist, but they used me as an extra on sets. I realized I was an extra.[65]

Having jobs in the nightlife of Beyoğlu was quite common for artists featuring in the Yeşilçam movies. An article from November 1972 in the *Milliyet* daily discusses how, following the opening of the new nightclub or *gazino* season, an ever larger amount of names of Yeşilçam stars was featuring in the neonlights.[66] The *Milliyet* indicates that this is a trend despite some *gazino* owners' claims that there would be no place anymore for movie artists in their *gazino*.[67] The relationship between Beyoğlu's nightlife and cinema, significant because they reinforced both its reputation as a centre of escapism and a centre of production of cinematic escapism, thus appears to be an inevitable one, though there are some signals of a certain unease with this relationship. In contrast to the apparent reluctance of some *gazino* owners indicated in the *Milliyet* article, Dilek Kaya Mutlu indicates that in the years preceding film producers had preferred hiring girls who had no experience in the nightlife sector. She quotes an article from the *Perde ve Sahne* magazine in which film-makers lament about their difficulties in finding female actresses. They indicate that the profession has a bad image because of the large number of 'pub women' (*bar kadını*) and belly dancers working as actresses.[68] An announcement in *Perde ve Sahne* from 1954 therefore explicitly asks for the following: 'a family-girl type of lady of 1,65 m tall, with a symmetrical body, pretty face, sufficiently acculturated, between the age of 22 and 26, with no working experience in places like public nightclubs or bars is sought'.[69]

A discursive dichotomy of moralities determined by spaces – in this case more particular space of occupation – stretches beyond the borders of film-making into its narratives. Dönmez-Colin makes an interesting remark with regard to the establishment of place in cinema that makes up the spatial binary of the 'typical Yeşilçam movie'. In it we find a 'here': the poor (but honest) environment of the countryside, the cradle of the protagonist. 'There' is Beyoğlu: 'the cradle of evil, home to the degenerate with slippery values, a trap for innocent country boys (and naïve young women without male protection'.[70] A recurring stereotype about the area as a place of moral deprivation is reproduced in Yeşilçam, somewhat contrasting, however, with the more 'positive' and recurring stereotype of Beyoğlu as the place to be in Istanbul and Turkey.

Despite the rosiness of many of the productions, driven by commercial, rather than artistic, motives, Dönmez-Colin's remark and the fierce censorship, it is peculiar to see that a considerable amount of productions focused on the issue of class discrepancies. This leads to a rather different interpretation of the Yeşilçam industry by one of the crucial names in Turkish cinema production, the director Yılmaz Güney (1937–84). He argued that all of the productions in the Yeşilçam genre are essentially about the struggle of classes. Such an interpretation seems much inspired by Marxist sympathies that were also particularly en vogue among the left wing of the ideological spectrum in Turkey. Yılmaz Güney himself is considered to be one of the frontmen of Turkish 'revolutionary cinema' and had been imprisoned for his work and ideas.

The credits of more than 100 movies hold Güney's name, a large portion of which was censored by the authorities. The director-cum-actor was crowned the *çirkin kral* (ugly king) by the audiences who struggled to recognize themselves as working migrants from Anatolia in the characters played by Göksel Arsoy, the handsome blond and blue-eyed actor who was often casted as the archetypal hero or Ayhan Işık.[71] The movies of the short-lived social realist movement in the early 1960s paved the way for Güney's movies that communicated political messages and put social issues at the forefront, in contrast with the bulk of contemporary commercial Yeşilçam productions.[72] He was imprisoned twice; the first time on charges for assisting a leftist organization and the second time for killing a prosecutor. He managed to escape from prison and died in exile in Paris. Arslan argues that Güney was exceptional in Yeşilçam since he managed to bind both female and male audiences to his movies. He – as actor, or director and screenwriter (or all at the same time) – struggled against the system in his movies as an anti-hero, with righteous or bad strategies. Arslan concludes that Güney instrumentalized reality and fiction to reflect on the desire of the audience. He quotes a brothel worker stating: 'His best film is *Baba* (Father, 1971). In that film, he cleanses (*kırklamak*) his daughter and saves her from prostitution. We all wait for someone to cleanse us.'[73] To a certain degree this particular representation also shows how different ideologies struggled with the squalor of society, a very significant part of Beyoğlu's representation.

Through the work of Güney and others before and after him, the block's fame would spread all over Turkey. Yet reflections on Yeşilçam as an 'actual place' on the map of Beyoğlu, beyond its reputation in cinema production are scarce. The actor Ahmet Mekin describes Yeşilçam Sokak, adjacent to the Cercle d'Orient parcel, in a very colourful way, indicating the discursive importance invested into this particular space in Beyoğlu:

The people of our street (. . .) do not live on their own street (. . .) the mornings are wild on our street. Yelling, shouting, conversations, and excitement . . . Cars, cameras, projectors stand in front of the offices of producers, and boxes and boxes of raw film are carried about. Stuntmen (. . .) snack on whatever they can find (. . .) Directors, reviewing their work plans for the day, determine the cast of players. At such moments there is nothing to say to the anxiety or the annoyance of the producers if one of the main players has not been seen yet (. . .) this is the cacophony just about every day on our street. No doubt one day, we will have big studios and a housing complex setup for the artists around it. And in this manner OUR STREET will become history. Even if this is a *hayal*, I like it.[74]

Mekin's narration of the street gives an insight in the vibrance of the street and area. It also communicates what this place is, both in fiction and in reality. It is exciting, lively, the place to be for anyone who wants to feature in a Turkish movie or wants to be part of this very particular place in Turkey: Yeşilçam as the cultural signpost for Beyoğlu, with Beyoğlu itself signifying Istanbul's position as the beating heart of Turkey's culture and economy.

A new dynamic in the continuously changing profile of the surrounding area becomes clear in a 1976 article from the movie critic Atilla Dorsay in *Cumhuriyet*.[75] Here, Dorsay complains how Istanbul's cinemas are being transformed into shops and passages. He in fact opens with the sentence that there has been talk for years about closing Emek Cinema and turning it into a passage. He states that the trend in Istanbul is to close art galleries, concert halls, cinemas and theatres, replacing them with shops and passages in order to gain higher rents.[76] In addition he states that books, movies, stage plays, *tuluat* theatre (improvisational theatre), ideas, thoughts, modernity and patriotism have been forbidden. What is left is only 'the worst of the worst, the most banal of the banal, the most disgusting of the disgusting, promoted under a guise of "film" or cinema'.[77] This remark is interesting as it echoes similar notions of what Beyoğlu should or should not be as a place of social gathering and cultural capital in comparison to those described by Kaya Mutlu in advertisements from the 1930s. The connection he establishes between cultural production and notions of modernity and patriotism – highly charged terminology in the context of the tumultuous Turkish 1970s – makes an implicit judgement about the 'newcomers', retailers and consumers, of Beyoğlu as well. Dorsay appears to be demarcating in this article the boundaries of what not only cinema, or arts and culture in broad terms, but also Beyoğlu, should be defined by.

Arslan notes that during what he defines as the 'late Yeşilçam era', that is, the late 1970s and early 1980s, cinema started to lose ground to television as more families were able to buy TV sets. Nijat Özön states that while the grand total of ticket sales in 1970 was 250 million, with sold number of TV sets at 30,000, these numbers contrast sharply with 1984, when the numbers are 56 million and 7 million respectively.[78] In consonance with the comments of Dorsay in the 1980s, Arslan points out that one of the direct effects was that cinemas in the city centre (so first and foremost Beyoğlu and its direct surroundings) were closed down or transformed into small shopping malls, meaning the passages that Dorsay talks about disgruntledly. He also argues that the decrease of families going to the movies after 1975 causes a shift of producers towards their new core audience, an urban male one. As a result Dorsay's 'banal of the banal' – action and sex – became the new mainstay in Yeşilçam's production pattern. Cinemas saw their visitor rates declining nonetheless, though the Yeşilçam industry managed to persevere through the introduction of videotapes.[79] One of the most crucial remarks of Arslan is the high regard of Yeşilçam movies and, more importantly, the nostalgia with which it is conceived: it allegedly represents a Turkish cinema industry not affected by the global economy, pure, naïve and innocent. Yet Arslan rightly criticizes this narrative, since these years, particularly the 1970s, were marked by political violence, major socio-economic change and the increasing visibility of urban labour migration on Istanbul's urban landscape.[80]

It is also important to stress once more in this context that, as shown also by Dorsay's article, these are the years in which Beyoğlu's sociocultural shifts are becoming most sharply noticeable and represented, contrasting the idea of a naïve and innocent Turkey, Istanbul, Beyoğlu or cinema industry.[81] With the eventual demise of the Yeşilçam industry, cinema production would leave the area for new studios in the newly developing business centres of the cities, though in fact one of the main players in the television production, the state channel TRT, would stay in Beyoğlu and invest in setting up its headquarters in Tepebaşı, only a few blocks away from Mekin and others' vibrant spatial centre point for their careers, lives and imagination.[82] Despite Dorsay's remarks it appears that Emek Cinema screened a diverse programme and also participated in film festivals, together with institutes such as the new Atatürk Cultural Centre at Taksim Square during the late 1970s and early 1980s, putting his representation of the vulgarization of Beyoğlu's cinematic culture into perspective.

Struggling for the right to cultural memory and informality

The Cercle d'Orient's main building meanwhile witnessed a different trajectory. A major fire had made parts of the floors used by the club practically unusable and in an article in *Cumhuriyet* from 13 November 1983 Yalçin Pekşen states that the Cercle d'Orient building had become a storage facility for a clothing brand.[83] The ground floors, however, were still used by shops, entrance to cinemas and the İnci Patisserie. The first floors were in use by the SESAM cinema owner's association by the 1990s, while the parts damaged by fire (of *Büyük Kulüp* and İpek Cinema) were still empty due to fire damage.[84] A first proposal of the *Emekli Sandığı* states that the building of the comedy theatre on Yeşilçam Sokak had been severely damaged and that a project including a new passage and business centre was suggested which would conserve the façade.[85]

Another occupant of the building was also faced with *Emekli Sandığı*'s discontent about its properties' revenues. Salim Alpaslan for *Cumhuriyet* daily reported on 29 March 1980 (page 7) that the State Gallery for the Fine Arts, Turkey's biggest art centre, opened only five years before on 1 March 1975, risked closure. The owner, *Emekli Sandığı*, had filed a lawsuit following an increase in the rent charged to the gallery. In the article it is stated that *Emekli Sandığı* had set up a company called the *Emek Turistik Tesisleri İşletme Ltd. Şir.* (Emek Touristic Establishments Operating Company Ltd.) to control the real estate properties of the *Emekli Sandığı*. The gallery had for a longer time struggled to pay its rent and deal with the rent increase. The chamber of accounts of the Ministry of Culture – the institute controlling the gallery – had argued that the rent might rise with 20 per cent. On top of that the *Emekli Sandığı* took the gallery to court demanding the evacuation of the gallery before June. The Ministry of Culture claimed that a favourable solution would be found for the issue. If the decision was taken, however, the author concludes, Istanbul would be without a state gallery for several months as a new location would be prepared.[86] In the *Cumhuriyet* issue of 17 June 1985, an advertisement for a painting contest for youngsters is announced in the gallery, with the address stated as İstiklal Caddesi 122/A. On 18 February 1990, however, the address is stated as İstiklal Caddesi 209/49, with the remark that the gallery is located above the Atlas cinema. Granted that street numbers on İstiklal Caddesi have changed various times, it seems assumable that the gallery moved from its old premises in the second half of the 1980s to its most recent location above Atlas Pasajı.[87] Until its recent renovation the property reserved by the gallery would be used by SESAM, the cooperative of cinema owners, with the tympanum occupied by the cooperative rather than the gallery's name.

As early as the 1970s, files from the TMMOB archives show that the Council for Historical Real Estate and Monuments had in a decision from 13 June 1971 demanded that practically all buildings on both sides of the axis between Tünel and Taksim – being İstiklal Caddesi – be subject to protection and conservation. A halt was thus made to any prospective changes. This decision was further solidified on 14 July 1978 when the Council decided that the entire area – as well as other historical areas in Istanbul – should be subject to protection and conservation legislation. The ultimate purpose of the council was to pave the way for reinvigorating the Beyoğlu area and turn it into an area for tourism.[88] The Ministry of Culture and Tourism's Tourism Bank proposed the Beyoğlu-Galata Tourism Development Project. The TMMOB, however, noted in a publication from the late 1980s titled '*Beyoğlu nasıl kurtulur?*' (how to save Beyoğlu?) that rather than adhering to these plans municipalities decide to start destroying historical properties illegally.[89] It should be noted that the decision by the Council was made around the same time when one of the most intrusive interventions in the İstiklal Caddesi's urban landscape was made, namely the construction of the Odakule office building. The intervention that would result in public outrage was, however, the destruction of major parts of the Tarlabaşı neighbourhood in order to construct a motorway in the mid-1980s. Although conservation and protection legislation was applied from a legalistic point of view, it seems that the Council lacked at least the financial and legal means to effectively enforce legislation in a uniform manner. It seems likely that influential stakeholders, such as municipal governments, moreover held a particularly strong sway over the direction the protection and conservation of the urban landscape would take, even more so after the restructuring of Istanbul's administrative governance structure in 1984.

This would start to have a notable effect on the Cercle d'Orient parcel when the *Emekli Sandığı* decided in 1993 to grant a concession for twenty-five years to a businessman, Kamer Tosun, and his construction firm Kamer İnşaat. Plans to turn the group of buildings into a hotel, business, entertainment and art centre had been forwarded for approval already in April 1991 by Süzer Holding, who would have been a prospective candidate for a '*Yap-İşlet-Devret*' (Build, operate, transfer) construction that was eventually granted to Kamer İnşaat. Soon after the concession was granted to Kamer İnşaat a group which feared closure of the cinema started a petition titled 'Let Emek Cinema exist' (Emek Sineması yaşatılsın). The group was fronted by the İKSV (İstanbul Kültür ve Sanat Vakfı – Istanbul Foundation for Culture and Arts) festival director Hülya Uçar. The petition was started on the same date as the thirteenth International Istanbul Film Festival, organized by İKSV, and managed to collect thousands of signatures during the first days of the campaign.[90] It would be one of the first steps in a long-lasting stalemate between the owner, the prospective developer, local government and civil society organizations.

The documents of the TMMOB show that various actors start to actively claim a position in the process of place-making. In a letter by three architects associated with the TMMOB from 17 January 1995, it is indicated that the buildings' future should not be only up to *Emekli Sandığı* to decide on as the Cercle d'Orient buildings are not only in a decent state from the perspective of engineering, but also since these buildings are among the most crucial symbols of nineteenth-century Istanbul.[91] It should be noted that no mention is made of the significance of more recent episodes in the history of the Cercle d'Orient parcel as a place of social and cultural gathering, distinguishing it from other activist representations of the block's significance, particularly in recent years with initiatives such as *Emek Bizim İstanbul Bizim* (Emek is Ours, Istanbul is Ours).[92] It moreover displays a quite limited interpretation of what these buildings (should) signify, namely a symbol of late-nineteenth-century vernacularized neoclassicism rather than a place with a rich sociocultural history. In a sense this is also the way the restoration of the Cercle d'Orient's main building was approached in the 2010s, as a placeless shell that ought to be restored with an obsession for authenticity. Istanbul's First Council for the Preservation of Natural and Cultural Objects decided that a report and layout sheet should be prepared to assess the state of the building. One of Kamer İnşaat's owners, Veysel Tosun, stated about the same time in 1995 that 'there are six architects taking measurements in the building. (. . .) After this, we will apply to the Council for Monuments and bring the project into operation. Everyone is going to thank us when this project is finished. We are changing Beyoğlu's appearance. Of course we are making profit from this project. No-one can execute a project like this for nothing, but we will definitely not touch the historical construction.'[93] Again, there is no mention whatsoever of the past and present users of the building and the remark simply ignores, wittingly or unwittingly, the position this particular place holds in the social memory of many Istanbulites and Turkey's citizens. The plans at the time, however, indicate that the plot was supposed to house a three-floored parking space, three theatre spaces, fifty-two meeting rooms, four exhibition halls, 200 stores and offices for a total price of 112 billion Turkish liras, with a total monthly rent revenue of 330 million Turkish liras (the Turkish lira to US dollar exchange rates were extremely volatile at the time, nearly doubling from 38,687 TL to $1 on 30 December 1994 to 59,501 TL to $1 on 29 December 1995).[94] It therefore seemed inevitable that the construction firm would severely damage the historical properties.[95] The first steps towards the process of spatial cleansing that had been successfully executed in the 2010s were thus already prepared in the early 1990s.

The fact that any future changes or projects in or around these buildings were subject to the approval of the Council for the Preservation of Natural and Cultural Objects, together with lawsuits opened by the TMMOB, hindered further steps by Kamer İnşaat. That changed, however, when in 2005 a notorious new law on urban renewal passed through the Turkish Parliament. This 'Law on the Protection of

Deteriorated Historic and Cultural Heritage through Renewal and Re-use' is most well known by its number, 5366. As İclal Dinçer, Zeynep Enlil and Tolga İslam argue the law grants extensive powers to local municipalities. From 2005 onwards local municipalities can declare any given site, regardless of its protection status, as a space for urban renewal.[96] In the case of historical sites this can be done based on the criterium specified in the law as 'protection of deteriorated historic and cultural heritage through renewal'.[97] The law thus does not specify this as renovation but rather as renewal. For projects to be granted a green light, however, several actors have to grant their accord. It is interesting in that context that the Council for the Preservation of Natural and Cultural Objects is basically sidelined in this process. Moreover, the political climate in Turkey since the early 2000s, dominated by the Justice and Development Party (*Adalet ve Kalkınma Partisi* – AKP), has effectively annulled the 'obstacle' of oppositional forces.

The parcel on which the Cercle d'Orient buildings were situated subsequently were designated as an urban renewal area in 2006. Despite an ongoing lawsuit opened by TMMOB in 2010 which obstructed any kind of work on the buildings on the Cercle d'Orient parcel, public outcry and several attempts to mobilize to protest the destruction of the buildings, Kamer İnşaat started the destruction of Emek Cinema and the surrounding buildings on the parcel in 2013. Contrary to its previous decisions, the Council for the Preservation of Natural and Cultural Objects had agreed with the project proposal already approved by the Council for Renewal. Possibly due to the fact that the destruction of Emek Cinema, more than other buildings on the parcel, had been the subject of public outcry, the Beyoğlu municipality and Kamer İnşaat presented the destruction of the cinema as a renovation. Elements from the old cinema hall were allegedly taken from the old building, restored and placed in an entirely new space in the shopping mall that had been erected on the parcel. The Beyoğlu municipality, fronted by Mayor Ahmet Misbah Demircan himself, took great pride in this 'restored' facility and the 'new' Emek Cinema has since then regularly been used for public events sponsored by the Beyoğlu Municipality as well.[98] The only remaining building on the parcel is the Cercle d'Orient building itself, well restored, though its function in public space has been effectively marginalized to the role of a – securitized – entrance of a shopping mall.

The recent history of the Cercle d'Orient parcel gives insight into the evolution in time of Istanbul's debate on public space in a location that features prominently in cultural and social memory through Beyoğlu's exceptionally rich history in Ottoman and Turkish movie production and screening. More than anything it reveals on a micro level how the city has been remade by government policies inspired by Turkish nationalism and later by increasing exposure to economic liberalization. Although the starting points may differ, the outcomes are in fact surprisingly similar as has been demonstrated in this chapter. The successive transfers of ownership in the case of the Cercle d'Orient building show that in all cases little to no attention was attributed to the – judicial and arguably moral – rights and needs of tenants and users of the buildings. From the transfer of a private party to the municipality in 1942, from the municipality to the *Emekli*

Sandığı to the concession granted by *Emekli Sandığı* to Kamer İnşaat: the first priority of the owners and concessionaries has been maximizing profit. The preservation of the site's complex historical legacy does not appear to be a concern of the various stakeholders, and, if it does, then only after consistent public pressure as demonstrated by the 'restoration' of Emek Cinema. The rich history of movie production described in this chapter was based here for nearly a century, yet – except for a few small cinemas – virtually nothing is left which can possibly serve as a reminder of this important marker in Turkey's, Istanbul's and Beyoğlu's history. The 5366 legislation has indeed granted local authorities with executive power that they could have only imagined just ten years before, but historically one might argue that there is an apparent urge to gain something from Beyoğlu or the Cercle d'Orient which seems stronger than the urge to enable citizens or conserve cultural heritage for the sake of it. The quote from Veysel Toşun, manager of Kamer İnşaat is telling in that context: 'no-one is going to do anything for nothing.' The case of the Cercle d'Orient also shows that the municipality as well as conservation authorities, due to their reluctance or inability to act until at least the 1990s as well as their eagerness to act after 2005, have historically had little interest in making efforts to preserve a unique part of the city's heritage. This has led to a situation in which Beyoğlu's tangible and intangible heritage is left to the grace of its speculative value and the potential interest of business corporations. This is particularly problematic since this block holds such a prominent position in the cultural and social memory of those who grew up with Yeşilçam cinema, in Turkey and beyond.

Chapter 4

GALATASARAY/GALATASARAY LISESI

TURKISHNESS *ALAFRANGA*

The *Lycée de Galatasaray* or *Galatasaray Lisesi* (Galatasaray High School) is situated right in the middle of the İstiklal Caddesi, where the street's pedestrian circulation takes a pause, making a slight turn en route from Taksim Square to the Galata neighbourhood. The early-twentieth-century neoclassicist building is largely hidden from the view of passers-by due to the imposing school gates, fences and tall trees in its front garden, making it one of the few – secluded – green spaces in the district. The Francophone school prides itself on its long history and reputation, currently holding 711 students with a teacher cadre of 68.[1] The former high school building at the Bosporus in Ortaköy has, since its foundation in 1992, housed the Galatasaray University. Similar to the high school, however, the historical description of the university makes claim to the earliest known history of tradition in the location of Galatasaray, claiming the historical ties of the high school with its Ottoman predecessor and even the Ottoman fifteenth-century palace school. The university is part of the Galatasaray Education and Training Institution (*Galatasaray Eğitim Öğretim Kurumu*) which consists of the Galatasaray Primary School, the Galatasaray High School and Galatasaray University.[2] The initiative to set up a university came in 1992 from a number of Galatasaray High School graduates, and the institution was founded as a French-Turkish University, with a French vice-rector and Turkish rector. Through the Galatasaray Education and Training Institution the primary school and high school adhere to the university's rectorate. The objective of the foundation was to establish an integrated line of education from primary to higher education.[3] With that idea in mind, the primary school was established in 1993 and currently resides in Şişli. Middle school-level teaching also takes place within the high school's premises.[4]

The focus of this chapter will be on the high school and its building in Beyoğlu, the roots of which lie in the second half of the nineteenth century, though claims to a longer history hold some value, if only for the etymology of the high school's name. As an effect of the *Tanzimat* reforms in the Ottoman Empire, the state's educational apparatus was subjected to an extensive metamorphosis. Carther Findley points out that the major focal points of the *Tanzimat* reforms were legislation, education, elite formation, expansion of government, intercommunal relations and the transformation of the political process. These focal points are interconnected and though Findley is right to argue that legislation was the reform movement's main instrument – with the introduction of the Gülhane decree of 1839, the reform decree of 1856 and the 1876 constitution, as well as integrating codes based on French models and religious (Islamic) legislation – the bases for the new Ottoman state were built in the new academies and colleges. Although earlier attempts at educational modernization had been made, the reforms of the *Tanzimat* resulted in the need for unprecedented changes in the educational system. These proceeded beyond the previously established engineering, medical and military schools aiming to bring the Ottoman Empire up to speed with its European counterparts. Zürcher argues that the *Tanzimat* also included a secularization campaign which had a major impact on the Ottoman judicial system. In 1839 Sultan Mahmud II decided to found secular schools, the *rüşdiye*, which aimed to link the traditional Quran-school, or *mektep*, to professional schools and vocational training.

It seems valid to argue that secularization posed a crucial reform of the Ottoman state's educational system. Further nuance is provided by Findley's agreement on the fact that it was in education that the loss of influence of the religious elite was most noticeable and Zürcher's indication that the goals of the reformists were utilitarian, reflected by the absence of a university until 1900, although the *Dar-ül Fünun* had existed since 1845 as a 'proto-university'. Before that education was directed towards training bureaucrats and army officers in colleges and academies.[5] These initial attempts to bring Ottoman education in accordance with that of the other major powers in Europe, however, did expose the growing Ottoman civil elite to foreign ideas and knowledge production. It is therefore not surprising that the first Young Turks were in fact graduates of the Ottoman military medical schools.[6] Further exposure to foreign education would in various instances consist of sending promising students abroad to Prussia, France and Great Britain.[7] Many of them would turn out to become leaders in political, military, bureaucratic or scientific reform.[8]

The dramatic growth of the bureaucratic apparatus – from approximately 2,000 scribes in 1770–90 to 35,000–70,000 civil officials in the Abdülhamidian era at the end of the nineteenth century – necessitated the expansion of teaching facilities in an empire where literacy levels were still very low. The most important example of a school which aimed to train officials was founded in 1859, the School of Civil Administration or *Mekteb-i Mülkiye-i Fünun-u Şahane* or simply *Mekteb-i Mülkiye*, which would be, following the foundation of the Turkish Republic, the basis for the Faculty of Political Science at Ankara University. Findley argues that the initial educational reforms resulted in elite formation, though there could be rather large differences within the degree of education or, as he points out, westernization marked by the officials' mastery of French. The rüşdiye were complemented with the equivalent of middle schools, the idadiye, from 1845 onwards.[9]

A new school in a new system: The Mekteb-i Sultanî

It would take another twenty-three years before the first high school, or *lycée*, was then opened, the *Mekteb-i Sultanî* at Galatasaray, right at the heart of Pera.

Historically, this area had already been the location of a school since 1481, when Sultan Bayezid II opened a palace school at the site. The foundation of this first school is the subject of various legends and even described by the author of one of the most famous pieces of Ottoman travel literature, Evliya Çelebi in his *Seyahatname*, as well as by the nineteenth-century Ottoman historian Tayyarzade Ata Bey in his *Tarih-i 'Ata*. Fethi İsfendiyaroğlu states that Ata Bey describes how Sultan Bayezid II travelled around the area of Galata and Tophane which was used as a hunting ground when he encountered an old man, who is sometimes claimed to be a dervish, known by the name of Gül Baba. The encounter is reputed to be linked directly with the building of a new school: as the capacity of the three palace schools, at Edirne, Topkapı Palace and the Old Palace at Beyazıt was not able to provide the required numbers of officials and clerics, Gül Baba recommended to Bayezid to set up another palace school in the area. This encounter is immortalized on a plaque commemorating the foundation of the school that was installed in the garden of the Galatasaray High School on the occasion of the school's 100th anniversary in 1968.[10]

Formally, the school founded during Bayezid II's reign would be called the *Galata Sarayı Enderun-u Hümayunu* (Imperial Palace School of Galata). For purposes of analysing identity formation and tradition making, however, it is salient that the school and site were already referred to by the name 'Galata Sarayı' (Galata Palace), long before that name would become the formal name of the high school. İsfendiyaroğlu claims that it was used long before it was coined as the high school's official name after the foundation of the Turkish Republic in the 1920s.[11] The contraction of the proper noun and the word 'Galata' and 'Saray', respectively, was made under the vernacularizing influence of foreigners: French speakers would refer to the school as *Galata-Sérai* or *Galata-Sérail*, whereas English and German speakers opted for *Galata Saray* (excluding the mandatory adjective suffix -Sİ in Turkish) or simply *Galatasaray*.[12] This school would have been an extension of the palace schools at Topkapı and Edirne providing training to the *devşirme* (the collecting of non-Muslim boys as tribute) as Janissaries, palace officials or servants.[13]

It should also be noted that the Ottoman rulership presented the site as the palace at Galata, despite the fact that the school's location was well beyond the former Genoese and Venetian settlement known as Galata and its walls, positioning it in what would become known as Pera. The Ottoman rulership referred to the area, at least initially, as Galata at large (being one out of four *kadılık*s, together with Istanbul, Eyüp and Üsküdar).[14] Louis Mitler indicates that the names Galata and Pera were used interchangeably until the early eighteenth century and considered to be the same district until the mid-seventeenth century.[15] The palace school's establishment would provide the name of the area around it and the name of the *lycée* during the republican period. In the period between the opening of the page school in 1481 and the founding of the *Mekteb-i Sultanî* in 1868, the school was allegedly used as a medrese from the reign of Sultan Selim II's reign onwards. It is said that his father and predecessor Süleyman I had more interest in the school, although the education of the *devşirme* was largely concentrated at the Topkapı during his reign. All activities related to the court, from statecraft, to the harem and page training were brought to the direct vicinity of the sultan due to the development of Süleyman I's meticulous court culture during the second part of his rule.[16]

With regard to the historical usage of the school, it is interesting to consider İsfendiyaroğlu's reference to Earl Paul Rycaut's *The Present State of the Ottoman Empire* (1670). Rycaut was special envoy of Charles II (1630–85) to Mehmed IV (1642–93). He writes that during his posting formerly Christian boys, to whom he refers as 'Ichoglans' (*İçoğlanı* – page), were educated at the Seraglio of Pera, Adrianople (Edirne) or the Grand Seraglio of Constantinople (the Topkapı Palace. He writes:

> But these Youths before they are admitted, are presented before the Grand Signior, whom according to his pleasure he disposes in his *Seraglio* at *Pera*, or *Adrianople*, or his great *Seraglio* at *Constantinople*, which is accounted the Imperial feat of the *Ottoman* Emperours. For these are the three Schools or Colledges of Education. Those that are preferr'd to the last named, are commonly marked out by special designation, and are a near step to degrees of Preferment.[17]

He thus indicates that the best pages were placed at the Topkapı Palace and simultaneously points out that the Galata Sarayı was around the second half of the seventeenth century, during Mehmed IV's reign, indeed used as a Palace School. According to sources published by the Galatasaray High School the premises were used as a medrese and palace school in an alternating fashion for 144 years until 1714.[18] A library, comparable to those found in the Fatih and Hagia Sophia libraries, was added by Mahmud I in 1741.[19] Joseph von Hammer mentions in his *Constantinopolis und der Bosporus* (1822) that with Galata-Serai the second half of Pera's main street begins, showing that despite many city fires and urban renewal in the nineteenth century, the integrity of the urban plan has largely remained the same.

The school's building was initially a timber construction, which was destroyed in 1819 during Mahmud II's reign as a consequence of one of the many city fires in Istanbul. Mahmud II ordered the reconstruction of the building, and, when it was reopened in 1838, it housed the *Tıbbiye-i Adliyye-i Şahane*, combining a hospital with a medical school. The school burned down once again during the reign of Abdülaziz in 1862, after which it was decided to build the reconstruction in stone. This building would house the *Mekteb-i Sultanî* from 1868 until 1873, when it was assigned to the Medical School again. The *Mekteb-i Sultanî* moved to a building in Gülhane, but after three years moved back once again to the building in Galatasaray. The wooden inner construction was destroyed again in a fire on 6 March 1906 or 22 February 1907 (different dates are used in different sources), when a fire in the kitchen of the French director's apartment broke out and would destroy the library that was a gift from Napoleon III, as well as the museum, which allegedly held the skeleton of a mammoth.[20] Lessons were transferred to the premises of the Beylerbeyi Palace, while the building was reconstructed, this time entirely in stone. The reconstruction that was finalized in 1909 is the building that stands on the spot today. It is particularly interesting to note how the continuity from the Palace School to the present-day high school is continuously stressed in the history writing on the high school in general and in the publications linked to the institutions of the Galatasaray Foundation and High School in particular. The roots of the present-day educational institution are continuously retraced back to the fifteenth century, although there is in fact little in common between the buildings and objectives of the Enderun school and the current high school.

After the opening of the first *sultaniye*, another comparable high school was opened in Darüşşafaka. A year after the opening of the Galatasaray *sultaniye*, a new system of educational legislation was introduced with the *Maarif-i Umumiye Nizamnamesi* (General Education Regulations). These regulations introduced a new system of primary education, high school education in every province and plans to open a university. The prospective plans projected in this legislation introduced a hierarchy of education from the primary to the university level and resembled to a significant degree that of the Ottoman Empire's counterparts in Western Europe. With some exceptions these regulations would set the framework for the public school system until the dissolution of the Ottoman Empire in 1923. Similar to the delay between legislation and execution of the plans to open a university, it would take a significant amount of time until Ottoman high schools were indeed set up in every Ottoman province.[21]

The high schools at Galatasaray and Darüşşafaka would thus constitute the only materializations of the Ottoman state's aim to introduce the *lise* level of education for a considerable amount of time. Yet even when other schools were introduced in different parts of the empire, the quality of education provided at the *Mekteb-i Sultanî* was unrivalled. Roderic Davison argues that this was in part a consequence of the French involvement with which the school was set up, with the help of an expert of the French Ministry of Education. As had been the case in earlier examples of educational reform, such as in the case of military academies, the school's model was based on the French system. The curriculum of the School of Military Sciences (*Mekteb-i Harbiye-i Şahane* – opened in 1834) in Constantinople, for instance, was in French and based on that of the French military academy Saint-Cyr.[22]

Also in the case of the Mekteb-i Sultanî the curriculum was based on the French model and entirely in French, with the exception of additional classes in Turkish and other local languages.[23] The French part of the diploma would designate the school as *Lycée Impérial de Galata-Serai*.[24] The headmaster and teachers were also in majority French when the school was opened. The school in Galatasaray would particularly cater to the children of the burgeoning Ottoman bourgeoisie and have a significant impact on the expansion and intellectual cultivation of the growing class of Ottoman bureaucrats.[25] Fatma Müge Göçek makes the ironic observation that the exponential growth of the Western-style schools in the Ottoman Empire, initiated by the Ottoman dynasty, would in fact cause the radical transformation of the Ottoman state apparatus, transferring power from the Ottoman dynasty's palatial household to a bureaucratic apparatus. It would be wrong to attribute this entirely to the upsurge in the foundation of schools from the second half of the nineteenth century onwards, since, as Göçek argues, it was a process that had essentially its roots before the second half of the eighteenth century. With the foundation of schools like the *Mekteb-i Sultanî*, however, the basis for institutional reform, that is, education, started to reach its apex.[26]

Davison notes that the school at its opening had 147 Muslim students against 194 non-Muslim students. Davison states that most of the Muslim students were 'presumably Turkish', but it should be noted that these categories had at least not formally crystallized yet within the Ottoman context.[27] That is further confirmed by the desire of the Ottoman government to desegregate education, which was, on the one hand, considered necessary to retain the loyalty of the non-Muslim Ottoman population and, on the other hand, bring the literacy levels of Muslims up to the level with that of non-Muslim Ottomans. The number of schools of the Ottoman millets had been expanding in the nineteenth century, and their quality of education was well beyond that provided to the Ottoman Muslims. Often supported by the University of Athens, Greeks abroad, Armenians in Russia and the *Alliance Israélite*, these schools would contribute to a growing dissonance in literacy levels between the Ottoman Muslims and non-Muslims.[28]

It is therefore hard to understate the importance and the need the Ottoman rulership felt to create a new 'Ottoman' high school, which would later become the Galatasaray High School. The school's graduates, particularly in the years of the late Ottoman Empire and the early years of the Turkish Republic, would grow up to become the administrators, diplomats and politicians of the late Ottoman Empire and early Turkish Republic – not to mention the legacy it would create as one of the most prestigious institutes of education to date.[29] Lewis argues that as much as it may have been initially set up as a school which would bring different Ottoman communities together, the school's profile started to change, becoming increasingly favoured by the ruling elite in the capital.[30] He argues that this is a phenomenon that became apparent during the Hamidian period (1876–1908) in which the school became more Turkish in character, dropping Latin from the curriculum and with an increase in Turkish students. Apart from the complications of the anachronistic usage of Turkish ethnicity as a 'national' category in this context, the names of the graduates provided in the yearbooks and other publications of the Galatasaray Alumni Association render a much more complex impression of the school population at the *Mekteb-i Sultanî* until well beyond the end of Abdülhamid II's reign, following his deposition in 1909. This counters Lewis's rather essentialist representation of the school's student population beyond the Young Turk Revolution. In 1873 the first Muslim Ottoman name – Abdurrahman Şeref – is registered, among a total of fourteen graduates, thirteen of which – considering their names – represent different millets, mostly Pontic Greek, Armenian, Jewish or Levantine. Most notable is a change in 1885 where the graduation cohort is split into three groups, those who graduate with both French and (Ottoman-)Turkish degrees and those who graduate only with the French or (Ottoman-)Turkish degree. In that year five Muslim Ottomans, one Armenian and two Persians get a dual-degree, four Muslim Ottomans get a Turkish degree, and a total of nine – three of which can be identified as Armenian, two as

Greek and two as Jewish – graduate with a French degree. It is only by the time of the First World War that the composition of graduates starts to change and by the time the Turkish Republic is founded and the *Mekteb-i Sultanî* is transferred to the Turkish school system, the frequency of non-Turkish names drops drastically.[31] In any case, considering the names of the school's graduates, it is hard to draw general conclusions about the school population at the high school at all, or even observe a rapid 'Turkification'.

The left wing of the school's building was used as a hospital by the Ottoman Red Crescent during the First World War, while lessons resumed in the other parts of the building. Until 1924 classes at the *Mekteb-i Sultanî* would consist of three-hour classes in French and two-hour classes in Turkish. After 1924 the French and Turkish cohorts were brought together and only the science and literature classes in the final year were separated. Considering the names of the graduates from the 1920s onwards it appears that the school was no longer following the earlier mission of the *Mekteb-i Sultanî*, that is, to bring the different Ottoman communities together. The names of graduates from the transformation of the *Mekteb-i Sultanî* to the *Galatasaray Lisesi* onwards are nearly exclusively Turkish. It should be noted, however, that apart from an occasional Levantine name in the graduation registers, some of the remaining members of the Ottoman millets chose or were forced to adopt Turkish names.[32]

The high school at the old palace school would educate many and employ many illustrious figures from Ottoman history. It is in this legacy that the Alumni Association of the High School takes particular pride. At the pinnacle of the production of the imagined and embodied *Galatasaraylı* community and its history features Tevfik Fikret. A poet and thinker, Fikret is oftentimes together with Yahya Kemal presented as the founder of modern Turkish literature. Fikret was born in Istanbul in 1867 and would become a prominent figure in the revolutionary Young Turk movement to such a degree that Ebru Boyar and Kate Fleet cite him as a major influence on the founder of the Turkish Republic, Mustafa Kemal.[33] Some of his poetry allegedly was among the favourite work of Mustafa Kemal. Vangelis Kechriotis, Maciej Górny and Ahmet Ersoy describe Fikret in equally praising terms and add, importantly, that Fikret's philosophy of life centred around the secular, materialist and progressive ideas that would be framed by state ideologues in the 1920s as some of the founding principles of the Turkish Republic.[34] Kechriotis, et al., however, also present Fikret as someone who looked down on nationalism and was an editor at the *Servet-i Fünun* (The Merit of Sciences), the Ottoman literary journal that was marked by its anti-establishment attitude as well as its liberal and progressive views. Within that setting, moreover they argue that Fikret was one of the most vocal critics against authority, conformism and tradition. As a consequence Fikret was celebrated as a 'recurrent target of conservatives and an enduring icon for generations of Republican modernizers'.[35]

Fikret was himself a student of the school who graduated as the best of his class in 1888 and would become a teacher at the high school not long after. He would part ways with the *Mekteb-i Sultanî* for a while and started teaching at Robert College, a high school and university founded by American missionaries (nationalized as

Boğaziçi University in 1971). His former house overlooking the Bosporus – the present-day Aşiyan Museum – still bears witness to that period. In 1908 he would return to the *Mekteb-i Sultanî* as the director. Not long after the building would be largely destroyed by a fire and Fikret would witness the building's renovation while the students moved to Beylerbeyi. In one of the sources this is presented as if it was Fikret's effort that enabled the renovation and the students' moving to Beylerbeyi, yet considering the year in which the fire took place – 1906 or 1907 – it seems unlikely that it was only Fikret who initiated these steps.

It is more generally interesting how in the publication on the history of the school, prepared for the occasion of the institution's centenary, Fikret's work as the director is so strongly emphasized. It is all the more remarkable considering the short period that he would be present at the school as its director: he would start on 20 December 1908 and leave the school again, after some cited discord with his superiors, on 28 February 1909. Considering the many other directors the school had in its relatively short existence, this is not necessarily remarkable, but even directors who stayed on for more than ten years were not credited as much as Fikret.[36] He is credited with giving the school and its students order and discipline as well as for the expansion of the building with a conference hall, laboratories and a library.[37] The authors go on: 'Mr Tevfik Fikret of all the directors of the *Mekteb-i Sultanî* in history, he was at the top of those who left a good reputation.'[38] In a short historical overview of a book published in 1996 on the occasion of the class of 1936's sixtieth anniversary, Fikret is described as a 'symbol of Galatasaray'.[39] The school cultivates and memorializes him with an oil painting in the school's conference hall – named the *Tevfik Fikret Salonu* – a bust in the front garden, and a commemorative stone.[40] Considering the remarks of Kechriotis et al., however, it seems less surprising that an institution which prides itself in being strongly embedded in a tradition of modernity and positivist education would choose Fikret as its main figurehead.

The continuous association of the school, in both formal and informal history writing, with its most illustrious alumni and institutional legacies is understandable. The school, for many decades, would educate the children of the elites, so it may seem as a logical outcome that the school or its alumni desire to share in the glory of legacies. Even in the educational context of Turkey where so much value is already attributed to the prestige of a school or university, the Galatasaray High School may be considered to stand on a different level. To say that one is 'of Galatasaray' (*Galatasaraylı*) invests many of its graduates with pride to be part of this community. This is clearly expressed in the Galatasaray High School's Anthem, the so-called *Galatasaray Marşı*:

> Our path follows the tracks of Ekrem and Fikret
> Our first goal is an advanced civilization
> We are the pioneers of knowledge, work and innovation
> We are western-minded, Turkish-hearted youngsters
> We are from Galatasaray, we are from Galatasaray
> with unmatched confidence and unmatched speed in service of the motherland

Our souls, our bodies are healthy
Our love, our knowledge, our compassion are profound
We came together, broke away and came from four parts of the homeland
We are western-minded, Turkish-hearted youngsters
We are from Galatasaray, we are from Galatasaray
with unmatched confidence and unmatched speed in service of the
   motherland.[41]

The lyrics of the song navigate the *Galatasaraylı* community's identity between Turkish nationalism and a community-bound elitist and positivist discourse of 'Westernized' cultural and intellectual supremacy. As such it may be interpreted as heavily influenced by Turkish state ideology.[42] This can also be observed in the memories of graduates, particularly of those who left the school during the early years of the Turkish Republic. What is significant, moreover, is that the song stresses the healthy minds and bodies of those who are from Galatasaray. The importance of the healthy body and sports for that matter are, in fact, frequently stressed in the identity and history writing on Galatasaray. The connection between the *Mekteb-i Sultanî* and the Galatasaray High School on the one hand and sport culture on the other in the Ottoman Empire and Turkish Republic, respectively, is an apparent one. A long legacy of sport clubs who hold their roots in the school exists. The pride towards this legacy is actively cultivated: in a special issue for the fiftieth anniversary of the graduates of 1933 prepared by the Galatasaray Educational Foundation (*Galatasaray Eğitim Vakfı*) several pages are attributed to the renowned ties of the school with sports.[43]

The roots of one the top teams in the Turkish premiere football league, *Galatasaray Spor Kulübü*, lie with the school. In the catalogue of an exhibition which was on display in 2010 at the Galatasaray Art and Cultural Centre in Beyoğlu, the football club's founder Ali Sami Yen explains how the club was founded in 1905 on the initiative of Ali Sami, Asım Tevfık, Emin Bülend, Celal, Bekir, Tahsin, Reşat Şirvani, Cevdet, Abidin, Kamil, Milo Bakiç and the Robenson brothers. Ali Sami, son of the Albanian Ottoman writer and philosopher Sami Frashëri who was a key figure in the Albanian National Awakening Movement, attended the school between 1902 and 1906.[44] Together they would found the first Turkish football club, which was admitted to the Istanbul Football League or Constantinople Football Association League in 1906, founded by James La Fontaine and Henry Pears as the Istanbul Sunday League.[45] The club would win three of seven titles in the Istanbul League following the introduction of Turkish professional football in 1952, twenty titles in the Turkish Super League since 1959 and sixteen titles in the Turkish Cup since 1962. Its greatest success was winning the UEFA Cup and UEFA Super Cup in 2000. Nowadays the *Galatasaray Spor Kulübü* is represented in a wide range of sports from basketball and volleyball to water polo, judo, motorsport and chess.[46]

The connection to club sports has contributed considerably to the feelings of pride and adherence to the *Galatasaraylı* community some graduates undoubtedly experienced. In the fiftieth-anniversary edition of the 1934 graduates, the authors write that 'sports is the most important of everything at Galatasaray and a

Galatasaraylı is from all perspectives a true sportsman.'[47] They go on by claiming that Western-style sports in Turkey started at Galatasaray. Demet Lüküslü and Şakir Dinçşahin retrace the origins of modern physical education back to Selim Sırrı Tarcan, who they argue was indeed inspired by the gymnastics classes he took during his short period of attendance at Galatasaray High School. It thus seems justified to make the claim that the *Mekteb-i Sultanî* had an important role in the development of a Western-style sports culture in the Ottoman Empire and Turkish Republic, although it should be stressed once again that it would take a significant amount of time until physical education became commonplace in other schools around the country as well.

The emphasis on body culture in the imagining of the *Galatasaraylı* reflects a broader phenomenon rooted in nation building projects. In the Ottoman context, Cüneyd Okay describes processes initiated by the Committee of Union and Progress (CUP) in 1913 to promote physical education with the aim to 'improve the health of Turks, reinforce their physical strength, and raise active generations as a contingency in times of hardship'.[48] The efforts were organized in a paramilitary substructure of the CUP, called the Association of Turkish Strength (*Türk Gücü Cemiyeti*). The association focused on promoting national sports which seem to reflect some of the contemporary historical imaginings of ethnic Turks; Okay mentions horse riding, archery, shooting exercises, wrestling and sword fighting. Additionally he also mentions the prescription of a 'national costume' in the associations by-laws.[49] The association's mission is quite similar to Friedrich Jahn's initiatives of the *Turnverein* in nineteenth-century Germany. Jahn developed training sessions in the first half of the nineteenth century, which would form the basis for radical nationalist militia. Leerssen shows that many nationalist movements in the decades to follow would copy his model.[50] In the context of English public schools, Sudipa Topdar argues that there was an intricate relationship between school games and ideas of discipline, masculinity, militarism and patriotism. In the colonial setting of British India, however, it served three different purposes: bringing improvement to the 'weak' bodies of native children; disciplining bodies for purposes of combating lack of hygiene and order; and finally depoliticizing bodies through obstructing them from participation in political activism.[51] As such they fit into broader schemes of colonial suppression and disciplining on the one hand and conceptions of a *mission civilisatrice* on the other.

Vladimir Tikhonov points out how beyond a colonial context European ideas on body culture and manhood would also trickle down to, for instance, Korea as an effect of the country's modernization efforts. He argues that, quite similar to the German situation, the Korean nation would be represented primarily as a group of healthy, strong and disciplined men.[52] It should be noted, however, that, for instance, in the German context from the years of the German Empire onwards initiatives were developed to also combine physical education with the arts, described by Christine Mayer as efforts to emancipate and educate rather than to drill.[53] Marion Kant, in addition, emphasizes that the roots of twentieth-century modern dance in fact lie within nineteenth-century gymnastics and *Turnen*.[54]

The body culture of the *sultaniye* thus represented a contemporary transnational phenomenon.

Galatasaray Lisesi *and* Galatasaraylılar *in the* *second half of the twentieth century*

The official name-change of the former *Mekteb-i Sultanî* took place in 1924, with the integration of the school in the newly established Turkish school system. By 1930 the school building at Galatasaray had proven to have insufficient capacity to provide for all the students and part of the Feriye Palace in Ortaköy – other parts being used by the Kabataş High School for Boys – was taken into use by the school as well. The school was visited by dignitaries such as Mustafa Kemal and several decades later by France's president Charles De Gaulle in 1968 to celebrate the school's centennial, cultivating a continuity between the Ottoman and Turkish institution. On the occasion of De Gaulle's speech then director Muhittin Sandıkçıoğlu prepared a speech which bears testimony to the belief of Galatasaray's community in being the champion of Turkey's modernization and progress. Parts of the director's speech also displays the feelings of indebtedness the director felt, or at least wanted to present to have felt, towards French culture:

> Mr. President, (. . .) we are honored and take pride in your visit, which illustrates the centenary celebrations of this Lycée, with a past that is synonymous with the very history of our culture. I spoke of modernization in the Western sense, but for us the West equates with France. (. . .) It is in French intellectual and social life that the intellectual, literary and social movements of our country found their raison d'être. (. . .) Because of its preponderant role in the development of education and social movements in Turkey, our school has been aptly called an open window in the East facing the West.[55]

Given the considerable amount of studies, popular and academic, regarding Galatasaray's history until the first half of the twentieth century, and until the 1920s in particular, it is remarkable how little material has been produced on the school's more recent history. This is particularly intriguing considering the importance the school and its community attribute to its role as forebears of modernity in Turkish society.

That being said, the publications of the Galatasaray Foundation provide a rich source corpus for studying Galatasaray High School's position and history in Beyoğlu from the 1930s onwards, since its alumni association, the *Galatasaraylılar Derneği*, has made considerable efforts to protect, collect, archive and make sources available to its alumni and, partially, the public as well. The Galatasaray alumni can, through the association's website, check the school's yearbooks up to the 1930s; the magazines published at the school – the *Galatasaray Dergisi, Akademi, Tambur* and *Le Tambour* – are available to the public. The *Galatasaray Dergisi* would typically contain short stories, poetry, essays and reports about news on the school. The association itself as well as the publications is an example of the importance and prestige that are attached to being a student at or graduate from the high school. The objective of the publications of the alumni association seems to be to cultivate and preserve the legendary status of the school, by emphasizing its role in sports and, through its graduates, politics, economics and culture. The yearbooks in particular provide valuable insights into what it meant to be a student at the high school and, significantly, what it meant to be a student in Beyoğlu from the 1930s until the 1990s.

The publications also provide insight into Galatasaray's position in a national context which was dominated by Kemalist nationalism, the school being an example of the complicated nationalist discourse in which the supremacy of the Turkish nation was negotiated with an admiration for a positivist interpretation of 'the West' and its achievements. A graduate of the year 1942 describes how Galatasaray to him was a place where nationalism was always upheld.

> I think that Galatasaray, in the Beyoğlu neighbourhood, which was the last to Turkify, was not just a hearth of knowledge where the most important and bravest sons of the nation were educated. At the same time, it was a sacred place where the masses who spoke with a variety of languages passed the iron fences were obliged to lower their voices. Yes, a sacred place. Even on the darkest days and the worst moments the children of the motherland were worshipping Turkishness there without losing any of the spirit and fire in their hearts.[56]

Others, at a later age, had different thoughts about this. A graduate of 1955 reminds his fellow graduates about the pogroms against non-Muslims in Beyoğlu and other parts of the city on 6 and 7 September 1955. He recounts how the diploma ceremony was delayed to October due to the pogroms, which he felt had turned out to be a huge plunder and campaign of destruction, describing it as 'disheartening'.[57]

The memories of the graduates in the yearbooks and commemorative editions of the earlier years recurrently remind of the darker episodes of Beyoğlu's history, including episodes of nationalist violence and the involvement or attitudes of some students in it. In phrasing which leaves little to the imagination, a former graduate explains how on 3 March 1929 they attacked a Rum newspaper in Istanbul. The author starts that he wishes to explain how sensitive the students from Galatasaray were to national issues. He narrates how one of them decided to gather a handful of friends 'to teach a lesson' to a Rum newspaper which was hostile towards Turkey. On 8 March 1929 they were in class together discussing a newspaper called *TaHronika*. The author describes it as 'a Rum newspaper which could not accept the trashing [of the Greek army] in Anatolia and exploited our incredible tolerance and was a piece of junk that did not let an opportunity slip to produce hostilities against Turkey in our lands'.[58] The newspaper had published an article regarding 'an episode about Anatolia'. The author and friends got agitated at a phrase which stated that 'when Izmir changed hands to the Turks, a civilization was ruined'. The author goes on to say that a Turkish columnist had countered these words in another newspaper, but emphasizes his agitation at the fact that no response came from the government. A former graduate and student at the Medical School then gathered eight to ten 'nationalist' friends (*8-10 milliyetçi arkadaşı*[. . .]) to 'resolve the matter themselves'.[59] They found out that the newspaper had their offices on the Şişhane Yokuşu and took the matter into their own hands: 'they went to the printing house and destroyed and threw out machines, devices, tools, printer cases, documents and furniture, while giving 5 or 6 Rum who were inside a good beating as well. The Ta Hronika rag was no longer published after that day and its owner pissed off to Athens' (*sahibi de Atina'ya defolup gitti*).[60] Gürhan Yellice indicates that the newspaper was closed on 3 March 1929 on the decision of the Council of Ministers, since the word 'agriotera' had been used, which was translated as 'brutal'. Later, however, the court case against Ta Hronika's owner was reopened and it was decided that the word had been intended as 'violent' and would therefore not be considered as an insult to Turkishness. He argues that considerations on bilateral levels between Turkey and Greece, which tried to mend their ties, were at play in the case. In 1930 the newspaper was able to resume publishing.

The graduate's testimony in the commemorative volume, however, does not need to be adjudicated based on its historical veracity. What is fascinating is that it is narrated by the author without remorse or embarrassment, but simply as a nostalgic story from his younger years as a student at Galatasaray High School, highlighting the profound tensions between different communities in the late 1920s and 1930s and the degree to which individuals felt at liberty to be vigilant. At the same time and at a different level – since this particular publication dates back to 1982 – it may also reflect the rising tensions between Greece and Turkey. Following the generals' junta of Kenan Evren, instated after his 1980 coup, vitriolic nationalisms were flaring up and possibly seeped through to a commemorative publication of this elite Turkish high school. Apart from these sentiments, however, more light-hearted encounters also occurred when the basketball team of Galatasaray had a special match in 1949 with the team of the Greek Zoğrafyon high school around the corner on Turnacıbaşı Caddesi. The team of Galatasaray lost with 11–13. The cited reason was that the team of Zoğrafyon was composed of players from the youth teams of the predominantly *Rum Beyoğluspor* and *Kurtuluş*. Also in some of the yearbooks match results of the Galatasaray sport teams and the Zoğrafyon High School's teams are cited, indicating that this was indeed not uncommon.[61]

Elsewhere students of graduation year 1933 argue against the occurrence of racism in the school. When one of the boys was running around in the class room he bumped into another boy, who – judging from the narration – was Jewish. The boy who struck the other boy then exclaimed: 'what are you afraid of you coward Jew?' The author writes that all of the boys then stood up for the Jewish kid and the boy who made the racist exclamations then felt obliged to make 'a thousand apologies'.[62] Another alumnus recounts how they would not understand their Armenian biology teacher to be Armenian when he was speaking French, but that they would get it when he was speaking in Turkish. He goes on by saying, 'He was entirely Turkified. He was a person who adopted Turkishness.'[63] A graduate of 1955 recounts: 'we were all Kemalist, but none of us were racists. We never looked down on the minorities. We did not differentiate between Turkish-Kurdish, Sunnite-Alevite, Jew, Rum or Armenian. We were raised without the pressure of faith.'[64] Nonetheless, some of the boys at times also referred to ethnicity or religiosity, without realizing the implications of making such statements. Another graduate of 1955 tells an anecdote about a teacher who would collect some cents from every student who spoke a word of Turkish in the French class. The teacher would collect the cents in a box and the boys would guess during their breaks how much money was in there. After some arguments one boy supposedly exclaimed: 'Give me a break, the Jew opens the box and steals from it!' The author then explains: 'When he said Jew, he meant no-one but our teacher Arditi, whom we had learned was Jewish.'[65] In the yearbook of 1959 it is explained that a boy was often called 'Salomon' by his friends since he was so good at doing impressions of Jews.[66] It is important to note that in these reflections there never seems to be any doubt about Galatasaray High School's right to have its place in this district. It appears that despite the eb and flow of nationalism in the students' imagining of their community, they did not think that they were in any way out of place in Beyoğlu. The school belonged in Beyoğlu, but Beyoğlu – at least partially – also belonged to them. This is particularly important considering the representation of post-1950s Beyoğlu as a place of perpetual change, loss and deterioration. Galatasaray, to the contrary, has remained both a place and a symbol of elitist continuity.

As has been explained in Chapter 1, the 1950s, and to varying degrees the preceding decades as well, were marked by racism and discrimination towards Turkey's non-Muslims and others who were not considered to be 'ethnic Turks'. The fact that the graduates feel the need to express that they were in fact not racists in itself is a revealing indicator of the general attitude towards these communities in Turkey. Discrimination and racism had always been common in the Turkish Republic and was actively encouraged by the state.[67] In his memoires, Bensiyon Pinto, the former chairman of the Jewish community in Turkey, gives an insightful account from the days when he was training to become a professional trainer at the Galatasaray football club:

> I was having a training session at the Hasnun Galip Street venue of Galatasaray Club. I was hopping along the narrow corridor after the match, still wearing my studded football boots. I was not supposed to do that, but I sometimes walked as far as the changing room before taking my shoes off. The adults never complained about it. That day there were maybe ten other players walking along with me. One trainer came along and said: 'Don't walk with these on, Jew! Take them off!' This was the second time I heard this word: 'Jew!' This time, I did not need explanations. I was old enough to understand what calling me a Jew with this tone of voice meant. It was discrimination itself. It was racism. (. . .) What bothered them were not my studs, it was my being Jewish.[68]

Sources from the high school also provide more light-hearted examples of the feelings of pride Galatasaray High School instilled in its students. In an issue of the

Galatasaray Dergi from August 1947, a student explains how they felt obliged to defend the reputation of their school when an American group came to Istanbul and visited the school. The author writes that he thinks the Americans were misguided by preconceptions about the city and explains that he and his classmates showed what an imposing place the school and Beyoğlu were. 'Our school is a centre like Beyoğlu, it is a place where foreigners wander around the most.'[69] They showed them around the school, and the author indicates how impressed the Americans were by the building, the gardens, the school's facilities and the prizes won by the various sports teams connected to Galatasaray. It seems that the students aimed to showcase how great a school Galatasaray High School was and that the school and its students were successful examples of modernity. He concludes with a letter he received from the American visitors: 'You taught these Americans who thought they knew everything that there are many things that they do not know and should learn (. . .) with your being a *Galatasaraylı* to us you are the best specimens of Turkish schools and Turkish youth. If all your schools resemble Galatasaray, Turkey can boast about its schools and youth.'[70] The author appears pleased with these compliments, adding that Tevfik Fikret once stated that Galatasaray was the first window of the East to the West.[71]

In the article numerous references are made to the quality of the school's building by the author and the impression it made on outsiders:

> A large building which rises up in the middle of a well-cared for and orderly garden, which a majestic gate and thick walls work to surround as if they do not want to show it to the outside world out of jealousy, took the American sailors' attention and these guests, who disembarked with the intention to not let anything slip their eyes anyway, wanted to understand what was going on here.[72]

These and numerous instances in various publications of institutions related to Galatasaray show how the building's quality is a common thread. One student, a graduate of the class of 1937, remembers what kind of an impression the school building had on him when his parents took him there for his admission:

> One day they took me by the hand and said: 'you're going to take an exam' and brought me in front of a big building. From between the high fences, it was a building which only revealed a big clock towering over the green trees. We went into the garden, and the school now lay fully in front of my eyes. This majestic building left me in awe. I thought to myself: 'I suppose I will grow up in this big city's schools'.[73]

Elsewhere in the yearbook of the graduates of 1968 an equally colourful memory is brought to the fore in a description of one of the graduates:

> If you enter the Galatasaray Sultani through the gate you will see the school building with all its majesty across of you. (. . .) Sometimes, you will see someone playing football in grand toilette, with brand new polished shoes, with a suit,

starched shirt and tie. Don't be surprised. This person who stands next to the other players in shorts is no-one but (. . .). (. . .) Despite him being from Kayseri he dresses chic.

Beyoğlu and the Galatasaray building as an ambiguous place of memory, nostalgia, recognition and belonging is a recurring theme in the yearbooks of the imagined and embodied community of Galatasaray graduates. One of the graduates of 1942 remembers how imposing or even terrifying an experience it was for the young boys to be in the school. The building's giant classrooms, dark corridors and restrictions, its crowdedness and sheer size scared them. They were, among other things, not allowed to approach the gates and tall iron fences, secluding the school grounds from the rest of the area. He explains how they felt much more at ease when they were moved to the school's building in Ortaköy, presently the building of Galatasaray University.[74] Elsewhere in an issue of the *Galatasaray Dergi* from March 1949, Metin Toker, renowned journalist and graduate of 1942, explains that they in fact found the building very appealing. They were still young students, and the school's gardens, *Grand Cour* and flower gardens were reserved for the older students. Yet, he explains, 'forbidden places appeal to people and these forbidden gardens attracted us like bees to honey.'[75]

The gate and fences separating the school from what happened around them are something that features prominently in the place-making of the students, as it recurs throughout the years and memories. It is noteworthy that this is in fact quite similar to the way Beyoğlu itself is represented in the context of Istanbul: an integral part of both the city and its urban identity, yet also something distinctively different from everything and everywhere else. In one of the reunion albums for the graduates of 1955 most of the students were boarding students until around the 1950s and would not be able to go anywhere else during the week: 'they could not even watch Beyoğlu from afar.'[76] From the other side of the fence memories also grew as graduate of 1964 and author İlhan Eksen writes:

> in the early moments of my boarding school years, far from home, I sought solace in the advertisement lights and sounds of the tram. To my surprise, my recently retired father would go to Beyoğlu every evening around nine to stand in front of the post office across the school, waiting for the lights of the dormitories to go out. After returning he would report to my Mom: 'I put our son to bed and came back.'[77]

The gates and fences facing Beyoğlu therefore seem to have become a metaphorical anchor point for some of the Galatasaray students. A picture in the yearbook of 1969 shows seven young men climbing the fences of the high school, with a caption that reads 'the place where colourful Beyoğlu nights started and ended ([. . .] what are you doing here, you're a married familyman)'. It appears that the policies regarding the crossing of fences of students became less strict through the years allowing the students to familiarize themselves with the nightlife of Beyoğlu. The reference of the caption's author to their friend's marital obligations (irony or not) is significant as it reveals the perception of the author, and possibly his friends, regarding the district. Beyoğlu at night was not a place for families, but for bachelors and, quite likely, male bachelors.[78] When, during the weekends, the students were able to go out, the district provided the students with opportunities for experiences they would not have been able to acquire in any other part of the city. One graduate of 1955 states: 'at Beyoğlu's heart we had the chance to learn about the tests of life at an early age. (. . .) We did not miss the chance to be a gentleman of Beyoğlu when we left the school during the weekend. Nothing was exempted in the warnings of our teachers about the responsibility of being a student of our school.'[79] Graduates of the year 1958 share insight into what this might mean while discussing one of their comrades: '[he] played the saz, but not with [eyes for the] scores. Always with a side-eye for the girls in Beyoğlu.'[80] Others seem to have been slightly more direct in following the impulses of their burgeoning sexuality, as a graduate of 1962 made it a habit to stick his head through the window of every car in Beyoğlu that would pass him and had a woman in it.

Accounts like these in which Beyoğlu and the school's building feature as a point of reference and setting, for the memories of the boys, and from 1965 onwards girls, indicate what strong an imprint the building's site left on the students of Galatasaray. In 2002 three graduates discuss the results of a forum that was organized by the Galatasaray Community Cooperative. The first question that is discussed is: 'what is the significance of the school's presence in Beyoğlu for being a *Galatasaraylı*?' The authors ask the reader whether the school could move to a new campus in a site outside of the old city? Those present argued that the school's presence in Beyoğlu was of prime importance. They state that the outcome was that the graduates concluded that Beyoğlu was a symbol of their shared past and unity.[81]

> The 'Point Zero' is this district, this building. Beyoğlu is one of Istanbul's, or even Turkey's, most prominent and important cultural and social places. (. . .) The students of those schools [which moved outside of the city centre] only know the city and the society from the windows of the school buses that bring them to school. The students of Galatasaray High School learn the realities of society through living them.[82]

They express the wish that the school will stay in the same place for the coming centuries and moreover feel indebted to the school. In conclusion they state that the school's presence in the area of which it is the namesake is quintessential. They thus make a strong claim to the school's right to be in its current place and the interconnectedness of school, building and site. Elsewhere, in a publication titled *Bitmeyen Mektep* (ever-lasting school) of the *Ankara Galatasaray Birliği* (Ankara Galatasaray Union), the issue of girls being admitted to the school is discussed. From 1965 onwards girls were accepted to the high school, which caused major upheaval at first. The girls who reached the high school level initially stayed at the building in Ortaköy, but gradually started to be admitted to the Beyoğlu building as well. The author states that this was significant, for 'to be a 'true *Galatasaraylı*' one needs to study in Beyoğlu'.[83]

The graduates of the high school thus felt their memories to be strongly connected to the place that is Galatasaray and Beyoğlu. Also in earlier instances than the quoted summary of the meeting organized by the Galatasaray Community Cooperative a strong connection to the school as a material site is visible. A picture featuring the back garden of the high school is accompanied by a comment describing its former beauty as a 'flower heaven at the heart of Beyoğlu' which was due to indifference turned into a ruin and a garbage dump. According to the authors it was waiting for the help of their foundation since the Ministry of Education would not provide the school with a gardener and allowance for it.[84] Elsewhere it is indicated that the building had by 1986 not received any substantial renovations apart from the parts that were repaired by the state. In 1982, however, İnan Kıraç, a prominent businessman at Koç Holding, philanthropist and himself a Galatasaray graduate of 1959, would set up the Galatasaray Education Foundation which in four years' time would donate 861 million liras to the school, which was complemented with 700 million liras from the state. With initiatives like these the many associations and foundations set up by graduates of Galatasaray High School try to preserve the school's legacy for the future, cultivating ties with alumni through formal and informal networks. The most notable is the annual Pilaf Day, in which a rice dish is served for the school's alumni on the school's grounds. Alumni associations moreover exist in other cities, notably Ankara, and abroad as well, in France, Belgium and the United States.[85] For all these alumni the Galatasaray building and 'their Beyoğlu' remain as the setting and point of reference for their childhood and adolescent memories. As much as they cherish the memories from their days at the high school, the presented cases also show that the students of Galatasaray

Figure 2 Enno Maessen (2018) – The fences of Galatasaray High School seen from Galatasaray Square.

reflected the shifting attitudes towards multiculturalism that existed within the framework of Turkish nationalism. Whereas some feel the need to stress that they were not racists, or cherish memories regarding their 'Turkified' Armenian teachers, other (older) graduates felt instilled with pride recounting memories or stories on attacks against Rum citizens. Such diversity in attitudes also makes the school a telling microcosm of more general tropes of representation of Beyoğlu, Istanbul and Turkey, ranging from multiculturalist nostalgia to xenophobia through the decades.

Chapter 5

İSTIKLAL CADDESI/ENGLISH HIGH SCHOOL FOR GIRLS

Historically Pera housed a great number of foreign or foreign-language schools, with some of the most prominent examples being the German High School, the Austrian Sankt Georg High School, the French Saint Benoit Lyceum, Sainte Pulcherie and later Pierre Loti High School, the Italian Schools and the English High School for Girls.[1] These schools were usually founded for the purpose of providing children education in their native language and adopted curricula that would relate at least in part to those of their 'homelands'. From a geopolitical point of view, however, it is significant to note that most schools would admit children from the local bourgeoisie as well. As such they had, and have, a significant role in building connections and spheres of influence between the Ottoman Empire or Turkey and notably France, England, Italy and Germany. As I will show in this chapter and further on in Chapter 7, this also had strong implications for Beyoğlu, marking it as the one of the most significant centres for education and British cultural diplomacy in the country.

The initial contact between Great Britain and the Ottoman Empire had been established through trade, organized in 1581 through the Levant Company's monopoly granted by Elizabeth I's charter. Christine Laidlaw and Geoff Berridge argue that trade would be the dominant mode of interaction between Great Britain and the Ottoman Empire for many years to follow.[2] Changes in Europe's balance of powers started to take shape. These shifts were partly driven by the Ottoman Empire's power reaching a status quo around the eighteenth century. The empire retained most of its possessions, but no longer posed an acute threat to the major European states as it had in the centuries before. British foreign policy became increasingly directed towards sustaining the Ottoman Empire and protecting its own interests in the Levant trade. Laidlaw indicates that particularly after the invasion of Ottoman Egypt by Napoleonic France in 1798, the British and Ottoman shared a common geopolitical interest against France. The British Embassy's significance would expand considerably as a consequence, and the Crown took over the responsibility for financing the British representation in the Ottoman Empire from the Levant Company, the responsibility it bore for over 200 years.[3]

The decades following would be marked by an increasingly close connections of the Ottoman Empire with Europe. Edhem Eldem argues that the Crimean War (1853–6) was of particular significance in that sense from a political point of view – the Ottoman Empire struck an alliance with the British Empire, French

Figure 3 Enno Maessen (2017) – Exterior view of the former English High School for Girls, currently Beyoğlu Anadolu Lisesi.

Empire and the Kingdom of Sardinia against the Russian Empire – but also from an economic point of view. As the Ottoman government became aware that it would need foreign loans to finance its endeavours, it embarked on a programme geared towards the acquisition of loans from Western European powers, notably France and Great Britain.[4] Eldem points out that the first loans in the mid-1850s were acquired at highly favourable rates, a result of the French and British interest in sustaining the Ottoman war efforts against the Russians.[5] This process culminated in a formalized dependency of the Ottoman Empire on foreign powers. Following its bankruptcy in 1875, the Ottoman Public Debt

Administration was founded in 1881, in order to structurally settle the Ottoman Empire's public debt. As Eldem points out this resulted in a 'state within the state', in which the Ottoman state was forced to accept the control of foreigners over substantial parts of its finances. He goes on, however, to indicate that this dependency took the shape of an economic, rather than a political, dependency, since the relation was between creditors and the state, without a structural formal role for the foreign powers.[6]

Effectively, the financial and strategic dependency of the Ottoman Empire on its Western European counterparts meant that the significance of the foreign presence, political, economically and culturally speaking, increased dramatically. One notable effect in the Ottoman capital was the increase of organizations geared towards providing in the needs for Europeans, notably churches, clubs, banks, companies and schools. One of the earliest examples of a school, which was set up to educate a growing number of children in Istanbul/Constantinople, is the English School for Girls. In a memorandum from the British Consulate General, from approximately 1968, it is stated that the English School for Girls was founded in 1860 and established in a building that was granted by Sultan Abdülmecid to the wife of the British ambassador, Lady Stratford de Redcliffe.[7] She transferred the school properties to the British Embassy in 1881 and established a general committee for the administration of the school.[8] A yearbook of the English High School for Girls (EHSG) from 1960 holds an extract from an article by Miss Thompson, headmistress of the Girls School, for the *Journal of Education* from 1944. In this extract the school is said to be founded as early as 1849 by Jane Walsh, who died in 1872. The epitaph on her grave at the former Crimean Cemetery in Tarabya stated that she had, with help of her sister, worked for twenty-three years in an institution established under the protection of the British ambassador at the time Stratford Canning. The author of the article deduces that the institution thus must have been established in 1849. After the Crimean War, according to the author, Sultan Abdülmecid granted to Lady Stratford de Redcliffe the plot on which the present-day school building stands today at İstiklal Caddesi 185.[9] The 'Trust Deed of Girls School at Constantinople' from 12 October 1881 indicates that the buildings presented to Lady Stratford de Redcliffe in 1858 were Grande Rue de Pera 347, 349, 351, 353, 355, 357 and 359. The document indicates that this consisted of 'a large Stone House and six Stone Shops commonly known as "The Casino"'.[10] Barrister and historian Edwin Pears wrote in his book *Forty Years in Constantinople* that the school was originally housed in an old timber building with cafes on the ground floor. This building was then required to be demolished when the Ottoman authorities claimed a part of the building's parcel for the expansion of the Grande Rue de Pera.[11]

A new building was constructed around 1901 or 1902, with the bottom floors reserved for shops rented out by the school committee, in charge with the administration of the school. The article by Miss Thompson, however, indicates that a stone building had already served the school before, which corresponds with the information of the cited trust deed. She also states that the school served mostly children of British nationals and other foreign members of the bourgeoisie in Istanbul/Constantinople during the final years of the Ottoman Empire, with numbers of around 200 pupils at the turn of the century. The school was closed in 1914 for six years due to the First World War.[12] Following the dissolution of the Ottoman Empire and the foundation of the Turkish Republic, the status of the school as an 'established foreign school' was recognized in 1923 in an exchange of letters between the British ambassador and Prime Minister İsmet İnönü.[13] This was particularly significant considering the stipulations of the Lausanne Treaty. Following the discontent among the Turkish National Movement with the Treaty of Sèvres from 1920, in which what remained from the Ottoman Empire's territory was divided into Armenian, Greek, Kurdish, Turkish, British, French and Italian territories, a large-scale conflict erupted, commonly presented as the Turkish War of Independence. Eventually this led to the Turkish National Movement and Atatürk's government in Ankara to push for the negotiation of a new treaty in 1923, known as the Treaty of Lausanne, which would essentially define the borders of the Turkish Republic.

The English High Schools as a spearhead of British cultural diplomacy

For the existing foreign schools that were suddenly within the borders of the Turkish Republic rather than the Ottoman Empire the Treaty of Lausanne would be of pivotal importance. Nimet Hadimoğlu argues that the status of foreign schools is hardly regulated and that the continuation of foreign schools in the Turkish Republic was dependent on the letters of İsmet İnönü to the English, French and Italian governments, which can be considered as an addendum to the actual Treaty. In the letters it is stipulated that 'religious, educational, health and welfare institutions of these states, which were recognized until October 30, 1914, will continue to exist, that these institutions will be treated the same as Turkish schools, that they will be faithful to public order and laws and regulations and will be controlled in good will.'[14] With that the existing rights of the schools, no more or less, were preserved. As will be shown in this chapter, this rigid result of international diplomacy would lead to ongoing legal problems for the English School for Girls.

It was indicated by the Turkish government that any changes in the location of the buildings or reconstruction of the buildings would mean that the schools would lose their special status as protected foreign entities under the stipulations of the Lausanne Treaty and that their status would have to be renegotiated if such changes were to be made. The British side disagreed with this rigid interpretation, yet also decided to remain within the boundaries of the status quo, which meant that profound financial and practical problems within the schools endured.[15] One of the reasons of the British government's hesitance to act may have been that despite the talks that were held at the highest level, the government appeared to have not been certain about what its legal ties and responsibilities were to the school. According to diplomatic cables from the 1960s, this led the British Embassy to investigate its ties with the English Schools in 1926, with no result except for the fact that the British government had made a donation of 5,000 pound sterling to have a new building for the Boys' School constructed in 1911.[16] Elsewhere, in documents of the Foreign Office, the previously cited text of Thompson is provided in full, yet here there is a lack of clarity regarding the legal ties between the British government and the Girls' and Boys' Schools. In the text it is argued that the school after its reopening in 1922 was based entirely on the model of an English high school, with teaching in English – except for foreign languages – by British teachers, primarily for British and other foreign girls as well as – once again – girls from the non-Muslim upper and upper-middle classes.[17] Following the Kemalist reforms of the educational system and the earlier quoted stipulations from İnönü's letters, the school had to start operating within the boundaries indicated by the new regime, although Thompson indicates that the school did not lose its 'character as an English School'.[18]

Certain subjects were from then onwards taught in Turkish and children of Turkey's citizens joined the school population. She narrates that the years following 1922 were difficult in terms of finances for the school, which nearly caused its demise. Although the school was self-supporting at first – possibly through the rents that were gained from the shop owners on the ground floor of the school's building as well as the financial assets the school had in its possession – it became reliant on subsidies from the British Council, similar to the English School for Boys in Nişantaşı, to the north of Beyoğlu. She does state that considering the small amount of applicants that could actually be admitted to the school, the British school system was appreciated in Turkey at the time. Contrary to the English High School for Boys (EHSB) the girls' school offered education only at the middle school level (orta), including three years of education preceded by two years of English prep school. This meant that the girls would be required to enrol in a different school once they reached the lyceum (lise) level. Several girls would continue their education at the American Schools or Robert College, though in the final years of its existence in the 1970s, female students were also admitted to the lyceum cohorts of the Boys' School.[19]

An influential actor in the organizational structure of the English High Schools in Istanbul was the British Council. Founded in 1934, the British Council stood and stands at the core of Great Britain's cultural diplomacy. Tamara van Kessel argues that this 'soft power', a significant branch of international relations, has received increasing attention in recent years, triggering research into the historical dimensions of cultural diplomacy. The British were relatively late in recognizing the significance of an organized effort towards cultural diplomacy. Van Kessel points out that in 1929 the Foreign Office made estimates of their foreign counterparts' spending in cultural diplomacy: £500,000 by France, £300,000 by Germany and close to £300,000 by Italy. She describes a lack of political will as a significant reason as to why the British were unable to organize similar efforts, with cultural affairs considered as a task that was to be beyond the realm of the state. She quotes the British diplomat Harold Nicolson, whose description of the general opinion is indicative: '[it was thought that] the genius of England, unlike that of lesser countries, spoke for itself.'[20]

Van Kessel points out, however, that not geopolitical, but rather economic considerations were the primary incentive for establishing the British Council. She does add that growing concerns of the British about control over their empire were another significant reason to invest in cultural propaganda and diplomacy, particularly in the Middle East. It was reasoned that good relations with Egypt were necessary to ensure stability along the Suez Canal, crucial for connecting Great Britain with India, and a robust standing against Italian and French competition could be partially attained by cultural diplomacy.[21] Van Kessel notes that the British Council differed from its Italian, French and German rivals since it was a private entity, although under the supervision of the Foreign Office and with the Prince of Wales as its patron. The reasoning according to her was that projections suggested that the council could eventually become independent from governmental subsidies. The reality turned out to be different: it would become fully dependent on the state. The objective of the Council then became 'to promote a wider knowledge and appreciation of Great Britain and the English language abroad, and to develop closer cultural and commercial relations between Great Britain and other countries.'[22] Van Kessel argues that although the British Council always denied during the interbellum to be involved in cultural propaganda and rather provided information and engaged in cultural diplomacy, the strategies of the Council were reminiscent of the former War Propaganda Bureau. She concludes that this was an outcome of the ties of both organizations with the Foreign Office and the involvement of the Council's founders in both. Representatives such as Lord Lloyd, chairman of the Council between 1947 and 1941, however, made statements that are significant in understanding the Council's involvement with the EHS in Istanbul: 'We do not force them to "think British"; we offer them the opportunity to learn what the British think.'[23] It is in that light also that the British Council's involvement in the EHS should be considered. The schools were essentially appreciated by the British Council as a way to exert influence over the outlook on life of potentially influential Turkish citizens, particularly with regard to their attitude towards anglophone culture.

This led around the time of headmistress Thompson's writings, in 1944, to a mixed school population with twenty nationalities, although most pupils were Turkish girls. It is unclear if she means Turkish nationals or 'ethnic Turks' in this case, or if the twenty nationalities she refers to also include the Pontic Greek, Armenian, Jewish and other populations that constituted an Ottoman millet before the regime change.[24] The Foreign Office and British Council in the meantime appeared to have shown great interest in the school, for both reasons of required financial investments and the potentially beneficial impact to Anglo-Turkish relations through raising and educating Turkish citizens as anglophiles. Angus Gillan, representative of the British Council in London, writes the following in 1946: 'On general principles, I feel strongly that an efficient British school which is open to and really used by the natives, is in any country the very best propaganda we can do and should have a very high priority.'[25] The amount of non-British students in both the girls' school and the related Boys' School in Nişantaşı is estimated to be 75 per cent, with long waiting lists, giving a clue of the impact that this school had on the local population, particularly considering that many of the schools' graduates would be able to attain established careers.[26]

The importance of this observation can also be appreciated in the light of iron curtains that were being drawn up. As Turkey was aligning itself with the Western bloc and being actively persuaded to do so by, among others, Great Britain and the United States, the significance of Gillan's words should not just be understood in a local, national or bilateral context, but also in a world of shifting geopolitics. Great Britain feared the possibility of growing influence of the Soviet Union in Greece and Turkey. With the aggressive rise of a communist party in Greece, the British government feared that Greece's sympathies could shift towards the Soviets, which would have a detrimental effect on the position of the United States in the region. Former US ambassador to Turkey George McGhee argues that the British government, which had become aware that it could no longer bear the economic burden of supporting the Greeks and Turks, pushed the United States to take up the responsibility of providing aid.[27] The Truman administration became quickly aware of the potentially hazardous situation and decided in no more than two days that it would support the Turkish and Greek governments and armed forces. McGhee points out that the US government considered Turkey to be a natural barrier against the Soviet Union and expected that the Soviets would not aim to invade the country, but rather to cripple its economy by provoking it just enough to push Turkey into upholding a sizeable standing army.[28] The US government therefore realized that an aid program would require to surpass the boundaries of military aid and also accommodate the Turks in building a robust economy. This should be considered one of the prime reasons as to why Turkey would receive Marshall Plan aid. Indeed, the Truman Doctrine, the pre-eminent geopolitical statement of the Cold War era, was formulated with this goal in mind: halting the potential impact of communism to Greece and Turkey.[29]

Within these circumstances the significance of cultural diplomacy on the side of the British, which could no longer provide aid on the same scale to Turkey and had to proxy the responsibility to the United States, becomes apparent. When issues of finance and the necessity for a transfer or adjustment of the schools' legal status became more pressing in the 1960s, it is pointed out in a memorandum of the British Consulate that the schools' committees opposed a transfer of the schools to the Turkish state, as the *maarif* (Turkish educational system) would 'inevitably result in the Schools losing their special nature as "English Schools"'.[30] The documents indicate that this special nature does refer not only to the language of instruction but also to the entire character of the school. Reflecting the discourse of a post-imperial Britain struggling to find its role in the world, it is suggested that the appeal of the schools was generated by its deviation from the Turkish educational system, along 'liberal English lines' which would 'develop a personal and intellectual discipline that is not found elsewhere in Turkey'.[31]

In a report on the activities of the British Council in Turkey, two decades earlier in 1944, the fourth year that the Council was active in the country, the importance of English-language education is stressed. The report explains that the British were in fact last to join Nazi Germany and France, which was reflected in the low numbers of Turkish students going to the UK for education in comparison with, for instance, Nazi Germany. The report boasts a significant increase in the interest of 'British culture', particularly since the diplomatic rupture between Turkey and Nazi Germany. In the years since 1940 the total number of English-language books, 188,000 distributed by the British Council, surpassed the amount of books that had reached departments and bookstores in the entire period before 1940 according to the report. Still the demand was much larger than the supply, which led the Council to introduce library loan, which was a novelty to Turkey. In addition, Turkish translations of English classic novels and other works were on the rise, both through efforts of the British and through separate endeavours by the Turkish Ministry of Education.[32] Another medium used as a means of 'cultural propaganda' were educational films screened at *Halkevleri* (People's Houses), military colleges and schools. Council teachers were moreover teaching English to over 2,000 students in fifty-five *Halkevleri* (People's Houses) spread over Turkey. English was also taught through initiatives of the British Council in civilian and military schools, companies and the Turkish Foreign Ministry.[33] Travelling exhibitions of photography portraying 'British graphic art and scientific achievement (. . .) architecture, countryside and educational institutions' aimed to familiarize people around Turkey with Great Britain and British culture (defined as an 'unpopular but convenient omnibus term').[34] Other topics which the Council involved itself in were science, medicine, agriculture, sports and archaeology. The Council meanwhile was able to execute its tasks, which is particularly noteworthy considering the fact that it was forced to close its branches in numerous communist countries and that it was severely curbed in Nasserian Egypt.[35] As such it can be considered as a clear sign that post-war Turkey was strongly embedded in the Western geopolitical sphere of influence. Slightly before the end of the Second World War, the report on the council's activities in Turkey indicates that the efforts of Germany had been gradually collapsing, which may have also given additional room for the British to operate within Turkey. Additionally, the authors think that the lack may have also helped launching the Council's efforts with unprecedented success: 'Even those with the longest memories find it difficult to think of other foreign organisations that have been allowed to make the same progress in the same or indeed in any lapse of time.'[36]

Cables from the British legations in 1944 show that the EHSG's school population was gradually changing, with the amount of 'Moslem Turkish girls' increasing to 47 per cent of the total. British dignitaries reflect on this development as somewhat worrisome, primarily because they feared that an increase in the amount of local students would decrease the quality of English-language education and hinder its own goals. Others, however, argued that the rise of local girls would increase 'in conformity with the wishes and policy of the British Council, if not to the full satisfaction of some of the Teachers and Committee members'.[37] The document suggests not to let the amount of 'Moslem Turks' increase beyond 55 per cent, citing the total amount in absolute numbers as 104, while it was 94 at the time of writing. The quality of English speech is explicitly cited as the reason for this recommendation.

It becomes clear, however, that there was a divergence between the aims of the British Council and the EHSG. Whereas the British Council aimed to spread British culture exclusively among 'Moslem Turks', the EHSG's board felt that it could only go as far along with the Council's objectives as it had until that year. Twenty-seven girls from the minorities versus ninety-four Muslim Turks are cited as being among the school population with fifty-four Muslim-Turkish girls admitted to the school since 1941 against ten girls from the minorities.[38] The Committee is said to have pointed to its Trust Deed as indicative for its own objectives, namely 'to show no prejudice or preference for any race or creed'. The report assesses the Charter of the Girls' School (as well as the Constitution of the Boys' School in Nişantaşı) to be incompatible with the Lausanne Agreements of 1923, although both documents had no legal standing in a Turkish legal context. They did, however, for the British government.[39]

The Committee moreover was not registered as a legal entity in Turkey, but functioned as such according to the British government and Embassy. The author of the report questions whether the High Schools would sustain the 'Turcising policy' at all if they were not dependent on the subsidies of the British Council. He also stresses that it would be difficult for the high schools to regulate the inflow of the student population so that the 55 per cent margin of Muslim Turks would be sustained, since the schools would maintain the principle of first come, first serve.[40] It appears, nonetheless, that around 1944 a certain degree of antipathy towards the British Council existed among the schools' management, that is, headmaster, headmistress and members of the school committees, which was principally caused by the British Council's effort to get more Muslim Turks into the schools' ranks.[41] The number of British pupils meanwhile was dwindling and not expected to increase, while the school became increasingly popular among Turkish nationals (Muslim and others) and non-British foreigners.[42] The British Council would eventually cease to subsidize the schools in 1968 (elsewhere it is claimed that the Boys' Schools funding had been terminated already by 1966 and that of the Girls' School in 1967), when it was decided that the sponsoring was 'no longer justified'. It seems that the funding of a number of British teachers in the schools by the Council, however, continued. It is suggested in diplomatic reports that the British Council and the British government had considerable disagreements over this matter.[43] The official instigation of the British Council to withdraw its support at that point were the ensuing budgetary difficulties of the schools, though no further explanation as to the exact nature of the disagreements between the two British parties is given. However, diplomatic communication from 1962 also shows that the British Council and Foreign Office seemed to be in agreement that it would be best for the council to 'entrench themselves in the educational system of a foreign country', rather than seek to maintain extra-national institutions which were exposed to pressures of various kinds. We were inclined to agree with the Council that we could not accept a solution that would put the schools at the mercy of the Turks'.[44] The duality of the Turkish position is remarkable, because the Foreign Office appears to have been of the opinion that closing the schools would have severe negative effects on Anglo-Turkish relations and was therefore to be avoided.

The Foreign Office and the British Council thus were actively engaged in what Sarah Davies describes in the context of British cultural diplomacy in the USSR as 'the struggle for men's minds'.[45] Nevertheless, considering the significant efforts that were deployed in other countries, the British initiatives at the onset of the Cold War seemed to have lacked a clear strategy. J. M. Lee argues that if there was any kind of coherence in what the British were doing on a global scale, it was centred on the question of what would happen to the 'British presence' in the post-imperial age.[46] Another issue mentioned by Lee was Arab nationalism and the priority that the UK should retain access to oil reserves. His argument in that context is essentially that objectives of cultural diplomacy in Davies's 'war for the men's minds' could be generally easier attained in 'informal empire and UN mandate' than in colonial settings. It is the specific context of the 1950s Middle East which pushed the British to compose a more organized strategy of cultural diplomacy Lee concludes.[47] James Vaughan adds, moreover, that British Council schools in the Middle East were often considered to be the most important branch of British cultural diplomacy. A quote from the Council's staff members is telling in that sense: 'their character building reputation' lent them a level of prestige which enabled them 'to attract the children of important families and to build up understanding of Britain both by their impact upon the pupils and by their contact with the parents'.[48] Yet, Vaughan also reaches the conclusion that cultural diplomacy in the Middle East essentially failed due to setting wrong or unrealistic targets by policy makers; cultural diplomacy typically takes much time to bear fruit, whereas the impact of political and economic diplomacy can have quick and drastic (or even dramatic) effects.[49]

In Istanbul the policies of the British appear to be marked by confusion as well, although within the Istanbul schools the freedom of the British was also severely limited. Nonetheless, the schools were appreciated, very popular and thus successful in their effort to be 'flagbearers' of Britishness in Turkey. From a local perspective, however, the schools appeared to have been on the expensive side in comparison with some of the French Schools, such as St Benoit, St Michel, St Joseph (in Kadıköy) and the German School, but in relative consonant with the American College for Girls and Robert College. A report found in the National Archives, however, notes that the facilities offered by EHSG and EHSB are insufficient and not comparable to those of the other schools, making the school fees much too high. The report therefore pushes against increasing the fees, because it would result in a further socio-economic asymmetry in the school's population or the increase of bursaries. In addition, the report suggests that the schools' curricula deliberately stray from the rules set by the Turkish authorities in line with 'various evasions and extensions to the curricula to which the Schools are entitled'.[50] The author suggests that these 'irregularities should be condoned if not encouraged' and argues that considering the circumstances in Turkey at the time efforts should be made to limit the amount of Turkish-language classes and other classes taught in Turkish, while pushing to increase the amount of classes on social subjects in English as much as possible.[51]

The author clearly seems to want to praise the schools' relative liberty (compared to Turkish high schools), as they offered an alternative world view and curriculum to students, thus offering a counterbalance to the growing nationalist grip on the educational agenda of the Turkish Republic.[52] More suggestions and recommendations are made to push back against the increasingly nationalist influence on foreign education in Turkey. The schools, however, are not considered 'unfavourably' by the Turkish state, due to the influence of the British Council on the Turkish Ministry of Education and the 'skilful, even Machiavellian negotiations' of the schools' management. Elsewhere it is stated that several British representatives did not have a 'high opinion of the value of (. . .) support' of Minister of Education, Hassan Ali. Further communication between the British and the Turks appears to have balanced awkwardly between flattery and insult. The minister stated that 'the English Schools are the best of the foreign schools, but foreign school as a whole are not very good'.[53]

The shadow of Lausanne: The EHSG's destiny in Beyoğlu

The building of the EHSG is described as being inadequate and inconvenient: 'The Girls' High School (exclusively for day girls) is a tall six-storeyed building in the middle of the shopping centre [i.e. Beyoğlu] of Istanbul. It is surrounded by commercial buildings and blocks of flats, the noise of traffic is continuous and loud, and there is little access of fresh air or sunlight.'[54] In the documents of the Foreign Office British officials comment on the peculiarity of the buildings in Beyoğlu and Nişantaşı (of the Boys' School) and claim that the buildings of both schools were expensive and difficult to maintain and run. The girls' school is cited as being 'full of safety hazards', which is probably in reference to the steep staircases and the recreational area on the rooftop that students would refer to as 'the Roof'.[55] A British English teacher who started working at the school after its transferal to the Turkish Ministry of Education recounts how he would be very strict about the way girls would go up and down the staircases, since a girl in the past had fallen from the staircase and died.[56] A more frivolous example of the peculiarities of the school building is narrated by one of the former girls who had fond memories how they would cross over the fenced area at the rooftop in order to sunbathe.

Visitations to the school by British dignitaries usually sum up in complimenting the staff and questioning how the staff managed to keep up a school in the building. In a telegram from a tour through the Middle East between February and April 1946, Angus Gillan reports that he was not happy about the institutions and their management, more due to financial shortcomings than the management itself. He was content with the way the girls' school was run, considering it 'is as well run internally as it can be in a building which is only excelled in unsuitability by the Boys' School'.[57] In another cable from the Ankara Embassy to the Foreign Office it is stated that the conduct of the schools is not up to standards, though the schools can on the grounds of prestige never be allowed to be closed down.[58] These matters appeared to have cleared up to some extent, as the tone of following cables regarding the girls' school is considerably more positive, though the enduring main problem appears to be the lack of sufficient funding.[59] The statement of accounts from 1961 to 1962 therefore indicate that despite the age of the building, which is described as old, only the most necessary repairs are executed.[60]

The issue of funding was a recurring one, which was essentially caused by the school's legal status (or rather the lack of it). In a cable from 1960, a lawyer named Ayhan Unler, lawyer of BP, explains the complications of registering the school building in name of the embassy. It becomes clear that the building and the school were separate legal entities.[61] The consul general appears to have, pressed by the Embassy, contacted authorities in Istanbul. The consul points out to the British Embassy that this is rather pointless, but necessary nonetheless. He explains that the only motivation to keep in touch with the local authorities in Istanbul was to avoid that the governor of Istanbul at some point would feel at liberty to take definite decisions regarding the school and its properties, in which the governor would claim that he could have intermediated in a more positive fashion to solve any problems of the school if only he had known about them.[62] The consul general contacted his German counterpart to see if they had experienced similar problems with the German School in Galata. The German consul general confirmed that the German School indeed had also considerable problems with the Turkish authorities, but he also explained to the British side that taking up the problem with the *Vali* (governor) of Istanbul would not help a great deal.

In a cable from 1962 new problems appear to arise, now connected to the buildings of both schools, which – according to the cable – urgently need repair and improvements requiring 're-building on new sites'.[63] Later in the 1960s, however, it became clear that new Turkish legislation forbade the enlargement of the existing building or developing new properties elsewhere. This restricted the freedom of movement for the schools even further. The documents suggest furthermore that the law also required foreign schools to become private legal entities. The Turkish authorities appear to have wanted to get rid of these independent schools in their current format, which is in a sense remarkable since the 1960 coup had introduced a constitution that was in essence more liberal than the previous one, and Zürcher points out that in general people and ideas in Turkey were becoming increasingly mobile.[64] This may also be one of the reasons as to why the Turks retained the status quo, but did not make fundamental efforts to entirely curb the freedom of the EHS. The Foreign Office also notes that there was discord within the Turkish state, which may have had a positive impact on retaining the status quo. The British Embassy's cultural attaché notes:

There seem to be two trends of thought within the Turkish Government. There is the usual anti-foreigner approach, which is evident in the desire that all foreign aid should be handed over at the frontier, including that for schools, and the more broad-minded approach of some Ministries who would like to see us giving technical aid, including, for instance, the running of technical schools.[65]

Nevertheless, statutes were drawn up to ensure a relative independence from the Turkish state, proposing to turn the schools into 'Anglo-Turkish entities under Turkish law'. It was hoped that the schools would become foundations, retaining the characteristics of the British educational tradition while conforming to the Turkish system. 'A war for the minds of men', offering an alternative (or in the minds of some: superior) outlook on life, thus also appeared necessary for the British Council and the Foreign Office in Turkey. The British appeared reluctant to consider closing the schools, since it may have incited legal action from parents and the necessity of sale of the properties which would have been 'extremely complicated', since the buildings and schools' status was so diffuse.[66] This resulted in a dragging legal case in 1962, in which it was made clear that the properties could not be turned over to the British Embassy as the grounds would require to be granted diplomatic immunity in that case which was impossible as the lot was designated for educational purposes. In the meantime it also proved impossible to move the properties away to sites in Tarabya or other parts of Istanbul owned by the British state.[67] The Turkish state appeared hesitant to allow the schools to be allowed to become foundations (*tesisler*) rather than associations (*kurumlar*), but the school committees insisted that the schools should become foundations since otherwise there would have been a serious risk of losing control over the distinct British character of the schools and their educational programs. At the same time officials from both the Turkish and British sides, up to the levels of the Turkish Minister of Education, stressed how important they considered the British contribution to the Turkish educational system to be and how closure of the schools would negatively impact the Anglo-Turkish relations.[68]

A noteworthy observation is made in a communication from the 1960s. In it the question of the school's embedding in the Turkish school system is brought up again, with particular regard to the relevance of the provisions indicated in the school's trust deed. Was the school committee legally obliged to conform to it or was it by now more a guideline than a legal document? The author, who signs as D. F. Duncan and is most likely working at the Foreign Office, wonders whether the school should be 'Protestant' and part of the 'Church of England', since this is indicated in the School's Trust Deed of 1881. As this would run against the legislations of the Turkish school system and considering the fact that there are very little to none Protestant girls in the school, he argues against taking too much notice of the considerations of the Trust Deed.[69] Despite this, several former girls who were students in the EHSG in the 1970s indicate that some of the English teachers asked the girls to say grace before lunch.[70] A math teacher who worked at the school in the mid-1970s puts this remark into perspective. She describes her decision to come to Istanbul to be inspired both by a desire for adventure as well as a Christian calling. She adds, however, that she was always very careful with regard to explicating her religious convictions and quickly understood she should not discuss these with her students at length. She did occasionally talk about her faith when her students asked about it, but she was always very careful, because she felt and feels that in Turkey people should not be evangelized under the age of 18.[71]

Most students were Muslims at the time, though in the mid-1970s approximately a third was still Christian or Jewish according to her estimates.

It also becomes clear that considerable confusion exists considering the exact prescriptions of the founding deed and the regulations in which the agreements were set up with the Ottoman government. In an investigation carried out by the British Embassy in 1956, which is cited in cables from the 1960s, it was found out that the founding deeds of the Boys' School from 12 April 1911 had permitted the school's premises to be listed in the name of the British Embassy's name. The cables point out that this became a problem only when on 1 March 1916 the Ottoman government decreed that no other land could be claimed by a foreign legation except for consulates and embassies, bringing the provision in the title deeds in conflict with Ottoman law. Consequentially the Boys' School officially had no owner. When the authorities pushed the school to have its properties registered in 1956 and 1957 it was only possible to do so in the name of the school. Interestingly also, possibly from a legal perspective as well, the British documents do not discriminate here between the Ottoman and Turkish governments, simply referring to the Ottoman Empire as 'Turkey' when discussing the acts of 1916.[72]

The British government did make efforts through the British Embassy to have the Girls' School's premises registered in its name when the 'local land commission' found out that it had no registered ownership, but the requests were refused by the Turkish Foreign Ministry several times. Eventually, similar to the Boys' School, the EHSG Committee had no other option than to allow the premises to be registered in its own name. Guarantees were given by the Turkish side not to interfere in the administration of the school: 'Fears that it would incur setting up an Anglo-Turkish Committee which might lead to embarrassing Turkish interference in the management of the Schools particularly of their finances were dispelled by the Turkish authorities.'[73] The documents further suggest that the Boys' School had been accepted by the Turkish government as a legal entity and was therefore entitled to own its building. When checking the registries in 1967 it was found out that the property was still without owner. Following the problems of registration of the Boys' School, which are cited confusingly to be in 1958, it was found out that registration was costly. This is cited as a possible reason as to why the building was still not registered. If the schools were to be closed the properties would therefore have no owner, which would imply the dissolving of the assets entirely and most likely being claimed by the Turkish authorities. The case for the Girls' School is claimed to be 'similar', although ownership of a playing field is suggested to be 'clearly registered in the [Girls'] School's name'.[74]

The situation that would unfold during the construction of the first Bosporus Bridge would counter that suggestion. The Trust Deed of the EHSG indicates, moreover, that the property was to be transferred from Lady Stratford de Redcliffe to the embassy's possession.[75] Apparently, that process was never finalized or at least not in agreement with the Ottoman authorities, leaving the building formally without an owner. This, as well as the uncertainty regarding the exact legal status of the school and the legal value of the deed, is confirmed in documents of the British legations from 1979.[76] The staff of the English High Schools and its school committees appear to have been caught in between the conflicting opinions of Turkish policymakers and politicians, one side wanting to preserve this prestigious institution of education, while other would rather see it disappear. This conflict may in part explain why it was so excessively difficult for the British representations or the schools themselves to break free from the impasse that they faced. The Turkish side seems to not have want to change anything regarding the school's status but preserve it nonetheless, whereas the British side for a long time did not dare to threaten with the school's closure fearing collateral damage to the diplomatic relations between the two countries and cause geopolitical fallout.

In cables from 1968 the issue still appears unresolved. Until the 1970s it had not caused severe problems that would risk dispossession by the Turkish state. In the early 1970s, however, the Girls School's plot of land that was used as a playfield in Şişli primarily by the Boys' School was disowned to construct a new road leading to the first Bosporus Bridge. Gwyneth Petter, the headmistress, writes in the yearbook from 1972 that the school held its last Speech Day in 1971 at the playfield since the Highway Authority claimed the property for the construction of the highway. She describes it as 'a fine scheme, but one which, in depriving us of our valuable playing area, is a great blow to the school'.[77] A year later she once again expresses her sadness with the loss of the playing field, but also narrates that the school was able to use the Tarabya Gardens of the British Consulate and the track facilities in the Dolmabahçe Stadium, the later Beşiktas JK stadium.[78] She hopes, however, that the school will at some point be able to use a small plot of land that was not dispossessed by the Turkish state. In cables from the British legations, it is found out that a compensation for the part of the land that was taken was paid, but when the committee of the school disagreed about the amount the authorities argued that there was no legal ownership connected to the plot.[79] This runs contrary to suggestions made in British memoranda that in fact the plot was registered in the name of the school on authority of the Beyoğlu Prefecture (*Beyoğlu Kaymakamlığı*) at the Land Registry of Beyoğlu. The estimated value in 1968 was 200,000 pound sterling and the British Consulate's documents state that it was expected that the value would increase once the Bosporus Bridge was constructed.[80] The exact amount granted by the Turkish authorities is not clear. The properties in Beyoğlu and Nişantaşı remained unaffected nonetheless, while plans for rebuilding on different sites and sale of the buildings appear to have been abandoned.

The stature of the school is still apparent in the documents of the late 1960s, with the committees stating that a closing of the schools would have a detrimental effect on the 'British standing in Istanbul'.[81] Despite all of its problems, the popularity of both schools was far from decreasing. It is suggested that both the boys' and girls' schools have a considerable reputation among businessmen, with the schools having trained many businessmen, and – showing the painful reality of a patriarchal society in the 1960s – 'hardly less important, many top private secretaries and wives of, for instance, important officials'.[82] It should be pointed out that this gender dichotomy in the career perspectives of the EHS graduates may not have been as black and white as the British reports suggest. In the interview with the math teacher of the girls' school, she narrates how she is often surprised how many of the girls would become professors, doctors and set up their own enterprises.[83]

To protect the school's legacy it is proposed once again by the British side, including the committees of both schools, to have the EHSG and EHSB turned into Turkish private schools. It becomes clear in the documents that an update of the statuses of the schools is required as it was by the late 1960s still based on the provisions made in the Treaty of Lausanne of 1923 which guaranteed the continuation of existing British institutions in the Turkish Republic. This would grant the schools more freedom to stipulate their own fees, which were already high in comparison with other comparable schools, and avoid the feared risks of losing the schools' 'Englishness' that a turnover to the *maarif* would entail.[84] Considerable confusion appears to exist on the British side about the legal connections of the UK with both schools and what plans for the future would mean in reality. At one point a British MP seems to have thought both schools are closed, in case of which the legation in Turkey has to explain this is in fact not the case.[85]

Another example of the ensuing misunderstandings is the suggestion of the Foreign Office to have the schools established on the line of the English-language Ankara College. This college was set up as a foundation by Mustafa Kemal Atatürk to push for education in English, in which – the British documents suggest – he pushed his circle to invest considerable funds.[86] The Foreign Office appeared to consider the school a state school, whereas in fact it was a foundation not under the direct control of the Turkish Ministry of Education. The Foreign Office then suggested to hand the schools over the Turkish authorities and have it run in a similar fashion as the Ankara College. This resulted in the British consul general, who was chairman of the Girls' School Committee in 1968, indicating that the school committees of neither the EHSG nor the EHSB were prepared to hand over the schools to the Turkish authorities for the reasons of losing the schools' British character.[87] The consul general added to this that he thought Anglo-Turkish relations would experience considerable harm from the schools' closures and 'have a highly adverse effect on our commercial prospects in Istanbul'.[88] The British Embassy appears to have disagreed and suggested that the consul general is to speak with the Turkish authorities only as representative of the School Committee from then onwards, since the committee has ignored the wishes of the Foreign Office, the ambassador and the British Council in London. He is also advised to resign as chairman of the Girls' School Committee. In an apparent shift of perspective compared to earlier decades, the embassy indicates that handing over the schools would not be damaging to Anglo-Turkish relations and that the embassy will do whatever it can to help the schools, although the British government decided not to support the schools with subsidies.[89]

The girls' school meanwhile housed 250 pupils in 1974, and a report notes that though the majority consists of 'Moslem Turkish girls', a total of eighteen different nationalities are represented at the school.[90] The math teacher, however, recounts:

> The girls who came were all Turkish nationals. The majority Muslim background, some, probably around a third Jewish and Christian.

She also notes the following on the quality of education at the school:

> it was called the English High School for Girls, but the education didn't really correspond with what it was like in England. We used English textbooks, but it was more like a grammar school really. Quite rigid really, because of being here in Turkey. (. . .) We didn't have permission to open the lise part, we only had the middle school part. There were always students who went to either the boy school, or Robert College or Üsküdar American High School. Some of the best girls went on to Robert College, they often were the top students. We had a two-year prep, which gave them a really good grounding. Üsküdar had, I think, one year of prep, so they had English, but not quite as good as our girls had got. That's what we used to tell ourselves anyway.[91]

The mixed population would remain a fact until after its transferral to the Turkish state and the math teacher narrates how girls would basically get along regardless of their background, with a third of the girls being Jewish in some classes, though occasionally the racist influences of Turkish nationalism would trickle down into the school lives of the girls as well, echoing stories from the Galatasaray High School:

> It was good academically and – I felt – a good atmosphere. Although I have talked to some students, one of the Jewish girls, she was actually harassed really because of her Jewishness. So there were a lot of things going on that we didn't pick up and that saddens me.[92]

Regarding the socio-economic divisions in the schools she recounts that most girls were from the 'old middle and upper middle classes' in Istanbul, reminiscing her of Orhan Pamuk's description of his family life in his memoir-like *Istanbul*. In this description she arguably establishes a synthesis between personal and cultural memory in a way quite similar to the process that has been coined by Marianne Hirsch as postmemory.[93] This ran contrary to the times when she taught in Robert College when a *nouveaux riche* class had started to develop in Istanbul. Despite the fact that fees for the schools were kept relatively low (though they were much higher than state school fees), the competition to get into the school made it particularly hard for children from less well-off families to get their children on the school. It is probable that the fees were also simply too high for some families as a report from 1960 discusses a visit by a Turkish inspector, who stated that the school fees of the English schools were above those of all other schools in Turkey. An ongoing quarrel between the Turkish and British side about these fees would ensue over the next two decades.[94] The math teacher mentions the following about this:

> They were from quite wealthy families, a lot of them. (. . .) There were some who were poorer, but mostly they were from quite wealthy backgrounds. (. . .) The school has been part and parcel of Istanbul and the mix that's here, it was obviously very elitist which I think is the downside of the school really.[95]

Despite this, the situation described in the archives of the Foreign Office makes clear that the schools were not allowed to increase their fees to a level that would allow for a healthy budgetary balance. The math teacher recounts how this would affect the lives of teachers in the schools on a daily basis:

> Eight years I taught there, I realized those were the best years of my teaching career. It was a very nice school and a very nice atmosphere. We didn't have much. The blackboards were awful and I got them painted and then in the end I had to do it myself, because they put green gloss paint on it. It has to be matte. There was a lot of do it yourself stuff, just to make it work. We had funding, but not a lot. The girls had to pay for all their textbooks. There wasn't a lot of money for doing things, so we did do some things ourselves. Mostly we had quite good foreign teachers who all worked together.[96]

Alumni from the years that the math teacher worked at the EHSG also shared fond memories of their years in the school. They also recounted the strict discipline that was upheld in the school. During a dinner at the EHS Alumni Association in Arnavutköy, a number of former graduates from the girls' school memorized how teachers were strict about the stairs routine. Saturday detention and other disciplinary measures were taken when girls would speak in Turkish during the breaks. School uniforms were mentioned as a matter of embarrassment for some as the girls would be required to wear hats which would inspire men on the streets to call them 'hostesses' on the street. Despite the apparent stringent regime of the school, the girls would occasionally be able to get away to spend time in a café near Galatasaray which was, according to the girls, also frequented by the Galatasaray football players. When a teacher found them they felt like they were walked back like a gaggle of geese.[97] The math teacher recounts how teachers and school administration was also quite strict about speaking English. She still wonders how some of the students managed to learn the language properly since the teachers in the prep school were usually not native speakers.

The school's status as a foreign school came to an end, following Margaret Thatcher's election as prime minister in the UK and her decision to close all foreign schools in 1979. The schools were nonetheless maintained as English-language institutions after the closing and reopened as Anatolian High Schools (*Anadolu Liseleri*), a selective public high school system. The change of attitude towards the importance of English-language education as a means of cultural diplomacy is reflected in a letter from the Foreign Office by Parliamentary Under Secretary of State Richard Luce, dated 21 November 1979. In this letter Luce points out that the British government has 'no responsibility for the education of British children living overseas; and certainly none for foreign children living in their own country'.[98] There was, however, considerable discord on the British side. In a letter in the National Archives Gasford Willis, former headmaster of the Boys' School and described in diplomatic cables as 'an extremely persistent correspondent', questions whether the ambassador was properly briefed on the matter since the closure would cause 'genuine hardship & distress and bitter anger against the

British which would be caused among all the 600 sets of highly influential Turkish parents as a result of the handover'.[99] He goes on by saying that 'did the CG [consul general] make it clear that we were *giving away* at least £2½ million sterling worth of British assets held by us for ¾ century – longer for the EHSG – without getting <u>anything</u> in return except a vast amount of odium and contempt' [emphasis in original].[100]

Though financial difficulties of the girls' school are frequently cited in the British documents, it does seem that the financial difficulties were primarily caused by the deficits of the Boys' School in Nişantaşı. The British ambassador, Derek Dodson, indicates that the Boys' School had been troubled by financial issues since it was founded in 1905. One of the main causes was in fact the lack of income, since, contrary to the EHSG, the EHSB did not have any shops in its buildings from which it could collect revenues.[101] Apart from that it becomes clear in the initial meetings of school committees and the British legations to discuss the transfer the school indeed had also financial reserves.[102] This is confirmed by the math teacher:

Actually the girls' high school was quite well off. They had not only some fees coming in, but they owned the shops as well underneath. So they had rents coming in. And then they must have had shares or even gold actually. Because I remember one of the heads commenting, and the head had to sell it. There was someone on the board who was quite astute and knew about investments, but then it was the head mistress, who had to take the action to sell or buy. So I think we had quite a lot of private investments or gold.[103]

In the Foreign Office's files concerning the transfer of the schools to the Turkish authorities it is indicated that the Boys' School was essentially about to go bankrupt whereas the Girls' School would only be able to sustain itself for another two years. An important reason was the rapid inflation which strongly affected the EHSG's financial assets on the one hand and the necessity to increase salaries of the British teachers if the school were to attract new teachers on the other.[104] Agitation was rising meanwhile among representatives of the Foreign Office. In one cable it was stated that the issues surrounding the schools had taken up far too much time of the consulate, embassy and British Council.[105] On the schools' side Mr Sharland, the headmaster of the EHSB, wrote a letter to an MP in the UK asking for support and indicating the sacrifices the staff had made financially to keep the school open, because they believed in its purpose.[106] Eventually, despite efforts, the properties were transferred to the Turkish Ministry of Education and the girls' school was named Beyoğlu Anatolian High School, or *Beyoğlu Anadolu Lisesi* in 1980.

Despite this, on the British side efforts were made by various parties to retain the links with Britain. In a protocol set up to facilitate the transfer it was indicated that the British Council would have a 'privileged position' in the policy of both the girls' and Boys' School. The continued use of English as the language of instruction was considered as another safeguard for preserving the schools' 'Englishness'.[107] This 'British experience' appears to have been one of the hallmarks of the school and its popularity. The math teacher recounts that the girls were influenced by the school, its teachers and curricula considerably. She wonders occasionally about what they were doing and whether this school system really helped them to establish livelihoods and cope in Turkish society:

> One thing that I often wondered about, because I thought about doing an MA in education. If I had done that I would have liked to have looked at the influence of the school on people culturally. I felt in a way – looking in retrospect – we were very British. There were lots of British teachers, even though you were not teaching British culture, it comes over. English literature and stuff like that. (. . .) I have often wondered whether we really helped the girls in some way. How able they were to fit into Turkish society. (. . .) They often went to English universities or universities in America and so on. (. . .) It wasn't obviously our fault, we were just part of a system. This is a long history of foreign education. (. . .) Those countries [France, Italy, Germany] would have probably fostered that. The influence it would have on the leadership of a country and so on. In a way it was a bit sad when the British government in 1980, didn't want to continue to have these schools here. It's sort of saying like we don't want a link with Turkey in a way. It was a time when we were having cuts, but I think it's a shame in a way. There wasn't that ongoing connection [anymore]. I mean you can't influence everyone, but I think there is value: it just gives a different viewpoint.[108]

After the school was turned into an Anatolian High School the school managed to uphold its reputation as an English-language institution for a number of years. A former student of the *Beyoğlu Anadolu Lisesi* recounts how classic English and American literature was part of their classes, with a prefect-system still in place. She also argues that the school remained very popular due to the increasing importance of English in Turkey. There was one British English teacher who made a particular impression on her at the school. The English teacher remembered by the student started working at the school in 1979, and he also narrates how the school appears to have retained its appeal among Turkish parents:

> When it became a Turkish government school suddenly it was flooded with pupils. We had inspectors coming round to see if even the little room where the tea was made could be turned into a classroom, because people were complaining that the school was not accepting enough pupils. Because a lot of parents wanted their pupils to get in, so we had lots of people trying to get in – shall we say the backdoor. Getting their girls into other Anadolu Lisesis and then transfer them to our school. We also got people who had been the daughters of Turkish diplomatic staff or military attachés abroad and so we had part from those, we also had a girl from India. I don't know how she managed to get in.[109]

His remarks in fact echo the reports of a school inspector who visited both the boys' and girls' schools in 1960 and complained about the small numbers of students in the classes of the Boys' Schools, describing it as 'a very expensive luxury'.[110] On a different note, the English teacher remembers that the population of the school still included significant representations of girls from the minorities. Regarding the student population he mentions the following:

> There were a lot of Armenian, Greek, Jewish girls at the school when it was the high school. But that carried on, after it had been taken over, we still had quite a lot of girls from the Christian and Jewish communities.[111]

The school would eventually, however, transform into a regular Anatolian High School, though at first British involvement continued through the funding of two British English teachers and one math teacher. The changing of the head mistress would have had a considerable impact, according to the English teacher:

> In the end, however, it appears that the school started to become integrated in the regular system of Anadolu Liseleri. (. . .) Well, we lost our head mistress, [. . .], she went off to be the head mistress of Darüşşafaka. Then we had a guy who stayed for about a year, then we had a lady from Kadıköy Anadolu Lisesi, but the new Turkish head mistresses and head masters had not been in the British system. The thing about [the head mistress who went to Darüşşafaka] was that she had been at the school when it was a British school, so she knew how things were run in the British system. And she knew what sort of things British people liked and didn't like. The people who came after were completely Turkish in their mentality, so it was very difficult for me in particular, because I was trying to hang on to some of the British traditions to get through to this lady. So that made life very difficult and it became very stressful, so I left.[112]

Regarding the British traditions he tried to uphold the teacher tells:

> First of all, the system of prefects. The teachers on duty and this going up and down the stairs in single file and quite quietly, because in the late seventies a girl killed herself by sliding down the bannisters, and of course there were six or seven floors. [. . .] What else . . . I think in general, discipline, because of course it had been a smaller school and it was easier to get people to go up and down stairs in single file and line up, cue up for instance in the canteen when they wanted food. That's a very British thing to cue up and the British are very strict about that. So that's the sort of thing that started to go.[113]

The Beyoğlu High School remains in its present building to this date, though education in English and its 'British character' have waned through the years as it became further integrated in the system of Anatolian High Schools. The most prestigious historical schools that offer education in English nowadays are embedded in an American, rather than a British, tradition, notably Robert College and Üsküdar American High School. The school was turned into a co-educational institution after 2002. In recent years there has been debate about turning the school back into a high school for girls only, which stirred a debate among parts of the general public as well as among students, both claiming it to be a move of the AKP government to push for separation of boys and girls in the educational system.[114] The director of the school claimed it was for 'historical reasons', since the school always had been a girls' school he had seen it fit to turn the school back to its 'original state', suggesting that he proposed it to the Ministry of Education which had granted him the go-ahead.[115] The ties with the historical institution that was once a standard-bearer of 'Britishness' in the city, however, have been severed and little reminds of the anglophone culture that was upheld in the EHSG and the early years of BAL.

Chapter 6

TÜNEL/THE GERMAN HIGH SCHOOL

PIVOT OF GERMAN CULTURAL DIPLOMACY

Down a steep hill at the intersection of Tünel square and the İstiklal Caddesi lies the German High School, currently a private school (*Özel Alman Lisesi* or *Deutsche Schule Istanbul*). Similar to the Galatasaray High School the building is secluded from its surroundings by a perimeter, in the case of the German School a wall, consigning little of the building's size. Since 1897 the school has held its premises here and functioned as a pivotal actor for German cultural diplomacy while providing a significant contribution to the Turkish education system which had a hard timing keeping up with the rapid increase of population, particularly in the city. That being said the German School was one of the elite high schools in the country, open only to the best students and historically with a considerable representation from the country's minorities among its student population. Set up in the same year as the *Mekteb-i Sultanî*, in 1868, the German High School was initially founded as the *paritätische Deutsche und Schweizer Bürgerschule* (German and Swiss civil school). It had earlier roots, however, as Anne Dietrich indicates, when she mentions a Protestant School that had already existed since 1857. Yet, the new 'German' school was deemed necessary by missionaries, who had complained that interconfessional marriages negatively affected the Christian upbringing of children in Istanbul. Again, Dietrich traces an earlier evangelical school in Smyrna, which was to be the model for the previously mentioned Protestant School in Istanbul.

The initial plot of land for its building was acquired in Aynalı Çeşme, where the first stone was laid in 1856 and which is presently still the site of the German Protestant Church. When the Protestant School also known as the Prussian School, opened in 1857 it had forty-four students of Protestant, Roman Catholic and Greek Orthodox descent. In 1867, part of the Protestant community suggested to lessen the Protestant character of education. Dietrich argues this was probably catalysed by new initiatives from within the Germanophone community in Istanbul, aimed to set up a new civil high school where Armenians, Catholics, Jewish and Protestants would benefit from the same type of education, with no religious discrimination or any particularly outspoken confessional orientation. Gerhard Fricke argues that efforts were initially made to merge the plans for this new school with the Protestant School, but were met with resistance of the Prussian representatives of the Protestant Church. The parents who took the initiative for the plans then decided to set up an entirely new school in a different building. This would be the *Deutsche und Schweizer Bürgerschule*, opened on 11 May 1868. Here, two teachers were responsible for twenty-three or twenty-four girls.[1] The foundational document of the school pointed out that the institution should match the standards of similar well-ranked educational institutions in Germany.[2] Not long thereafter the Protestant School and the *Bürgerschule* were merged, on 23 November 1873, continuing together as the *Bürgerschule*.

The paritätische Deutsche *und* Schweizer Bürgerschule *in Istanbul*

Another type of 'competition' coming from earlier German language education institutions was that of the national school (*Nationalschule*) of the Austro-Hungarian Empire, located near the imperial embassy in the vicinity of Galatasaray.[3] Ulrich Münch explains that, similar to the *Bürgerschule* which was about to be opened, the *Nationalschule* was under the supervision of Austrian-Hungarian clergymen, who were known to be liberal. They consequently opted to steer the school clear of religious education bound to a particular denomination. The main instigation behind this choice, Münch argues, was the multi-confessional background of the pupils.[4] He describes the observations of a visitor in the school around 1873, who noticed that the Jesuits had by then indeed 'conquered' the religious education, but that any kind of autonomy of the Jesuits inside the school was in the curriculum. This suggests that the school had maintained what could be seen as a liberal context. It reflects the broader philosophy of the Austrian school, which not only offered classes in four languages, but set an ambition for itself summarized as follows: 'to steer clear entirely from national identity and represent the Austrian-Hungarian government, from which only a few are German'.[5] Elsewhere Gerhard Fricke suggests that the language of instruction at the school was in fact Italian rather than German.[6]

In contrast to the Prussian Protestant School and the Austro-Hungarian *Nationalschule* the *Deutsche und Schweizer Bürgerschule* appears not to have had any clergymen or representatives of the North German Confederation involved in its establishment. This leads Münch to the conclusion that the school was a private initiative by parents.[7] Paradoxically, the *Bürgerschule* grew much more popular among the German-speaking community than the Prussian Protestant School. By the early 1870s, the German consul Gillet noted that the number of students at the *Bürgerschule* was double that of the Protestant School and its income and contributions moreover were thrice as high.[8] The secular character may have been a partial cause for this popularity. It should be noted, however, that the *Bürgerschule* was quite unique in the context of the German-speaking community in Constantinople: Marcel Geser argues that before the founding of the *Bürgerschule* most schools had been either Protestant or Catholic mission schools.

The *Bürgerschule* may be seen as representative of a new trend bearing similarities with the English schools and the Ottoman *Mekteb-i Sultanî*. As indicated in Chapters 4 and 5 these schools did not, due to the multi-confessional and multi-ethnic composition of their respective student populations, have obvious religious orientations as well. The *Bürgerschule* actively cultivated a disregard for any of the particular denominations as the head master of the school Engelking noted in 1872:

> The grounds for a lack of allegiance to denominations was more advantageous here than elsewhere. In the day-to-day lives of Germans the denominational differences are so little noticeable and disappear to such an extent that many do not know of their close acquaintances whether they are protestant or catholic. Of many of the parents of the children who attend our school, I do not know to which denomination they belong.[9]

Münch furthermore quotes the pastor of the Protestant community and consular priest in 1871 when stating that the school did not just disregard denominations, but religion altogether:

> The considerably larger number of German Catholics here only serves the Protestants as a suitable coverup for their aversion against all evangelical institutions and aspirations. Everything should be German, not something denominational! That way all things 'German' become synonymous with a-denominational or a-religiosity.[10]

Münch notes, however, that the pastor appeased himself by joining the school board, becoming a delegate of the German Empire's embassy on the school council and even teaching religious classes in the school.

The directors of the school actively transformed the *Bürgerschule* into a *Realschule* where children could learn Latin and Greek. Director Mühlman, however, suggested that the daily reality of Istanbul and the German-speaking community within it required a different kind of skill set than classical languages. According to him it would make more sense to teach children New Greek, Turkish, French and English. The book published for the 125th anniversary of the German School points out that most children were already familiar with Greek or '*Vulgär-Griechisch*' (vulgar/crude Greek) as Mühlmann calls it, likely due to their interaction with Greek nannies, and that consequently it would be a more logical choice for students in the higher groups to take grammar classes in Greek or Turkish. He goes on by stating that:

> The real needs of the school community with regard to the education of their sons were in a different area than those of a classical education. The doings and dealings in Constantinople demand of anyone who wants to make it in life, that he can speak and write modern languages, especially French, but when possible also English.[11]

Mühlmann takes concern particularly with the career path for boys, hinting at the distinct educational trajectories of boys on the one hand and girls on the other. Indeed the curricula of boys and girls differed: girls were allocated more time for education in geography, history, singing and English, as well as 'female handicrafts' (*weibliche Handarbeit*), while ignoring math altogether.[12]

Lothar Wiltmann of the German Foreign Ministry's Cultural Department indicates that the school was placed under the patronage of the German Empire in 1878 with the 'National School Fund'(*Reichsschulfonds*).[13] It rented a property for the German School, but it proved to limit the potential for growth of the school. The community needed 100.000 *Goldmark* to finance the acquisition and build new premises. Half of this amount was collected by the community itself, with 12,000 *Goldmark* donated by the small Swiss community. According to Fricke, the school community consequently changed its name to German-Swiss school community (*deutsch-schweizerische Schulgemeinde*). Fricke points out that the subsequent tradition of having one Swiss citizen on the German School's board endured up to the time of his writing in 1958. The rest of the amount needed to build the school was covered by the German Empire, which also made commitments to assist the school in its future development. Eventually a new site was chosen near the Galata Tower in 1871, where a three-storey school building was constructed.[14] Director Mühlmann describes the location of the building: near the Galata Tower where it would catch the healthy winds from the Bosporus and Marmara Sea from all directions and thus highly suitable for a school. He notes: 'There truly are few German schools that shows such a wonderful landscape through its windows.'[15] A heavy earthquake in 1894, however, badly damaged the building which led the *Kölnische Zeitung* to report in that year that 'the not very pleasant building of the school' had become a hazardous site for the children attending it to such an extent: 'That the children can no longer visit safely without risking of life and limb.'[16]

The school is described by director Mühlmann as two separate buildings, connected by a courtyard. The buildings were built in stone, with asphalted terraces and flat roofs. Both buildings had their own cisterns for water provision, while the school's playground was lined with ailanthuses.[17] It had a total of eleven classrooms, an apartment for the rector, two married and two unmarried teachers, and a housemistress. Furthermore, it possessed a gymnastics hall, which was rented by the local German gymnastics club. By the time of the new building's opening in 1872 the school had already 133 students; 71 boys and 62 girls of, as Fricke points out, 'exclusively German origin or German ethnicity', growing further to 200 students and 9 classes with 10 teachers in 1874.[18]

Fricke states that it remains unclear, due to the destruction of documents from the early years of the school in a fire, when the restrictions on the students' ethnicity were lifted to allow other non-Muslim and Muslim children to attend the school. Student numbers had by 1897 risen to 600, however, which indicates that by that time not much had been left of the school's restrictive access. In the 1880s already, director Mühlmann notes that besides German, Swiss and Austrian citizens, also Ottoman Turkish, Romanian, English, French, Greeks, Russians and others were attending the school. In the 125th anniversary of the school edition in 1993, Gerhard Nurtsch noted that Mühlmann in the 1880s tried to counter critiques regarding the mixed school population. He adds that if German language proficiency, rather than nationality of the parents, was to be taken as criterion, then most Turks, Romanians and Russians from the school's numbers could have been designated as Germans, inserting an ambiguous definition based on language proficiency rather than nationality.[19] The 1880s were a decade of quickly burgeoning nationalism and antisemitism in the German Empire, which may explain why sensitivities on nationalities became a topic of interest for the school's management. Nurtsch points out that the reason as to why Mühlmann felt the need to defend the school's policies regarding student inflow was the German Empire's burgeoning national consciousness and identity formation, the rise of racist identity politics and antisemitism. Nurtsch cites a message from a publication referred to as the *Kreuz-Zeitung* from 4 July 1903, which is probably the *Neue Preußische Zeitung*, later known as the *Kreuz-Zeitung*: 'If the German School in Istanbul wants to raise a justified claim to the high national grant in the future, it must calculate the tuition fees for non-German and non-Christian pupils in such a way that the expenses for these pupils are fully covered.'[20] The article moreover encourages the school board to limit the admission of Jewish students, because: 'Anyone who thinks that the foreign Jews could be Germanized by attending the German school or at least develop a friendly attitude towards Germanness, does not know the characteristics of the Levantine Jews, who are even more unreliable in national terms than their fellow believers in Central Europe.'[21] Looking at the admission statistics of the school, Nurtsch states that these sentiments had little effect on the admission policies of the school.

Partly due to the earthquake, authorities sought a different location for a new school building.[22] By the time the decision was made to leave the old building, the school had approximately 300 children under its roof. In 1895 it was decided that the parcel would be acquired through bank director Wülfing. The school moved from across the Müeyyedzade Mosque along Galip Dede Caddesi, to the site on which the German School presently is situated, near Tünel and at the top of the slope connecting Pera to Galata. Architect Otto Kapp, also responsible for the construction of the Teutonia building, was prepared to design and supervise the construction of the new school free of charge and provided the school's association with a loan of 200,000 mark, completed with another 50,000 by Wülfing.[23] The former building of the school was eventually sold to the Greek *millet* in 1909 and continued as a Greek school. Christa Lippold notes that by 1938 it was in the possession of the *Zoğrafyon Rum Erkek Lisesi*.[24]

Construction started in June 1896, with a plan including fifteen classrooms and an auditorium. The opening ceremony took place on 14 September 1897 and between 1901 and 1903 an adjacent parcel was bought for six additional classrooms for the girls' school. The school would be occupied by Allied forces in 1918, following the German Empire and Ottoman Empire's involvement in the Triple Alliance. The school would eventually be handed back in 1925 by France, with the building in a run-down state. Classes by then had already been resumed in the Polonya Sokak since 1924, in a building currently owned by the Grand

Lodge of Free and Accepted Masons. Once the school was returned to the German authorities, the renovation efforts brought new furnishings such as central heating. More significantly, however, the flat roof was replaced by a pitched roof and during that process the school's distinctive tower was demolished out of a practical need to connect the roof tops of the building's two wings.[25] Josef Joraschek indicates that the fundamental layout of the school would not change until 1944, when it was confiscated by the Turkish authorities.[26]

The Deutsche Schule *and Nazism*

Dietrich suggests that children who had emigrated from Weimar Germany would also be admitted to the German School from the moment the NSDAP seized power in 1933 onwards. She cites the message of director Scheuermann to his students on the first graduation ceremony after the end of the First World War, who said the following amid rising nationalist tensions in both Turkey and Nazi Germany: 'That they should understand and appreciate their fellow human beings as human beings, across all nations and religions, as they have done so far in class with their classmates.'[27] Nonetheless, the coming to power of the Nazi regime affected the Istanbulite German School as well, with the large number of Jewish children in the school declining rapidly: from 365 children (on a total of 828 students) in 1932–3, to 236 in 1933–4, 164 in 1935–6, 106 in 1938, 34 in 1939, 20 in 1940 and 7 in 1942–3. In those years, pressure from the school administration on the parents of its Jewish students was increasing. The headmaster explicitly requested parents to take their children away from the school.

An interesting insight in the contradictions of the dynamics in those years belongs to Adolf Hommes, teacher at the German School between 1942 and 1944, who also confessed his regret when he received orders to remove all Jewish students from the school in 1943 and 1944. He remembers with great regret one talented student in particular who was not able to do her exam because of these measures. When Turkey cut off diplomatic ties with Nazi Germany, the German community was given a choice between repatriation or being interned. Hommes himself managed to make it back to Nazi Germany, but he claims others who were interned were held on the premises of the German school. Such remarks from Hommes' are particularly interesting considering the fact that the German School was registered under the Turkish school system. Due to this, the school was implicitly following Turkish legislation, meaning the Nazi regime had no authority to send the children away from the school on grounds of antisemitic legislation. The rapid and dramatic decrease in the number of Jewish students in the German School, however, means that the 'problem' for the Nazi authorities in part resolved itself. The order Hommes claims to have been given also indicates the antisemitic fanaticism that was still at work when local Nazis decided to exclude the students from the school. Dietrich also explains that the presence of a Turkish vice-rector prevented the implementation of race theory education and broader antisemitism as well as, for instance, the usage of the turn hall by the local branch of *Hitlerjugend*.

She does not, however, address the inertia of the general context of rising racism and antisemitism in Turkey itself, at a time when Turkish Jews were also the victims of the national agenda of the Kemalists and the Jewish community in Istanbul was affected, particularly in 1942 with the Wealth Tax (*Varlık Vergisi*).[28] Dietrich does emphasize that among the Germans in the school there were few who openly distanced themselves from national socialism or antisemitism after 1933. Additional classes and meetings for the *Hitlerjugend*, moreover, were relocated to the premises of Teutonia. As explained in Chapter 1, Teutonia would allow the *Hitlerjugend* to organize various activities such as the *Heimabende* on its premises. Film screenings of national-socialist propaganda were also organized for the German students, who were also allowed to celebrate events such as the annexation of Austria in the school.[29] The German authorities apparently made efforts to avoid conflict with the Turkish educational officials and emphasized the similarities between the nationalisms of the two countries and its leaders. Concretely, this resulted in singing both national hymns, raising the flag of both countries during festivities and 'honouring' Mustafa Kemal with three cheers of '*Sieg Heil!*'[30]

Reinstation and rehabilitation: The Deutsche Schule *after the Second World War*

After the Turkish authorities confiscated the school, following the pressure of the Allied forces to join their side in 1944, its premises were used as a Turkish state school for girls, the *Beyoğlu Kız Lisesi*. Necla Altınok, geography teacher at the German School, writes in 1993 how she remembers being a student at the girls' school. They were students at the *İnönü Kız Lisesi* (İnönü High School for Girls) in Fındıklı and their school was transferred and renamed in the second school semester.[31] In July 1953 the school was returned to the *Bundesrepublik Deutschland* FRG or the Federal Republic of Germany (FRG) and on 1 October of the same year the school became the German School once again. Irrespective of the state of the building, admission to the German School was soon once again in high demand. At the moment of its opening, the school had 226 students, 55 students with German nationality and 171 others, 9 German-speaking and 162 with a different native language. The school's statistics provide an overview of the makeup of the student population during the first three years after the school's reopening (Table 1).

Though no precise explanation can be provided, it is remarkable that the category of Greek Catholics – possibly a *Rum* Istanbulite branch of the Eastern Catholic Church – is quoted separately here for the school years 1955 and 1956. All other Christian denominations (presumably including Greek and Armenian Orthodox) are assigned to a single 'other' category. If we are to follow Romain-Örs and Alexandris' observation that Greek speakers were typically distinguished formally on the basis of their nationality (Greek or Turkish), their religion may

Table 1 Deutsche Oberrealschule Schulerstatistik – 'Sammtlicher Schüler in den letzten fünf Jahren'[32]

	German nationals	Other nationals		Protes-tant	Roman Catholic	Greek Catholic	other Christian denominations	Jewish	Muslim
	German speaking	German speaking	other						
53/54	55	9	162	48	14	–	4	–	160
54/55	66	18	345	62	36	–	23	5	303
55/56	81	39	524	77	45	10	32	6	474

have been less of an issue. Particularly so as hardly any differentiation was made between Jews, Orthodox and Catholic Christians, especially at the time of the most violent outbursts of nationalism in Istanbul.[33] The identification considered Muslims or non-Muslims, regardless of whether the latter meant Orthodox, Catholic or Jewish. Apart from the possibility that this description may have been a mistake, or that they were in fact Greek Byzantine Catholics, it is possible that these students were, in fact, Romanians.[34] The Greek Catholic Church in Romania was historically a church that both accepted supremacy of the pope, and retained the rights to perform the Byzantine liturgy during mass. By the mid-twentieth century the church's community constituted a sizeable minority. When the communist regime came to power in 1948 in Romania the Greek Catholic Church was forced to merge with the Romanian Orthodox Church and its real estate was dispossessed.[35] Considering the mention of Romanian students in the German School in earlier decades, it is possible that this in fact explains the (deliberate) identification of Romanians as 'Greek Catholics'.

A report from April 1957, drawn up by the chairman and vice-chairman of the board of the German School, Dr Fricke and Hans Weidtman, indicates that the number of students had grown to 800, which was comparable to the student population before the Second World War. The reasons cited for this are, on the one hand, the overall prestige that the school had built up in the years preceding the war and on the other the overall high demand for admission into foreign schools in Turkey.[36] The reasons why the schools were popular may vary, but some of the most significant causes stem partly from socio-economic, and partly from political considerations. Foreign schools would give children access to foreign-language instruction, often by native speakers and additionally in some cases (such as the German School) a foreign system of higher education. In various instances, the diplomatic cables of the German and English consulates and embassies also suggest that the quality of education was better at the German School and the English High Schools, compared to the average of the Turkish public high schools. On the other hand, a relative independence from the nationalist Turkish schooling system would have been appealing for the members of the cultural minorities in Turkey.

It is clear that the management of the school was aware of the school's importance for the public diplomacy of the FRG from an early point onwards. Fricke and

Weidtman argue that the management of the school had decided to take in as many students as possible: 'This need should be taken into account as far as possible in light of the critical importance of a substantial broadening of German language proficiency in Turkey for the cultural, but especially also economic, German-Turkish relations.'[37] They explained that the class sizes, in the prep level, exceeded the boundaries of the pedagogical limits, with class sizes of fifty pupils on average. Even with classes of this size the management had to turn down numerous applicants. The management acknowledged it as an indication of the school maintaining a relatively intact prestige after the war and that the influence of German in Turkey was rising rapidly. Tenbrock argues that whereas in the first eighty years of its existence the student population was mostly composed of children from non-Turkish nationals and minorities, by 1958 at least 80 per cent of the school's population consisted of Turkish nationals (see also Table 1). Tenbrock therefore suggests that the German School should be a place of interaction for Turkish and German culture, where a fruitful dialogue between the two could grow.[38] As such, it can be considered as a space of cultural or educational diplomacy, a dynamic noticeable in the English High Schools as well. Fricke and Weidtman indicated that they wanted to limit the intake of students from 200 annually to 140 and reduce class sizes to 40 students. With those numbers they projected that the school would have 1,105 students in 1961, which would require 42 class rooms rather than the available 26.

In their plans to counter these structural challenges, they suggested three possibilities. The first was to cut back on the number of admissions, although they presented this solution as undesirable since it would be disappointing for far too many Turkish parents who had pinned their hopes on the German School for their children's' futures. The second option was to leave the old building behind and erect a new building elsewhere, which they presented as the best option due to the ever-increasing numbers of students and the position of the German School in the educational landscape of Turkey in the 1950s. It would also open the possibility of a boarding house so that students from beyond Istanbul, 'The very best students from the wide Anatolian hinterland,' would be able to attend the school.[39] They pointed out, however, that the Turkish authorities would likely make it difficult for the school to move and construct a new building since they were empowered by the Lausanne Treaty to obstruct the building of new foreign schools. Although it seemed as the most desirable option, they expected that it would also mean losing a great deal of independence, that is, a fully Turkish management would take over the school. These were concerns which would not have been an issue if the school decided to stay in the old building. The third option was to expand and renovate the present building. The solution would not enable the school to grow into a situation that would at least partially meet its potential, but at the same time it would not cause the sort of problems that would arise from the second option. The board thus requested that the German Foreign Ministry decide between the second and third option, arguing the first option could jeopardize the existence of the school altogether.

The representatives of the German legations in Istanbul and Ankara apparently shared the board's concern with rapid action on the issue and pressed their colleagues in Bonn to set in motion the necessary procedures and send a building expert to Istanbul. The Foreign Ministry was not able to allocate the necessary funds for the expansion of the school building in the same year, that is, 1957, after which the director of the school solicited the ministry to pay for the construction by means of a loan through the school board, so that the immediate future of the school would not be at risk.[40] Other plans were to reconstruct part of the existing building, which would entail moving the teachers who had been living on the school's premises elsewhere, for which the building of Teutonia was considered to be an option. The Consulate General kept on pressing the Foreign Ministry to make a decision on the matter since no students could be admitted as of 1958 without a new construction or reconstruction. It is worth noting here that the Consulate General emphasized to the German Foreign Ministry that the German School should not be left to wane away due to the limits of its building and should be granted all necessities in order to ensure its growth in the future since it was 'The core of our cultural policy efforts in Turkey'.[41] The German response was strikingly similar to the attitude of the Foreign Office and British Council towards the English High Schools until the 1970s. The potential 'cultural-diplomatic' function of the school was emphasized by the German Embassy in Ankara as well, indicating the significance of the school for furthering German interests.[42]

In the end, the school was refurbished in 1957, with a new gymnastics hall and music room. A more expansive modernization was obstructed due to the high tariffs the Turkish authorities would charge for building materials from the FRG.[43] Another plan, also cut short but mentioned in the documents of the consulate general, was to move the building away from Beyoğlu altogether:

'At a later date, however, the aim should be to relocate the German School in Istanbul, currently located in a very unpleasant part of the city, to the Bosporus, slightly outside the city centre as had already been planned before the war.'[44] The employee of the cultural department of the German Foreign Ministry went on to state that other schools already existed in the vicinity and claimed that additional stories would in the long term prove to be wholly inefficient and that plans for the expansion of the old building should not be considered. With the benefit of hindsight this has proven not to be the case, as foreign or foreign-language schools continue to be highly popular in Istanbul. As regards the interaction between the schools on the formal level, I was only able to find hints at the previously mentioned interaction in Chapter 7, from which we can deduce that the British consul general and his German counterpart appear to have occasionally briefed or consulted each other on the issues they encountered with the Turkish authorities with regard to the EHS and the German School respectively.[45] The concerns and plans for a new building elsewhere along the Bosporus were ignored and disqualified by the school's management as too expensive and not realistic due to traffic reasons.[46]

The Deutsche Schule *and cultural diplomacy between the FRG and Turkey*

The school meanwhile became a pinball of politics and competing bureaucracies. Director R. H. Tenbrock wrote a memo to the educational authority in Hamburg that the German School had been subjected to what appeared to be harassment by Turkish educational authorities and conflicting instructions from different officials. Moreover, he seems conflicted about the instructions from the German counterpart. The German Foreign Ministry appears to have explicitly instructed him to emphasize the German character of the school in order to prevent a further watering down of the school's character.[47] From a different perspective, German parents complained to the German Foreign Ministry about the burden that was placed on their children who were subjected to a significantly higher number of classes, particularly in the lower grades (27 hours versus 18 hours in the FRG in the first year and 32 hours versus 22 hours in the second year) due to the conflict between German and Turkish regulations. In their letter, they pressed for the opening of an embassy school in Istanbul. They explained that the discrepancy emanated from the Turkish Ministry of Education's push for 6 hours of Turkish language, 2 hours of history and 2 hours of geography, all in Turkish. The parents argued that it was hard for a child with no native proficiency in Turkish to catch up, but that particularly for children who joined the school at a different starting point as newcomers it was an absurd demand.[48]

Tenbrock's memo was forwarded to the Foreign Ministry in Bonn together with a letter of the German consul Mr von Graevenitz, who indicated that such problems were the consequence of 'the well-known Turkish mentality, especially its distinctive nationalism' ('*der bekannten türkischen Mentalität, vor allem des ausgeprägten Nationalismus*') which never waned or will wane in the future. He advises, however, to be cautious with pushing back against the Turkish side. Graevenitz, following Tenbrock, explains that the Turkish authorities were trying to overrule German educational regulations: 'To gradually replace tried and tested German guidelines with what we consider to be worse Turkish ones'.[49] Apart from that, he argued that Tenbrock suspected that this was also the effect of a personal vendetta against his persona pursued by unsatisfied parents or educational officials, which resulted in a 'policy of pinpricks' (*Nadelstichpolitik*).[50] The consul warned the Foreign Ministry that the letter received by the educational authority in Hamburg might prompt action from the German side in a way that may harm the interests of the FRG. He requested the Foreign Ministry to take action in such an event 'because of the primarily cultural-political'.[51]

The explanation provided by the German Embassy in Ankara to the Foreign Ministry in Bonn bore similarities with the situation of the English Schools in Beyoğlu and Nişantaşı: the Turkish officials strictly followed the reasoning and agreements stipulated by the Treaty of Lausanne regarding the existing foreign institutions of education. The officials at the German Embassy, however, explain that the foreign schools were considered private schools, which was – as explained in the chapter on the EHSG – different for the English schools. Despite that, the German School and the English Schools were subject to Turkish legislation and still considered, in legal terms, 'Turkish schools', regardless of the sponsors of the schools and their teachers. Interestingly the embassy official goes on by stating the following:

> This is justified through indicating that there are Greek, Armenian, Jewish and even Bulgarian schools in Istanbul and that these of course need to be kept under

control. This attitude no longer corresponds in any way to today's intellectual and political position of Turkey as reflected in the many dealings of the embassy. To the objection that there should be no concerns of this kind in light of the good German-Turkish relations, the answer is: 'We trust you Germans, but if we grant you concessions, the English, American and French schools will present the same demand and our cultural-political system will collapse.'[52]

Elsewhere a cable communication also argues that the foreign schools are treated in the same way as those of national minorities and, as a consequence, the students in the foreign schools are subjected to the same nationalistic pressure as their peers in Armenian or Greek schools.[53] Despite earlier messages from the German legations that the German School's situation should not negatively interfere or affect cultural relations between the FRG and Turkey, it appears that by 1959 the representatives at the consulate and embassy realize that the matter is too complicated for the school director to resolve alone. Particularly the situation of non-Turkish children in the school seems to have instigated the need for action on the side of the Foreign Ministry in Bonn. The aforementioned embassy official indicates that 80 per cent of the students at the time of writing in 1959 were Turkish, yet he argues against the Turkish authorities' claims to subject 20 per cent of the school's population (who did not have Turkish nationality) to Turkish educational regulations. He goes on to explain that a compromise should be reached, but that the Turkish authorities should understand that the German parliament can allocate funding to the school only if it can also cater to the needs of the German minority. The way the director deals with the situation, the official thinks, can affect the cultural relations of the FRG and Turkey or even the general attitude of Turkey to foreign endeavours. He believes, therefore, that the matter should be considered a 'political' one and a resolution to the issue should follow clear instructions of the German Foreign Ministry.[54]

The problems which director Tenbrock was facing resonate also in his opening words to the publication occasioned by the German School's ninetieth anniversary. He is at pains to stress how the path of Turkey is strongly intertwined with that of its European partners and that Turkey has established a very warm relation with the German people. He goes on by stating that the '*Sinn und Ziel*' of the German School should also be considered from this perspective.[55] The German School does not aim to alienate its students from their national character (*Volkstum*), but to educate them in Turkish and German, two languages which – Tenbrock argues – are significantly apart, but have much to offer to each other. Tenbrock is diplomatic in his choice of words, clearly conditioned by the problematic situation that the German School found itself in, and by his role as the school's key representative to Turkish authorities.

Tenbrock's veiled messages are clarified by reflections of some of the high school's students, who show what great an impact the school had on their personal and professional outlook. Barbaros Çağa explains how the greatest contribution provided by the school was in fact to learn to understand the Germans and their culture. It was particularly the work of Thomas Mann which made an impact on him and also showed him that the life problems of Germans and Turks are apart, arguing that Mann would have picked different topics had he lived in Turkey. Contrary to the Galatasaray High School, Çağa feels that the students at the school do not feel a very strong connection to the school: 'The students came to school in the morning and went home at noon.'[56] Similar to statements made with particular emphasis by alumni of Galatasaray High School from the 1950s and 1960s, he also argues that he and his fellow students took pride in the fact that no one was discriminated against on national grounds: 'We live like a family in our school, and in a family no one despises or hates the other.'[57]

Contrary to earlier years by 1962, it seems that the relations between the school and the Turkish Ministry of Education became slightly smoother. Director Hanz Anstock reports to the German Foreign Ministry that year that the Ministry of Education had agreed to shrink the school down to levels that would no longer tax the staff and facilities to the same degree it had since its reopening. A report in the archives of the German Consulate General in Istanbul indicated that the student numbers reached 1,000 at the time of writing, 17 May 1962. Elsewhere it is indicated that the school would provide students coming from the Turkish primary schools, with one year of prep classes, followed by two years of middle school and four years of high school. The school had 44 to 46 German teachers and 22 Turkish teachers.[58] There were 37 classes, of which it was expected that 27 classes with 650 students should remain after the reduction of the school's size. More significantly, the report indicates that of the 1,000 students in the school an approximate 70 students had German nationality, while all others were Turks. It seems unlikely that all of these students, however, were ethnic Turks, so considering the concise nature of the report Turkish here probably means Turkish citizens.[59] The report also indicates that the school was planning a new building.

The *Oberschulrat* (school inspector) Fritz Krog who visited the school in April 1962 argues that the school building, despite needing repairs and being too small for thirty-seven classes, was still suited for its purpose. The exception was, however, the facilities for physical education. A separate turn hall did not meet the demands of a large coed-school, in terms of both size and equipment. The girls did not have their own facilities, so had to do their classes outdoor and in the attic during the winter. Krog, probably taking up the school management's suggestion, proposes to build new and modern facilities on the second floor of the building, which the building, notwithstanding its modest size, would be able to lodge.[60] With regard to the plans of the school to reduce its size, Krog states that the school's management thought these would probably prove impossible to execute without the mediation of the German Foreign Ministry, given that the expansion of Turkish high schools already did not meet the demand of a rapidly growing population in Istanbul and Turkey. This seems highly probable in light of the remarks of Fricke and Weidtman in the 1950s who indicated there were long waiting lists for students trying to be admitted to the school. Krog goes on to explain that he also visited the director of national education in Istanbul 'Sayin Bay Halis Curtça' (Halis Kurtça). Following the suggestion of the German School's director Krog, he paid this courtesy visit which would potentially enhance the director and his office's willingness to accede to the requests of the school in the future. Kurtça appears to have been very forthcoming and stressed how important he considered the German contributions to Turkish education to be. He applauded the suggestions of the school to set up a bursary system for German-speaking Turkish teachers which indicates that his enthusiasm could have had positive effects for the German School.[61]

Director Anstock reports on 8 January 1963 that the measures to reduce the student population of the school had been approved by both the German and Turkish authorities. Krog later confirms the reduction of the school's population in a report from 16 July 1963 and makes a noticeable comment about the school's popularity among Turkish citizens:

> The reputation of the German School is of significance here as much as the fact that there is an insufficient number of Turkish high schools in Istanbul. It is noteworthy that the Turkish parents who register their sons and daughters at the German School by no means only belong to the upper classes but to a high degree belong to the middle class. (The school fee is 100 Turkish pounds per month = around 44 DM according to the official rate).[62]

Krog thus clearly points out that the school population from the Turkish side was no longer limited to the country's bourgeoisie, but that also citizens from the middle class were at pains to have their children educated in a foreign school with better perspectives for education and careers than a regular Turkish high school could probably provide.[63] A reflection on Krog's report in the German consular archives, however, also claims that the popularity was an effect of the shortcomings of Turkish high schools in Istanbul, which prompted Turkish parents to apply for the admission of their children at the German, English and French schools simultaneously.[64] The fact that the parents applied for various foreign or foreign-language schools may signify that these parents may have cared slightly less about which school their children would end up in as long as it was not a regular state school. Fatma Gök points out that from the 1950s onwards the Turkish state would establish *maarif kolejleri* (Educational Colleges) which had a better reputation than regular state high schools. These would pave a way to the later Anatolian High School system. Between the 1950s and 2000s the Turkish educational system would gradually become more and more competitive, with highly selective private schools (such as the German High School and the EHS) on the one hand and on the other hand a highly segregated system of public high schools. Within the public system Gök discriminates between the regular public high schools, the Anatolian High Schools and the so-called super secondary schools (such as Galatasaray High School). In the case of the latter two, instruction would be in English, French or German rather than Turkish and admission to these schools was (and is) subject to fierce competition. This holds true for the German School as well, although this is a private school (like all foreign schools) requiring tuition, whereas the Anatolian High Schools and 'super secondary schools' are free.[65]

Six years previous, moreover, the Consulate General reported that considerations of reducing the size of the school should be taken with caution as many of the parents who apply for their children's admission to the school are from the 'influential Turkish community'.[66] Refusing children would send a message that the FRG is disinterested in an important aspect of Turkey, which the consul general concludes is 'an aspect that is not only of a cultural-political nature'.[67] Meanwhile the usage of the building beyond school hours grew increasingly intense during the 1960s. By the mid-1960s the building was, for instance, also in use by the Goethe Institut, which used the classrooms for 39 German language courses with approximately 1,000 participants, teaching for 156 hours weekly, with another 400 students in 13 to 14 groups and 52 to 56 hours during the summer holidays. The Goethe Institut meanwhile made plans for a language lab in the school.[68] A new gymnastics hall was planned in 1965 thanks to the efforts of the Foreign Ministry.[69] A report from 1966 explains further concerns that were growing in the Foreign Ministry about the German School. Mr Von Dziembowski writes that the historical ties the FRG has in the field of education with Turkey are matched by few others, yet quotes the 'strong growth of contemporary Turkey's self-confidence' (*'sterk gewachsenen Selbstbewußtsein der heutigen Türkei'*) as a possible reason for concern. Particularly since the Cyprus crisis, he argues, this nationalism has grown to be increasingly anti-Western, and any foreign influence or effort is treated hostile. Attempts to expand existing schools or open new ones are blocked with reference to the Treaty of Lausanne.[70] Nonetheless, Dziembowski argues that every 'thinking Turk' (*'denkende Türke'*) is aware of the fact that speaking Western languages and connecting with Western research and technology are inevitable if the country is to move forward. He sees this as the primary reason as to why the great majority of students in the German School indeed consist of Turkish nationals.[71] Meanwhile director Heinz Anstock describes the relationship between the school and the Turkish officials as being good. The proof of that, according to the German side, are the many compliments by Turkish officials regarding the school. Interestingly, the observation is accompanied and explained with the following remark: 'in the Orient people like to praise ' (*'im Orient lobt man gern'*).[72]

A major tribute to the German School was furthermore the acknowledgement of the Turkish authorities of German and other non-Turkish students as guest students, exempted from the rigid education regulations that the school was subjected to.[73] In practice this meant that the non-Turkish students could opt for French, Latin or Turkish as a second language.[74] More significantly, the previous arrangements also imposed the teaching of subjects such as geography, history, literature, psychology and sociology in Turkish, which put significant pressure on the non-Turkish students due to the great amount of extra hours, learning material, instruction for non-native speakers and the Turkish teachers themselves whose classes are described as: 'unmethodical' (*'unmethodisch'*).[75] In addition, the school director did not formally have a say in the organization of these courses, since those were the responsibility of the Turkish vice-rector.[76] The new regulations also meant that the school could accommodate students from the FRG easier and synchronize their education with that of the German School.[77] The arrangements had immediate effect as in 1967, the parents of 110 students out of 113 eligible (non-Turkish) students at the German School and the consulary school registered their children as guest students. The remaining three consisted of one Austrian and two Israeli children.[78]

In a different report from 1966 the German Embassy in Ankara Mr Röpper mentions the significance of continuing the school, since 'it is becoming increasingly clear from year to year that the cultural work in Turkey is really paying off'.[79] Referring to the greater efforts that were made by the French and Americans in 1965, he recommends Turkey be ranked higher on the Foreign Ministry's priority, particularly considering the 'sincere friendship of the Turks' ('*aufrichtigen Freundschaft der Türken*').[80] It should be noted that while work-related migration from Turkey to the FRG had begun officially since 1961, its effects on the German School through the 1960s were still quite marginal, considering that the pool of potential students for the German School came from the middle classes and higher middle classes, whereas the working migrants were mostly low-educated migrants.[81] The effects of workers' migration, however, would start to have an impact in the 1970s, which will be discussed further on in this chapter. Again similarities to the case of the EHS also become apparent in the archives: with regard to the problems caused by the Turkish side's attitude towards the opening and expansion of foreign schools and the insistence of maintaining the status quo of the Lausanne Treaty is commented by him as follows:

> Insightful critics of this law pointed out that Turkey could not really afford itself the luxury of such a ban in view of the still completely insufficient number of schools.[82]

The rapid growth of the population and high levels of illiteracy (Röpper quotes 65 per cent) make for an unmanageable situation, even though schools are continuously built, he argues.[83] He suggests increasing the number of German teachers at Turkish schools, which will lead to improvement and expansion of German education at Turkish schools. He suggests, moreover, that half of Turks studying abroad are studying in the FRG, while the division of foreign-language education in Turkey is divided over English, French and German in a 5:3:2 ratio.[84]

A shift in the attitude about the school from the side of the German Foreign Ministry can be read in the answer of the Ministry regarding the possibility of opening a boarding house on the premises of the German Catholic Church community. Complications with achieving proper class sizes in the embassy school (*Botschaftschule*) in Ankara led to requests to open a boarding house for the German School in Istanbul.[85] The Ministry reports that it is interested in such a project, but adds that no financial support from the Ministry should be expected. The official suggests that German firms and parents should contribute to the endeavour since the Foreign Ministry is already keeping a very expensive high school in Istanbul.[86] The building of the German School and the obstacles for a renovation indeed seemed to have been a burden for the German Foreign Ministry. In 1976, the building is mentioned as a problem for the German side, since its poor condition would soon require an inevitable and costly renovation – a need that could no longer be ignored moreover.[87] The school building is described again as too small for a student population of 900, with maximum student numbers in many groups. Noticeably, the author Bernard Becker of the Central Office for Schools Abroad (*Zentralstelle für das Auslandsschulwesen*) reports applications from Turkish citizens in the FRG were refused on those grounds. He goes on to say that the need to have the building painted, which had been mentioned in 1971 already, has become even greater yet the growing costs make it increasingly unlikely that it would actually happen. Significantly, Becker also remarks that the building's exterior could not be changed anymore, an indicator that the Council for the Preservation of Monuments probably listed the building as a second-degree protected heritage.

Becker furthermore notes that the school had 900 students, with noticeably 110 non-Turkish students, 80 per cent of which were German and 10 per cent Austrian and Swiss. Forty-one German teachers were responsible for 75 per cent of the teaching. The numbers of applying parents were still very high: 2,400 applicants were tested, of which 102 were in the end admitted to the prep classes.[88] Meanwhile the report indicates that it was not easy for all German children, typically the children of expats who would have been in Istanbul for a couple of years, to get along in the school which is described as a 'Turkish elite school' ('*türkischen Elite-Schule*').[89] This is problematic for these children as their different talent and IQ levels would have placed them in different school levels in the FRG.[90] The author remarks how impressed he was by the rapid progress Turkish students made in the prepclasses and how motivated they were, so much that he remarks: 'I have not seen anything comparable during the many school visits that I have made so far.'[91] As regards the teachers in the higher groups he notices that they speak as if they were speaking to a native German group and that 'a little more discipline in speaking' ('*ein wenig mehr sprachliche Disziplin*') would be recommendable. It appeared to him that the teachers' professional engagement – most probably a euphemism for an excessive usage of colloquial or complex expressions – obstructed the capacity to remain aware that they were speaking to a foreign group. He thus seems to push for a more consistent usage of standard or formal German, enabling students to improve their language comprehension.[92]

A response of the consulate to Becker's report follows and takes stance towards Becker's description of the *Istanbul Erkek Lisesi* (Istanbul High School for Boys) – a Turkish state school with instruction in German – as being more significant for the FRG's cultural diplomacy efforts in Turkey.[93] In poignantly clear-cut language, the official at the German Consulate points out to the Foreign Ministry in Bonn how the difference between the school may not be as great as projected by Mr Becker. The official counters Becker's statement that the student population of the German School is determined by the socio-economic position since – as a private school – it asks for tuition, whereas the *Istanbul Erkek Lisesi* as a Turkish state school does not. The official argues against this by stating that 'needy and worthy students' ('*bedürftige und würdige Schüler*') are granted a scholarship.[94] A significant general comment he makes concerns the socio-economic position of the parents who send their children to the German School: 'There is a considerably larger middle class here than in other developing countries. This is where the students of the Alman Lisesi mainly come from, not just from the circle of the "rich". These children of today's middle class will, however, move into the leading classes tomorrow."[95] Finally, he also pointed out that the parents who send their children to the German School have already studied at German universities and expect to send their children to the FRG as well, which was generally possible since the children could be awarded diplomas which granted them access to both the Turkish and German School system (although problems had arisen in the mid-1970s with Turkish restrictions for dual diplomas). For students of the *Istanbul Erkek Lisesi* this was much less so the case, since the parents, the official argues, typically hoped that the mediation or recommendation of the German teachers at the school would make access to Turkish universities easier for their children.[96] He finishes with the statement that the children who continued their education at either of the schools would gradually lose their interest in upholding their German language skills, leading him to conclude that 'the cultural-political impact is therefore substantially dependent on studying in Germany.'[97] Thus the argument is made that the choice of higher education of the children largely determines their 'political value' for the FRG. Mr Becker on 20 October 1976 confirmed the official's statement, indicating that priority would be granted to the German School also in the future, pointing to its funding in 1975 which amounted to 3 million German mark, more than the great majority of other German schools abroad received.[98] The institution in Beyoğlu thus remained crucial for Germany, Turkey and their bilateral relations.

School director Franz Lippold explains in an article in the 125th-anniversary publication that by 1968 the inflow from Turkish students stabilized and the explosive growth of the school came to an end. He claims that the high esteem of the German School among Turkish parents was a continuous reason of concern for the school since, as indicated before, it attracted massive amounts of applicants. He explains that in 1968 1,343 applicants registered for the 90 positions in the prep classes, whereas those numbers had risen to 3,415 in 1977.[99] The school could no longer cope with the process, but he stresses that the school management was saddened by the Turkish decision to centralize the application process since they thought that 'the ability to learn languages is underrated, while crammed knowledge is overrated.'[100] Elsewhere he argues that this is the result of the Turkish school system which pushes for control of knowledge and 'nerves' during a multiple-choice exam.[101]

In the 1970s the effects of the increasingly complex ties between the FRG and Turkey due to workers' migration from Turkey to the FRG are becoming visible. By 1974, the number of legal Turkish working migrants in Germany had risen to 617,500.[102] The popularity of the school increased even further with the many Turkish families that returned from the FRG in the 1970s whose children had attended schools in the FRG and tried to register their child in the German School. Many were rejected, Lippold points out, while many of those who made it into the school in Beyoğlu had great difficulties. The school was also compared to regular German high schools, on a different level. German children who were and are admitted to the school did not have to participate in any of the Turkish courses and, therefore, also did not acquire diplomas that were valid in Turkey.[103] He also points to the problems with the building, which by 1993 still appear to have not been resolved in a satisfactory way. The limited space for sport facilities in and around the building at Tünel did not hinder the students from being quite successful in various championships. The technical installations, much of which dated back to the early years of the twentieth century, were due to be renovated in 1989 yet were postponed to 1995 because of the high costs of West and East Germany's reunion. Lippold expresses the hope that the vacant parcels next to the school would be acquired by 1995 so that the school would have more space for improving its building.[104]

Lothar Wittmann of the Foreign Ministry's Cultural Department meanwhile argued in 1993 once again how important the Beyoğlu school had been and is in the FRG's cultural policy. He argues that 'In addition to the pedogical task of stimulating interest in and enjoyment of the German language, we also want to convey an up-to-date image of Germany and deepen the bond with our country, its culture and its people.'[105] The mission and value of the school for the FRG meanwhile becomes clear in Wittmann's following statement: 'Many of the Turkish ALMAN LISESI graduates have close ties to our country and often contribute to shaping German-Turkish relations from responsible positions in politics or society.'[106] Currently the school is still a science lyceum with 640 students who can graduate either with a Turkish diploma with or without a language diploma or take the German *Abitur* exam which grants them the same rights as any other German High School graduate.[107] Generally speaking, despite the occasionally tumultuous relations between the FRG and Turkey, the educational ties between the two countries are strong and actively stimulated by public and private sectors in both countries. Although virtually all foreign-language education has lost ground to instruction in English, initiatives between Turkey and Germany are actively encouraged. Examples are the public Turkish-German University (*Türkish-Deutsche Universität/Türk Alman Üniversitesi*) and a campus in Berlin of the private Bahçeşehir University.

In the 2015 call, prior to the 2016 attempted coup d'état in Turkey, Germany received 144 Turkish participants from the Erasmus+ staff mobility programme, the highest number of incoming participants of all countries and 2,667 Turkish Erasmus students, making it fourth in the ranking of outgoing Erasmus students with Germany as their destination. Turkey, on the other hand, received only twelve participants in the staff mobility programme. Additionally, however, Turkey received 2,231 German Erasmus students, making it by far the most popular destination for German students.[108]

CONCLUSION

Following the collapse of the Ottoman Empire, the foundation of the ethnonational republic, two world wars, the Cold War, extensive and aggressive social engineering and mass labour migration, the five places in the Beyoğlu landscape witnessed effects to their populations, names, functionalities and representations. Yet despite this, these places retained their spatial integrity, as would the bulk of historical Beyoğlu in the direct adjacency of İstikal Caddesi. Beyoğlu's relative integrity would come to an abrupt end in the mid-1980s:

> Passing through Tarlabaşı over a six-way motor lane, we will drink coffee alongside the Golden Horn. (. . .) When we look at Tarlabaşı we see these narrow buildings with two, three, maybe four stories. We will grant planning permits of up to 15 stories, befitting to the width of this boulevard. After granting the permits for construction, we will knock everything over and increase the height of buildings to at least ten metres. That way the dirt will be gone. A new business centre will be born.[1]

This is how the mayor of the Beyoğlu Municipality Haluk Öztürkatalay described the destruction that would run through the Beyoğlu district between 1986 and 1988. As an effect, existing disparities in the district would be further exacerbated.[2] The described need to clear away the dirt in the Tarlabaşı quarter has been uttered in similar ways by the metropolitan mayor of Istanbul at the time, Bedrettin Dalan, further stating that the buildings in the quarter, historically known for its Greek and Armenian working-class population, do 'not belong to our culture'.[3] These and other statements indicate that the politicians of the 1980s wanted to push Istanbul and Beyoğlu into different directions, making it attractive for business, commerce and tourism. A magazine published by the Beyoğlu Municipality states that with Tarlabaşı Boulevard 'the dream of Adnan Menderes and Turgut Özal would become reality', drawing continuities between the interventionalist urban transformations in the 1950s and those of the late 1980s.[4]

The destruction of over 370 historical buildings in Tarlabaşı coincided with efforts by the municipality and associations to turn the area around İstiklal Caddesi into an open-air shopping centre.[5] Advocates of these efforts express the desire to return Beyoğlu to its former splendour and reverse the cycle of decay in which the area had allegedly been trapped for years. A prominent member of the Beyoğlu Beautification Association, Vitali Hakko, founder of the Vakko clothing chain, talks in an interview of the old Beyoğlu, that he discusses upon request. He suggests, somewhat ironically, that various 'more intellectual folks, columnists' have discussed this numerous times, but 'even if it is the thousandth time, I will say it':

> Before we would go to Beyoğlu we would stand in front of a mirror first. We would check whether our ties were straightened, our gloves and hats elegant. It was a big thing to raise one's hat to someone, or drink a tea at Lebon Patisserie.[6]

Vakko also reflects on how the Beyoğlu Beautification Association wants, with the help of the Beyoğlu mayor and chair of the Association, to turn the district into: 'the world's most beautiful shopping centre. (. . .) Through the constructive efforts of our mayor Haluk Öztürkatalay and the association of which he is the chair, the Beyoğlu we missed will be straightened out and return to its former beauty'.[7] Following the pedestrianization that was projected in the plans of the municipality and the association, gentrification in the area would accelerate and gradually spread to the surrounding areas.[8] As the quote by Mr Vakko shows, little attention was paid to the strong degree of continuity in Beyoğlu's core functions that had persisted over the years. Significantly also, as Edhem Eldem has argued, in the process of gentrification and the romanticization of the district's history the problematic or outright traumatic episodes of the district's past were ignored.[9] It is the kind of interventionalist attitude that Beyoğlu witnessed in the Tarlabaşı destruction which became a constant during the 1990s, 2000s, 2010s in Beyoğlu, culminating in the protests to halt destruction or contested redevelopment of Tarlabaşı, Emek Cinema, Narmanlı Han, but also the Gezi Park protests at the border of historical Beyoğlu in 2013.[10] To understand the effect and path towards dramatic ruptures such as 6–7 September 1955 or the Tarlabaşı destructions, it is necessary to subject mystifying representations of the area to critical scrutiny and carefully consider the continuities and discontinuities in the period between 1950 and 1990 in Beyoğlu. The book has made a step in this direction and contributes in a broader sense to historical research on contemporary European cities, in which most studies of urban history have focussed on the period preceding the Second World War.[11]

As Eldem has suggested in the context of Ottoman Pera and Galata, the abundance of sources on elite communities means that there is an overrepresentation of precisely these communities in academic and popular discussions of the area in the nineteenth century, ignoring Muslims and the working-class segments of non-Muslim populations. Although the problem of Beyoğlu during the second half of the twentieth century is considerably bigger, due to its absence in scholarly discussions, the underrepresentation of working-class communities is also a problem in the sources that date back to the second half of the twentieth century. Yet, this book has engaged with this problem in a more holistic way by focusing on what Eldem presents as 'coherent units of space', smaller segments of Beyoğlu that demonstrate how middle classes gain and retain influence in the area's usage.[12] This is particularly significant in light of pervasive representations of the area since, as has been noted in various cases, with the departure of large portions of its (non-Muslim) residents, Beyoğlu would also lose a significant portion of its cultural and social capital, aesthetic appeal and witness strong shifts in the balance of its functionalities by day in contrast to those by night. This means that the experience of the area could differ considerably between day and night when its core functionalities shifted (but not disappeared) from a centre for business, social gathering and education to a centre for 'cheap' nightlife. This is, in fact, similar to the observation Edhem Eldem has made about representations of Pera and Galata's history as an interplay between 'luxurious shops, brasseries, theaters, and *café-concerts*' and 'taverns, brothels and sleazy hotels' respectively. A 'silent majority', representing more mundane urban life, becomes obliterated in between.[13]

New light has been shed on the question how communities in and of Beyoğlu have imagined themselves in relation to their surroundings. Beyoğlu as a contested place has maintained a pivotal position in a variety of institutionalized or semi-institutionalized communities, at local, national and international scales. Diverse communities within the area coped with the changing reality of Istanbul's development from an imperial capital, to a semi-provincial city, to an ever-expanding 'global' metropolis. The book has put further emphasis on the problematic nature of the conflation of representations of loss and decay with historical developments in the context of Beyoğlu and shown the degree to which the district's identity and legacy have historically been contested. It furthermore demonstrates the diffuse nature of continuities and discontinuities in the urban landscape before and after the 1950s, which further counter essentialist representations of loss and decay. Such representations of decay, marginalization and perversion intersect with a decrease and change of functionality, demographic shifts and the dilapidation of architecture and infrastructure. The representations, however, also lead to anachronistic discourses on Beyoğlu's development from the 1950s onwards, replicated in mass media, by novelists, but also by civil society actors, academics, private enterprises and governments.

The three schools which have been discussed in this book can be considered as representative of the way in which foreign-language elite schools in Beyoğlu retained their reputation and influence during the decades in which Beyoğlu would gradually start sharing its core functions with new centres in the city.[14] The schools also reveal how closely interconnected Beyoğlu was with local, national and international contexts. In the case of the English and German schools their original purpose, that is, providing schooling for local Anglo- and Germanophone communities, had been diminished by the 1950s. In the context of a new geopolitical world order, increasing emphasis was placed in both the EHSG and the German School on their roles as instruments of cultural diplomacy, vital to building a positive impression of Great Britain and the Federal Republic of Germany among a local intelligentsia in Turkey. As such, international geopolitics and bilateral relations had, and have, a direct effect on the core functions of Beyoğlu. Through these institutions, local children were exposed to foreign languages and curricula and effectively creating hyphenated community identities. It is in part also for that reason that correspondence found in the National Archives in London and the *Politisches Archiv* in Berlin, respectively, repeatedly points to the need to resolve problems with finances, the location of the buildings in order to be able to effectively influence the education and development of future generations, in ways that were sympathetic to the Anglophone or Germanophone worlds. This shows how the stipulations of the 1923 Lausanne Treaty – in which existing foreign schools could remain in the Republic of Turkey, but not expand their premises – had a direct impact on local contexts and, importantly, how these schools grew out to be increasingly significant focal points in cultural diplomacy policies.

The chapter on the Galatasaray High School shows a different perspective on Beyoğlu that seems, in light of the pervasive representations on the Beyoğlu district that were discussed in Chapter 1, paradoxical and thus helps to critically review these representations. On the one hand it shows how a Turkish elite school that presented itself as a forebear of Kemalist nationalism could actively claim its place in the Beyoğlu area, which in its urban landscape, representation and demography countered the ethnonationalism of national ideology. Although as a state school it was not confronted with the limitations imposed by the intersections of local and geopolitical dimensions from the Lausanne Treaty, the decision was never made to move the school in its entirety to the school's Ortaköy premises. The representations of the school's belonging in the area would counter the argument that this was merely an effect of the limited capacity of the Turkish school system. To be a *Galatasaraylı* is to have studied in Beyoğlu according to alumni.

The histories of clubs and their buildings similarly show how various communities engaged their sense of belonging in the district. The Teutonia club's narrative demonstrates the significance of a 'national' meeting place in a small community gradually decreasing, in part due to the club's position during the years of the Nazi regime and partly because of the move of most Germans and other potential members away from Beyoğlu and adjacent areas. It is intriguing nonetheless that Teutonia remained, especially after the 1960s when activities where reduced to a minimum. The club assumed a role of caretakership for its premises in order to preserve the building for a German purpose in Istanbul. After the Teutonia gradually lost its significance as a meeting point for Germans in Istanbul, the building would be used for a variety of educational purposes, for which the location of the German High School was certainly significant in the later years of the club. Yet, the building also provided shelter for seamen and GDR refugees, showing the extent of its multifunctionality and how actors associated with the building's fate searched for new purpose. Through an arrangement with the German Consulate, moreover, it would be protected against a disownment by the Turkish state, should the club be unable to meet the minimal requirements of Turkey's legislation on associations. Although the days of skittle alleys, movie nights, concerts and carnival were mostly in the past, the building by Kapp and Semprini remained a significant node of activity in Beyoğlu, for German speakers and others.

Yet even the actual departure of a club would not necessarily mean that Beyoğlu lost its core functionality as a place of social gathering in a specific space. Quite to the contrary in fact: while the significance of Abraham Pasha's Beyoğlu building of the Cercle d'Orient diminished during the 1970s, the importance of the parcel around Yeşilçam Sokak would only grow over the years and attract new crowds to the area. The significance would in fact be so considerable that it has become synonymous with one of modern Turkey's most important centres of cultural production, the Yeşilçam film industry. The marked resistance against the destruction or redevelopment of the Cercle d'Orient parcel and particularly the Emek Cinema, moreover, shows that communities which felt attachment to this particular space had created their own sense of place in Beyoğlu, at times intersecting with older tropes of Beyoğlu nostalgia, yet also decisively different from a romanticized image of an upscale area. The remark of philosopher and novelist Kerem Eksen, a high school student at Galatasaray in Beyoğlu during the early 1990s, seems befitting in this context: he reflects on the way the novels of his father were imbued with a deep sense of nostalgia for the Beyoğlu of his youth, that appeared like a discourse of decadence to Eksen's generation growing up in the 1980s and 1990s. While this generation ridiculed the preceding one for their nostalgic stories about the well-ironed trousers they used to wear when going to Beyoğlu – since they wore blue jeans, or at least not the creased pants of the older generation – he noted that his generation has developed their own nostalgias of Beyoğlu, with the disappearance of movie theatres and bookstores that they came of age with and in.[15] Each generation has a Beyoğlu of its past to yearn for. This nostalgia is understandable, especially in light of the urbicides that have marked neoliberal Istanbul over the decades. Yet, the specific context of Emek Cinema also sheds light on the necessity to consider the troubling continuities of these spaces, in which historical legacies and ownerships were never the priority.

The analysis in this book further underscores the importance of studying recent urban history, to understand the development towards present-day situations and conflicts in urban settings and how they correlate with national and international events or trends. It furthermore counters conceptions of the dilapidation and loss of function of historic urban centres after the Second World War. What the case of Beyoğlu demonstrates is that the area was next to decline – primarily caused by the forced departure of significant portions of its residents – subject to a significant deal of continuity in its functions and on the other hand saw gradual shifts in its usage profile and users' profiles. As has been noted previously, this had a catalysing effect on existing representations of Beyoğlu as a place of squalor, moral decay, vulgarity and essentially a Janus-faced district; a space for business, education and culture during daytime and of shady nightlife at night. Identifying, analysing and critically commenting on these representations, their origins and correlation with historical developments retain its relevance in the Beyoğlu of today as well. Similar to other metropoles in which historical landscapes and rapid urban transformation come together, historical Istanbul and Beyoğlu are highly complex and palimpsestic historical landscapes and as such any major intervention to their landscape 'must negotiate these historical complexities, layers, and associations'.[16] This pertains equally to the layers of the first decades of the Turkish Republic and before, as it does to the periods between the 1950s and the 1990s. Acknowledging and investigating these layers never loses its relevance. As the 2016 *New York*

Times article quoted at the outset of this book shows, the trope of decay continues to be replayed in even the most recent popular representations of the city. This book is, in that sense, a critical call to reject dismissal of the right to place-making and history writing and representing the area through the lens of overdetermined nostalgia.

NOTES

Introduction

1   Tim Arango, 'On Istiklal, Istanbul's Champs-Élysées, Symbols of a City's Malaise', *The New York Times* website, 20 September 2016. https://www.nytimes.com/2016/09/21/world/europe/istiklal-istanbul-turkey.html (accessed 21 January 2019).
2   Ibid.
3   My understanding of space and place is primarily informed by cultural and political geography, notably Doreen Massey and John Agnew. See: Doreen Massey, *Space, Place, and Gender* (Minneapolis: University of Minnesota Press, 1994); John Agnew, 'Space: Place', in *Spaces of Geographical Thought*, ed. Paul Cloke and Ron Johnston (London: Sage, 2005), 81–96.
4   Dilek Güven, *Nationalismus und Minderheiten: Die Ausschreitungen gegen die Christen und Juden der Türkei vom September 1955* (München: Oldenbourg Verlag, 2012); Alexis Alexandris, *The Greek Minority of Istanbul and Greek-Turkish Relations, 1918-1974* (Athens: Centre for Asia Minor Studies, 1992). Sibel Bozdoğan and Esra Akcan have contributed extensively to understanding the architectural and urban environment of Istanbul in the second half of the twentieth century: Sibel Bozdoğan and Esra Akcan, *Turkey: Modern Architectures in History* (London: Reaktion Books, 2012). İpek Türeli explicitly and actively engages the lacunae in the historiography on Istanbul's recent history and the city's representations since the 1950s: İpek Türeli, *Istanbul, Open City: Exhibiting Anxieties of Urban Modernity* (New York: Routledge, 2018).
5   Moritz Föllmer and Mark B. Smith, 'Urban Societies in Europe since 1945: Toward a Historical Interpretation', *Contemporary European History* 24, no. 4 (2015): 475–91.
6   Denis Cosgrove, *Social Formation and Symbolic Landscape* (Madison, WI: The Wisconsin University Press, 1998, first published: 1984), xxx and 1–68.
7   Denis Cosgrove, 'Landscape and Landschaft', *GHI Bulletin* 35 (2004): 68.
8   Veronica Della Dora, 'The Rhetoric of Nostalgia: Postcolonial Alexandria between Uncanny Memories and Global Geographies', *Cultural Geographies* 13, no. 2 (2006): 207–38.
9   Svetlana Boym, *The Future of Nostalgia* (New York: Basic Books, 2002), 121–72.
10   Edhem Eldem, 'Istanbul as a Cosmopolitan City: Myths and Realities', in *A Companion to Diaspora and Transnationalism*, ed. Ato Quayson and Girish Daswani (Malden, Oxford: Blackwell Publishing Ltd, 2013) 212–30.
11   Ayhan Işık, 'The Emergence, Transformation and Functions of Paramilitary Groups in Northern Kurdistan (Eastern Turkey) in the 1990s', PhD Thesis, Utrecht University, Utrecht, 2020, 37–54. Şaban Halis Çalış, *Turkey's Cold War: Foreign Policy and Western Alignment in the Modern Republic* (London: I.B. Tauris, 2017), 87–132.

12 Begüm Adalet, *Hotels and Highways: The Construction of Modernization Theory in Cold War Turkey* (Stanford: Stanford University Press, 2018), 1–22, 159–92; Çalış, *Turkey's Cold War*, 71–86.
13 Joseph S. Nye, 'Soft Power', *Foreign Policy* 80 (1990): 153–71.
14 Föllmer and Smith, 'Urban Societies in Europe since 1945', 475–91.
15 Bozdoğan and Akcan, *Turkey: Modern Architectures in History*, 108–62.

Chapter 1

1 Afife Batur, 'Galata and Pera: A Short History, Urban Development Architecture and Today', *ARI: The Bulletin of the İstanbul Technical University* 55, no. 1 (2002): 1–2.
2 Edhem Eldem, Daniel Goffman, and Bruce Masters, *The Ottoman City between East and West: Aleppo, Izmir, and Istanbul* (Cambridge: Cambridge University Press, 2005), 144.
3 Ibid.
4 Paolo Girardelli, 'Architecture, Identity, and Liminality: On the Use and Meaning of Catholic Spaces in Late Ottoman Istanbul', *Muqarnas* 22 (2005): 233; Louis Mitler, 'The Genoese in Galata: 1453–1682', *International Journal of Middle East Studies* 10, no. 1 (1979): 71–91.
5 Eldem, Goffman, and Masters, *The Ottoman City between East and West*, 151.
6 Ibid., 152.
7 Paolo Girardelli, 'Sheltering Diversity: Levantine Architecture in Late Ottoman Istanbul', in *Multicultural Urban Fabric and Types in the South Eastern Mediterranean*, ed. M. Cerasi, A. Petruccioli, A. Sarro and S. Weber (Istanbul: Orient Institut, 2008), 114; Maurice Cerasi, 'The Formation of Ottoman House Types: A Comparative Study In Interaction With Neighboring Cultures', *Muqarnas* 15, no. 1 (2008): 146.
8 Cerasi, 'The Formation of Ottoman House Types', 120.
9 Girardelli, 'Sheltering Diversity', 114.
10 Shirine Hamadeh, *The City's Pleasures: Istanbul in the Eighteenth Century* (Seattle: University of Washington Press, 2008), 6.
11 Ibid., 12.
12 Ibid., 220.
13 Ibid., 236.
14 Erik-Jan Zürcher, *Turkey: A Modern History*, 3rd edn (London and New York: I.B. Tauris, 2004), 39.
15 Ibid.
16 Ibid., 51.
17 Ibid., 50.
18 Lorans Tanahtar Baruh, 'The Transformation of the 'Modern' Axis of Nineteenth-Century Istanbul: Property, Investments and Elites from Taksim Square to Sirkeci Station', PhD thesis, Boğaziçi University, Istanbul, 2009, 78. Baruh indicates that the letter was originally translated into French by Stéphane Yerasimos in: Alain Borie, Pierre Pinon, Stéphane Yerasimos, *L'occidentalisation d'Istanbul au XIXe siècle, Rapport de synthèse, septembre 1996* (Paris: École d'Architecture de Paris La Défense, Bureau de la Recherche Architecturale, 1996), 28–9.

19 Zeynep Çelik, *The Remaking of Istanbul* (Berkeley and Los Angeles: University of California Press, 1993), 49–81.
20 Girardelli, 'Sheltering Diversity', 114–15.
21 Çelik, *The Remaking of Istanbul*, 42.
22 Ibid., 43.
23 Ibid.
24 Ibid.
25 Ibid, 45; İpek Akpınar, 'The Rebuilding of Istanbul after the Plan of Henri Prost 1937–1960/ From Secularisation to Turkish Modernisation', PhD thesis, University of London, London, 2003, 38.
26 Çelik, *The Remaking of Istanbul*, 45.
27 Ibid.
28 Girardelli, 'Sheltering Diversity', 113.
29 Ibid., 118.
30 Çelik, *The Remaking of Istanbul*, 126–37.
31 Girardelli, 'Architecture, Identity, and Liminality', 258.
32 Girardelli, 'Sheltering Diversity', 118.
33 Ibid., 126–7.
34 Eldem, 'Istanbul as a Cosmopolitan City', 212–30; Edhem Eldem, 'Galata-Pera between Myth and Reality', in *From 'mileu de memoire' to 'lieu de memoire': The Cultural Memory of Istanbul in the 20th Century*, ed. Ulrike Tischler (Munich: Peter Lang, 2006), 18–38.
35 Eldem, 'Istanbul as a Cosmopolitan City', 223.
36 Stanford J. Shaw, 'The Population of Istanbul in the Nineteenth Century', *International Journal of Middle East Studies* 10, no. 2 (1979): 265–77; Çelik, *The Remaking of Istanbul*, 38.
37 Will Hanley, 'What Ottoman Nationality Was and Was Not', *Journal of the Ottoman and Turkish Studies Association* 3, no. 2 (2016): 277–98.
38 Paul Dumont, 'Freemasonry in Turkey: A By-Product of Western Penetration', *European Review* 13, no. 3 (2005): 481–93.
39 Orhan Koloğlu, *Cercle d'Orient'dan Büyük Kulüp'e* (Istanbul: Boyut, 2005).
40 See chapters 6–8 in this book.
41 Joep Leerssen, 'Nationalism and the Cultivation of Culture', *Nations and Nationalism* 12, no. 4 (2006): 573–4; Ann Rigney, 'Embodied Communities: Commemorating Robert Burns, 1859', *Representations* 115 (2011): 71–101.
42 Ulrike Tischler, 'Microhistorical Views of the Sociocultural Phenomenon of Pera Society in the Post-Ottoman Period', in *From 'mileu de memoire' to 'lieu de memoire': The Cultural Memory of Istanbul in the 20th Century*, ed. Ulrike Tischler (Munich: Peter Lang, 2006), 159–60.
43 Tischler, 'Microhistorical Views', 156–69.
44 Ibid., 168.
45 Çelik, *The Remaking of Istanbul*, 64.
46 Girardelli, 'Architecture, Identity, and Liminality', 254.
47 Çelik, *The Remaking of Istanbul*, 47–54.
48 Ibid., 47.
49 Murat Güvenç has been preparing a project that inventorizes the socio-economic function of addresses and the occupation of residents. Edhem Eldem refers to this project, entitled 'Continuity and Change in the Commercial Geography of Istanbul: Street Profiles in the 1910–1922 Oriental directories' at the time of his writing, in Eldem, 'Ottoman Galata and Pera between Myth and Reality', 25–6.

50 Barbara Radt, *Geschichte der Teutonia: Deutsche Vereinsleben in Istanbul 1847-2000* (Istanbul: Orient Institut d. Deutschen Morgenländischen Gesellschaft, 2001), 24.
51 Çelik, *The Remaking of Istanbul*, 93.
52 Girardelli, 'Sheltering Diversity', 126-7.
53 Sibel Bozdoğan, *Modernism and Nation Building: Turkish Architectural Culture in the Early Republic* (Seattle: University of Washington Press, 2001), 16-22.
54 Edhem Eldem, *Bankalar Caddesi: Osmanlı'dan Günümüze Voyvoda Caddesi - Voyvoda Street from Ottoman Times to Today* (Istanbul: Osmanlı Bankası, 2000), 77-83; 253-63.
55 Girardelli, 'Sheltering Diversity', 127.
56 Bozdoğan, *Modernism and Nation Building*, 28.
57 Ibid., 30-2.
58 Alexandris, *The Greek Minority of Istanbul*, 31.
59 Ibid.
60 Ibid., 45.
61 Vangelis Kechriotis, 'Greek-Orthodox, Ottoman Greeks or Just Greeks? Theories of Coexistence in the Aftermath of the Young Turk Revolution', *Études balkaniques* 1 (2005): 51-72.
62 Alexandris, *The Greek Minority of Istanbul*, 51.
63 Zürcher, *Turkey: A Modern History*, 100.
64 Murat Gül, *The Emergence of Modern Istanbul: Transformation and Modernisation of a City* (London: I.B. Tauris, 2012), 64; Stanford J. Shaw, 'The Ottoman Census System and Population, 1831-1914', *International Journal of Middle East Studies* 9, no. 3 (1978): 335.
65 Ayhan Aktar, 'Conversion of a 'Country' into a 'Fatherland': The Case of Turkification Examined, 1923-1934', in *Nationalism in the Troubled Triangle: New Perspectives on South-East Europe*, ed. A. Aktar, N. Kızılyürek and U. Özkırımlı (London: Palgrave Macmillan, 2010), 23.
66 Gül, *The Emergence of Modern Istanbul*, 65-70.
67 Ibid., 112.
68 Uğur Üngör, *The Making of Modern Turkey* (Oxford: Oxford University Press, 2012), 55-169.
69 For a discussion of denialist historiography: Fatma Müge Göçek, *Denial of Violence: Ottoman Past, Turkish Present, and Collective Violence against the Armenians, 1789-2009* (Oxford: Oxford University Press, 2015).
70 Üngör, *The Making of Modern Turkey*, 140.
71 Alexandris, *The Greek Minority of Istanbul*, 54.
72 Ibid., 63.
73 Zürcher, *Turkey: A Modern History*, 133-65.
74 Ibid., 160.
75 Ibid., 163-4.
76 Charles King, *Midnight at the Pera Palace: The Birth of Modern Istanbul* (New York: Norton & Company, 2014), 62.
77 Gül, *The Emergence of Modern Istanbul*, 79.
78 Özcan Altaban and Murat Güvenç, 'Urban Planning in Ankara', *Cities* 7, no. 2 (1990): 149-50; and Bülent Batuman, 'City Profile: Ankara', *Cities* 31 (2013): 578-9.
79 Türkoğlu Önge, Sinem, 'Spatial Representation of Power: Making the Urban Space of Ankara in the Early Republican Period', in *Developing EU-Turkey Dialogue - A*

Cliohworld Reader, ed. Guðmundur Hálfdánarson and Hatice Sofu (Pisa: Pisa University Press, 2010), 235.

80 Türkoğlu Önge, 'Spatial Representation of Power', 244; Bozdoğan, *Modernism and Nation Building*, 56–105; Zeynep Kezer, *Building Modern Turkey: State, Space, and Ideology in the Early Republic* (Pittsburgh, PA: University of Pittsburgh Press, 2016).

81 Akpınar, 'The Rebuilding of Istanbul', 43.

82 Ibid., 44.

83 Ibid.

84 Cana Bilsel, 'Remodelling the Imperial Capital in the Early Republican Era: The Representation of History in Henri Prost's Planning of Istanbul', in *Developing EU-Turkey Dialogue, A Cliohworld Reader*, ed. Guomundur Halfdanarson and Hatice Sofu (Pisa: University of Pisa Press, 2010), 260–1.

85 Carole Woodall, '"Awakening a Horrible Monster": Negotiating the Jazz Public in 1920s Istanbul', *Comparative Studies of South Asia, Africa and the Middle East* 30, no. 3 (2010): 574–5.

86 Ibid., 580.

87 Jeremy F. Lane, *Jazz and Machine-Age Imperialism: Music, "Race," and Intellectuals in France, 1918-1945* (Ann Arbor: The University of Michigan Press, 2013), 17.

88 Arus Yumul, '"A Prostitute Lodging in the Bosom of Turkishness": Istanbul's Pera and its Representation', *Journal of Intercultural Studies* 30, no. 1 (2009): 67.

89 Woodall, '"Awakening a Horrible Monster"', 581.

90 Sossie Kasbarian, 'The Istanbul Armenians: Negotiating Coexistence', in *Post-Ottoman Coexistence: Sharing Space in the Shadow of Conflict*, ed. Rebecca Bryant (New York: Berghahn Books, 2016), 209.

91 Search query '*Türklüğe hareket eden*'.

92 *The New York Times*, 'The Turkish Minorities', 17 September 1943, 20.

93 Üngör, *The Making of Modern Turkey*, 231–2; Meltem Türköz, 'Surname Narratives and the State—Society Boundary: Memories of Turkey's Family Name Law of 1934', *Middle Eastern Studies* 43, no. 6 (2007): 893–908.

94 Aysun Akan, 'A Critical Analysis of the Turkish Press Discourse against Non-Muslims: A Case Analysis of the Newspaper Coverage of the 1942 Wealth Tax', *Middle Eastern Studies* 47, no. 4 (2011): 605–6.

95 Ibid., 607.

96 Bilsel, 'Remodelling the Imperial Capital', 264.

97 Ibid., 267.

98 Bozdoğan and Akcan, *Turkey*, 161.

99 Ibid., 161–2.

100 Ibid., 108–10.

101 Ibid., 113.

102 Ibid., 116–17.

103 Ibid.

104 Sara Fregonese and Adam Ramadan, 'Hotel Geopolitics: A Research Agenda', *Geopolitics* 20, no. 4 (2015): 799.

105 Adalet, *Hotels and Highways*, 1–22, 159–92.

106 Ibid., 1–2.

107 Ipek Türeli, 'Heritagisation of the "Ottoman/Turkish House" in the 1970s: Istanbul-based Actors, Associations and their Networks', *European Journal of Turkish Studies* 19 (2014): 5.

108 Türeli, 'Heritagisation of the "Ottoman/Turkish House"', 5.
109 Sven Grabow, 'The Santiago De Compostela Pilgrim Routes: The Development of European Cultural Heritage Policy and Practice From a Critical Perspective', *European Journal of Archaeology* 13, no. 1 (2010): 91.
110 Yumul, '"A Prostitute Lodging in the Bosom of Turkishness"', 67–8 and Ali Şükrü Çoruk, 'Cumhuriyet Devri Türk Romanında Beyoğlu (1924–1980)', MA Thesis, Istanbul University, 1993, XXI.
111 Çoruk, 'Cumhuriyet Devri Türk Romanında', 79–80.
112 Ibid., XX.
113 Mark Wyers, 'Selling Sex in Istanbul', in *Selling Sex in the City: A Global History of Prostitution, 1600s–2000s*, ed. Magaly Rodríguez García, Lex Heerma van Voss, Elise van Nederveen Meerkerk (Leiden: Brill, 2007), 278–305.
114 Mark Wyers, *Wicked Istanbul: The Regulation of Prostitution in the early Turkish Republic* (Istanbul: Libra Kitap, 2012), 172–3.
115 Ibid., 168–213.
116 Çoruk, 'Cumhuriyet Devri Türk Romanında', 52–64.
117 Yumul, '"A Prostitute Lodging in the Bosom of Turkishness"', 68.
118 Translation by Arus Yumul, '"A Prostitute Lodging in the Bosom of Turkishness"', 68; original quote by Çoruk, 'Cumhuriyet Devri Türk Romanında', XXI–XXII.
119 Dilek Güven, *Nationalismus und Minderheiten: Die Ausschreitungen gegen die Christen und Juden der Türkei vom September 1955* (München: Oldenbourg Verlag, 2012), 16.
120 Ibid., 26.
121 Ibid.
122 Ibid., 30.
123 Ibid., 31.
124 Ibid., 31–2.
125 Ibid., 37–41.
126 Alexandris, *The Greek Minority of Istanbul*, 260–1.
127 Ibid., 258–9.
128 Güven, *Nationalismus und Minderheiten*, 170–1.
129 Ibid.
130 Alexandris, *The Greek Minority of Istanbul*, 271.
131 İlay Romain Örs, 'Beyond the Greek and Turkish Dichotomy: The Rum Polites of Istanbul and Athens', *South European Society and Politics* 11, no. 1 (2006): 79–92.
132 Alexandris, *The Greek Minority of Istanbul*, 283.
133 Ibid., 284.
134 Kasbarian, 'The Istanbul Armenians', 223.
135 Alexandris, *The Greek Minority of Istanbul*, 286.
136 Ibid., 287.
137 Çağlar Keyder, 'The Setting', in *Istanbul: Between the Global and the Local*, ed. Çağlar Keyder (Lanham: Rowman and Littlefield Publisher, 1999), 11.
138 Çağlar Keyder and Ayşe Öncü, 'Globalization of a Third-World Metropolis: Istanbul in the 1980's', *Review (Fernand Braudel Center)* 17, no. 3 (1994): 384; Bensiyon Pinto, Tülay Gürler, Nicole Pope, and Leyla Engin Arık, *My Life as a Turkish Jew: Memoirs of the President of the Turkish-Jewish Community, 1989–2004* (İstanbul: Bahçeşehir University Press, 2012), 49.
139 Keyder and Öncü, 'Globalization of a Third-World Metropolis', 384.
140 Zürcher, *Turkey: A Modern History*, 226.

141 Vedia Dökmeci and Lale Berköz, 'Transformation of Istanbul from a Monocentric to a Polycentric City', *European Planning Studies* 2, no. 2 (1994): 193–205; Vedia Dökmeci, Ufuk Altunbaş and Burcin Yazgı, 'Revitalisation of the Main Street of a Distinguished Old Neighbourhood in Istanbul', *European Planning Studies* 15, no. 1 (2007): 153–66.

142 Türeli, 'Heritagisation of the "Ottoman/Turkish House"', 5.

143 Ibid., 5.

144 Dökmeci and Çiraci, 'Pera', 359.

145 Hachette, *Les Guides Bleus: Turquie* (Paris: Hachette, 1969), 171.

146 Ibid., 171. *'Beyoğlu, l'ancienne Péra, quartier moderne d'Istanbul est, avec ses nouveaux faubourgs de Harbiye, de Şişli, de Maçka, etc., le quartier résidentiel par excellence. C'est là que se trouvent les hôtels les plus confortables, ceux qui, en général, sont fréquentés par les touristes étrangers. Ce sera donc le centre de rayonnement à partir duquel partiront les divers itinéraires qui permettront de visiter Istanbul et ses environs.'*

147 Çoruk, 'Cumhuriyet Devri Türk Romanında', XXII; Ayfer Bartu, 'Who Owns the Old Quarters? Rewriting Histories in a Global Era', in *Istanbul: Between the Global and the Local*, ed. Çağlar Keyder (Lanham: Rowman and Littefield Publisher, 1999), 36–8; Reşat Ekrem Koçu, 'Barlar', İstanbul Ansiklopedisi, 4 (İstanbul: Tan Matbaası, 1960), Özdemir Arkan, *Beyoğlu: Kısa Geçmişi, Argosu* (Istanbul: İletişim, 1988).

148 Çoruk, 'Cumhuriyet Devri Türk Romanında', XX.

149 Ayşe Öncü, 'Istanbulites and Others: The Cultural Cosmology of Being Middle Class in the Era of Globalism', in *Istanbul: Between the Global and the Local*, ed. Çağlar Keyder (Lanham: Rowman & Littlefield, 1999), 104–5.

150 Dökmeci and Lale Berköz, 'Transformation of Istanbul', 198.

151 Vedia Dökmeci and Hale Çiraci, 'Pera: A Threatened Historic European City within Istanbul', *Ekistics* 55, no. 333 (1988): 359.

152 Keyder, 'The Setting', 12.

153 Ibid.

154 Örnek and Üngör, *Turkey in the Cold War*, 10.

155 Zürcher, *Turkey: A Modern History*, 263.

156 Ayşegül Baykan and Tali Hatuka, 'Politics and Culture in the Making of Public Space: Taksim Square, 1 May 1977, Istanbul', *Planning Perspectives* 25, no. 1 (2010): 58–64.

157 Kerem Öktem, *Turkey since 1989: Angry Nation* (London: Zed Books, 2011), 56.

158 Öktem, *Turkey Since 1989*, 57.

159 Zeynep Çelik, 'Urban Preservation as Theme Park: The Case of Soğukçeşme Street', in *Streets Critical Perspectives on Space*, ed. Zeynep Çelik, Diane Favro and Richard Ingersoll (Berkeley and Los Angeles: University of California Press, 1994), 83–4.

160 Bahar Sakızlıoğlu, 'A Comparative Look at Residents' Displacement Experiences: The Cases of Amsterdam and Istanbul', PhD thesis, Utrecht University, Utrecht, 2014, 163–6.

161 Dökmeci, Altunbaş and Yazgı, 'Revitalisation of the Main Street', 157.

162 *Milliyet*, 'Beyoğlu çekidüzen veriliyor', 9 June, 1984, 3.

163 C. Nil Uzun, 'The Impact of Urban Renewal and Gentrification on Urban Fabric: Three Cases in Turkey', *Tijdschrift voor Economische en Sociale Geografie* 94, no. 3 (2003): 363–75; Nilgün Ergun, 'Gentrification in Istanbul', *Cities* 21, no. 5 (2004): 391–405.

164   Eldem, 'Istanbul as a Cosmopolitan City', 225–6. Duhani was a prominent Perote from a Christian Arab family.
165   Türeli, 'Heritagisation of the "Ottoman/Turkish House"', 6; Della Dora, 'The Rhetoric of Nostalgia, 209; Mercedes Volait, 'The Reclaiming of "Belle Époque" Architecture in Egypt (1989–2010): On the Power of Rhetorics in Heritage-Making', *ABE Journal* 3, no. 1 (2013): 1–36 (paragraphs).
166   Ibid., 228.
167   Ibid., 225–6.
168   Ibid.
169   Eldem, 'Istanbul as a Cosmopolitan City', 225–6; Asu Aksoy and Kevin Robins, 'Changing Urban Cultural Governance in Istanbul: The Beyoğlu Plan', *KPY Working Paper* 1 (2011): 4–7.
170   Eldem, 'Galata-Pera between Myth and Reality', 26.

Chapter 2

1   For the Prussian Embassy see: Carsten Meyer-Schlichtmann, *Von der Preussischen Gesandtschaft zum Doğan-Apartmanı: 130 Jahre Geschichte eines Grundstückes und Hauses in Beyoğlu – Istanbul* (Istanbul: Istanbul Kitaplığı, 1992).
2   Paolo Girardelli, 'The Renovation of the Società Operaia Italiana di Mutuo Soccorso (SOI), in Istanbul (1908–1910)', in *Değişen Zamanların Mimarı – The Architect of Changing Times, Edoardo de Nari (1874–1954)*, ed. Baha Tanman (İstanbul: İstanbul Araştırma Enstitüsü, 2012), 122–7; Paul Dumont, 'Freemasonry in Turkey: A By-Product of Western Penetration', *European Review* 13, no. 3 (2005): 481–93.
3   Joep Leerssen, 'Nationalism and the Cultivation of Culture', *Nations and Nationalism* 12, no. 4 (2006): 559, 578.
4   Ann Rigney, 'Embodied Communities: Commemorating Robert Burns, 1859', *Representations* 115 (2011): 71–101. Rigney provides a critique to Benedict Anderson seminal concept of imagined communities, by arguing that it were not just imagined communities which provided the foundation for national (and other communal), identities, but also the interaction between imagined and embodied communities; Benedict Anderson, *Imagined Communities: Reflections on the Origin and Spread of Nationalism*, Revised ed. (London New York: Verso, 2006), 6; Joep Leerssen, 'German Influences: Choirs, Repertoires, Nationalities', in *Choral Societies and Nationalism in Europe*, ed. Krisztina Lajosi and Andreas Stynen (Leiden, Boston: Brill, 2015), 9, 27–9.
5   Selçuk Akşin Somel, 'Die Deutschen an der "Pforte der Glückseligkeit": Kulturelle und soziale Begegnungen mit Istanbuler Türken zwischen 1870 und 1918. Almanlar Dersaadet'te: 1870–1918 Devresi İstanbul'unda Almanlarla Osmanlıların Kültürel ve Toplumsal Buluşma Deneyimi', in *Boğaziçi'ndeki Almanya / Deutsche Praesenz am Bosphorus*, ed. Matthias von Kummer (Istanbul: Generalkonsulat der Bundesrepublik Deutschland, 2009), 48.
6   Zürcher, *Turkey, A Modern History*, 41.
7   Ibid.
8   Particularly Prussian officers because Prussia was considered to be a role model by the Ottoman government. The Prussian state and army had successfully reformed

itself and had been able to occupy France in 1871 almost without the assistance of other German states, providing the Ottomans with a substantial source of inspiration for their own reforms. See: Malte Fuhrmann, 'Istanbul, die Deutschen und das 19. Jahrhundert – Wege, die sich kreuzen', in *Daheim in Konstantinopel / Memleketemiz Dersaadet: Deutsche Spuren am Bosporus ab 1850 / 1850'den İtibaren Boğaziçi'ndeki Alman İzleri*, ed. Erald Pauw (Neurenberg: Pagma Verlag, 2014), 38.

9   İlber Ortaylı, *İkinci Abdülhamit Döneminde Osmanlı İmparatorluğu'nda Alman Nüfuzu* (Ankara: Ankara Üniverstesi Basımevi, 1981), 58.

10 Erald Pauw, Sabine Böhme, Ulrich Münch, 'Vorwort', in *Daheim in Konstantinopel / Memleketemiz Dersaadet: Deutsche Spuren am Bosporus ab 1850 / 1850'den İtibaren Boğaziçi'ndeki Alman İzleri*, ed. Erald Pauw (Neurenberg: Pagma Verlag, 2014), 5–10.

11 Anne Dietrich, *Deutschsein in Istanbul: Nationalisierung und Orientierung in der deutschsprachigen Community von 1843 bis 1956* (Opladen: Leske+Budrich, 1998), 78.

12 Teutonia Archives, Istanbul (TAI from here onwards), Typescript of 'Geschichte der Teutonia 1847–1938' by Franz von Caucig, Istanbul 1957, 1.

13 Leerssen, 'German Influences', 14–23. Leerssen borrows the term and definition of 'embodied communities' from Ann Rigney in 'Embodied Communities', 71–101. Choral societies, the early Teutonia inclus, can be considered as prime examples of these embodied communities, which helped as well as actively aimed to disseminate cultural nationalism.

14 Ibid., 27–9.

15 Türkisch – Deutsche Wohltaetigkeitsgesellschaft Teutonia, '110 Jahre "Teutonia"', *Teutonia Mitteilungsblatt* 2, no. 15 (1957): 5.

16 Von Caucig, 'Geschichte der Teutonia', 1.

17 Radt, *Geschichte der Teutonia*, 24.

18 Dietrich, *Deutschsein in Istanbul*, 99.

19 Von Caucig, 'Geschichte der Teutonia', 10.

20 Ibid., 2–4.

21 Von Caucig, 'Geschichte der Teutonia', 2–4. Aynalı Çeşme, Asmalımescit and the old English embassy are mentioned as geographical landmarks of the first buildings.

22 Ibid., 13. 'Als ich am 6. Oktober 1870 durch Herrn Buchhändler Christian Roth daselbst als Gast eingeführt wurde, kam ich mir vor wie der Knabe im Märchen, dem ein glänzender, reich verzeichter Spiegelsaal versprochen wird, der sich aber plötzlich in einem Stallke befindet und nun neugierig und in banger Erwartung der versprochenen Zauberwirkung und Metamorphose umherblickt. Der Spiegelsaal erschien nicht und ich musste mit einem grossen Zimmer vorlieb nehmen, worin sich ein Billard und ein Lesetisch befanden und welches auch sonst sehr primitiv anzusehen war.'

23 Ibid., 13–14.

24 Ibid., 16–18.

25 Ibid., 16–17.

26 Von Caucig, 'Geschichte der Teutonia', 17. The architect is mentioned as being 'Barborini', being the 'Baumeister' (master builder). This is almost certainly Giovanni Battista Barborini (1820–91), a student of the renowned Fossati brothers. Barborini also designed the German Evangelist Church in Tarlabaşı and the Dutch Embassy or Palais de Hollande at the Grand Rue de Pera. He was a political exile and supporter of Italian unification fighting for the Roman Republic at Cornuda in

1848. See: Paolo Girardelli, 'Architecture, Identity and Liminality: On the Use and Meaning of Catholic Spaces in Late Ottoman Istanbul', *Muqarnas: An Annual on the Visual Culture of the Islamic World* XXII (2005): 233–64.

27 Von Caucig, 'Geschichte der Teutonia', 18.

28 Hoi-eun Kim, 'Made in Meiji Japan', *Geschichte und Gesellschaft* 41, no. 2 (2015): 288–320.

29 Radt, *Geschichte der Teutonia*.

30 Ibid., 29.

31 Ibid., 39.

32 Von Caucig, 'Geschichte der Teutonia', 21.

33 Radt, *Geschichte der Teutonia*, 39. Von Kapp had led the building of the German School shortly before. Von Caucig, 'Geschichte der Teutonia', 22.

34 Von Caucig, 'Geschichte der Teutonia'.

35 Radt, *Geschichte der Teutonia*, 41.

36 Von Caucig, 'Geschichte der Teutonia'. Von Caucig probably refers to Turkish-speaking Muslims here.

37 See Ortaylı, *İkinci Abdülhamit Döneminde*. For a study of the significance of the military and arms trade in the German-Ottoman relations see Naci Yorulmaz, *Arming the Sultan: German Arms Trade and Personal Diplomacy in the Ottoman Empire before World War I* (London and New York: I.B. Tauris, 2014).

38 Radt, *Geschichte der Teutonia*, 43.

39 Ibid.

40 Zürcher, *Turkey: A Modern History*, 133, 140.

41 Dietrich, *Deutschsein in Istanbul*, 144.

42 Radt, *Geschichte der Teutonia*, 64.

43 Ibid.

44 Ibid.

45 Von Caucig, 'Geschichte der Teutonia', 49: 'Indessen darf allerdings auch nicht übersehen werden, dass während der Jahre, die dem Kriege unmittelbar vorangingen, die "Teutonia" ein tatsächliches Sammelbecken aller Deutschen in Istanbul wurde und in ihren Räumen manch offenes wort gesprochen werden konnte, ohne dass es Jemanden zum Schaden geriet.'

46 Dietrich, *Deutschsein in Istanbul*, 214. 'Kamerad Walter sprach von den Juden, und wie wir uns gegen sie zu benehmen hätten und noch von allerlei Dingen, auf die wir hier achtgeben sollen.'

47 Ibid., 214, 402.

48 Ibid., 402–3.

49 Radt, *Geschichte der Teutonia*, 67.

50 Ibid., 68.

51 Azade Seyhan, 'German Academic Exiles in Istanbul: Translation as the *Bildung* of the Other', in *Nation, Language, and the Ethics of Translation*, ed. Sandra Bermann and Michael Wood (Princeton & Oxford: Princeton University Press, 2005), 276.

52 Izzet Bahar, 'German or Jewish Humanity or *Raison d'Etat*: The German Scholars in Turkey, 1933–1952', *Shofar: An Interdisciplinary Journal of Jewish Studies* 29, no. 1 (2010): 48–72; Carter Findley, *Ottoman Civil Officialdom: A Social History* (Princeton, NJ: Princeton University Press, 1989), 131–73.

53 Bahar, 'German or Jewish', 49; Lucy S. Dawidowicz, ed., *A Holocaust Reader* (West Orange: Behrman House Inc., 1976), 38–42.

54 Stephan Conermann, 'Die Lage jüdischer deutscher Hochschullehrer und die Einschränkung wissenschaftlichen Arbeitens während der NS-Zeit', in *Istanbuler Texte und Studien*, ed. Christopher Kubaseck and Günter Seufert, Vol. 12 (Würzburg: Ergon-Verlag, 2016), 65.

55 Kader Konuk, *East West Mimesis: Auerbach in Turkey* (Stanford: Stanford University Press, 2010), 84.

56 Ibid.

57 See also: Ayhan Aktar, *Varlık Vergisi ve "Türkleştirme" Politikaları* (İstanbul: İletişim, 2000), and '"Turkification" Policies in the Early Republican Era', in *Turkish Literature and Cultural Memory*, ed. Catharina Duft (Wiesbaden: Harrassowitz Verlag, 2009), 29–62. For an account of the experience of a prominent Turkish Jew, see: Pinto, *My life as a Turkish Jew*.

58 Bahar, 'German or Jewish', 55; Aykut Kazancıgil, Uğur Tanyeli and İlber Ortaylı, 'Niye Geldiler, Niye Gittiler? Kimse Anlamadı', in *Cogito-Türkiye'nin Yabancıları* (Istanbul: Yapı Kredi Yayınları, 2000), 130.

59 Bahar, 'German or Jewish', 57.

60 Seyhan, 'German Academic Exiles in Istanbul', 281–3.

61 Bozdoğan and Akcan, *Turkey*, 63.

62 Ibid., 50–9.

63 Zürcher, *Turkey: A Modern History*, 205.

64 Radt, *Geschichte der Teutonia*, 96.

65 Jörn Rüsen, 'Holocaust Memory and Identity Building: Metahistorical Considerations in the Case of (West), Germany', in *Disturbing Remains: Memory, History, and Crisis in the Twentieth Century*, ed. Michael S. Roth and Charles G. Salas (Los Angeles: Getty Research Institute, 2001), 252–70, 262–6.

66 Dietrich, *Deutschsein in Istanbul*, 402–3.

67 Ibid., 401–3.

68 TAI, 'Ordentliche Generalversammlung', 29 March 1957; 'Protokoll der Vorstandssitzung', 13 November 1952.

69 Rüsen, 'Holocaust Memory and Identity Builiding', 252–70, 262–6.

70 TAI, 'Richtlinien über die Aussprache mit Herrn Botschafter Dr. Oellers', 27 November 1956, 1.

71 Ibid., 2.

72 Ibid., 3.

73 TAI, 'Rückblick über die Tätigkeit der Teutonia nach Rückgabe des Vereinsgebäudes, undated – approximately winter 1956/57'.

74 Ibid.

75 Türkisch – Deutsche Wohltaetigkeitsgesellschaft Teutonia, 'Ein Rückblick', *Teutonia Mitteilungsblatt* 1, no. 1 (1956): 2.

76 Türkisch – Deutsche Wohltaetigkeitsgesellschaft Teutonia, 'Hauptversammlung der Teutonia am 29 März 1957', *Teutonia Mitteilungsblatt* 1, no. 12 (1957): 4.

77 Türkisch – Deutsche Wohltaetigkeitsgesellschaft Teutonia, 'Der Neue Badeplatz in Fenerbahce', *Teutonia Mitteilungsblatt* 3, no. 26 (1958): 6.

78 TAI, 'Rechenschaftsbericht für die Generalversammlung am Freitag, den 29. Marz 1957', 29 March 1957.

79 TAI, 'Opening address for the season of 1958/59', undated – approximately fall or winter 1958.

80 Türkisch – Deutsche Wohltaetigkeitsgesellschaft Teutonia, 'Über den Sinn unseres Vereins', *Teutonia Mitteilungsblatt* 1, no. 2 (1956): 1.

81   Radt, *Geschichte der Teutonia*, 2.
82   Türkisch – Deutsche Wohltaetigkeitsgesellschaft Teutonia, '1. Juni 1847 – 1. Juni
     1857', *Teutonia Mitteilungsblatt* 2, no. 14 (1957): 1–2 and 'Hauptversammlung am
     25. März 1958', *Teutonia Mitteilungsblatt* 2, no. 24 (1958): 5.
83   Teutonia, 'Hauptversammlung am 25. März 1958', 5.
84   Ibid., 4–5.
85   TAI, 'Rechenschaftsbericht für die Generalversammlung am 28.1.1955', 28 January
     1955, 8.
86   Radt, *Geschichte der Teutonia*, 100–2.
87   Türkisch – Deutsche Wohltaetigkeitsgesellschaft Teutonia, 'Veranstaltungen der
     Teutonia', *Teutonia Mitteilungsblatt* 8, no. 76 (1963): 15.
88   Türkisch – Deutsche Wohltaetigkeitsgesellschaft Teutonia, 'Zeichen und
     Wunder: Zum Umbau und zur Renovierung des Teutonia-Gebäudes', *Teutonia
     Mitteilungsblatt* 9, no. 80 (1964): 1–2.
89   Radt, *Geschichte der Teutonia*, 2.
90   TAI, 'Rechenschaftsbericht des Vorständes', 29 March 1964.
91   TAI, 'Rechenschaftsbericht für die Generalversammlung am 28 January 1955',
     28 January 1955, 8.
92   Türkisch – Deutsche Wohltaetigkeitsgesellschaft Teutonia, 'Ordentliche
     Generalversammlung der Teutonia am 29. März 1965', *Teutonia Mitteilungsblatt* 10,
     no. 82 (1965): 2–3; Teutonia, 'Hauptversammlung am 25. März 1958', 5.
93   Radt, *Geschichte der Teutonia*, 104, Thilo Schmidt, *Deutschland Radio Kultur
     Länderreport: Ich bin dann mal weg* (2011), 6.
94   Radt, *Geschichte der Teutonia*, 104.
95   Türkisch – Deutsche Wohltaetigkeitsgesellschaft Teutonia, 'Generalversammlung
     der Teutonia am 17. März', *Teutonia Mitteilungsblatt* 11, no. 83 (1966): 2.
96   Marcel Geser, '"Wir sind im Kleinen, was das Vaterland im Großen": Der deutsche
     Kindergarten in Istanbul von 1850 bis 2007', in *Facetten internationaler Migration in
     die Türkei: Gesellschaftliche Rahmenbedingungen und persönliche Lebenswelten*, ed.
     Barbara Push and Tomas Wilkoszewski. Istanbuler Texte und Studien 13 (Istanbul:
     Orient-Institut Istanbul, 2016), 124.
97   Teutonia, 'Ordentliche Generalversammlung der Teutonia am 29. März 1965', 3.
98   TAI, 'Rechenschaftsbericht des Vorstandes', 29 March 1965, 6.
99   Geser, 'Wir sind im Kleinen', 124.
100 Radt, *Geschichte der Teutonia*, 125.
101 Ibid., 106.
102 TAI, 'Mitglieder 1987', undated member list from 1987.
103 Hachette, *Les Guides Blues Illustrés: Istanbul et ses Environs* (Paris: Hachette, 1958), 66.
104 Radt, *Geschichte der Teutonia*, 106.
105 TAI, 'Letter about the Deutscher Club Teutonia to the German Consulate General',
     2 February 1971, Teutonia Archives, Istanbul, Turkey.
106 Radt, *Geschichte der Teutonia*, 123–4.
107 Cumhuriyet Gazetesi, 'Türk Alman Hayır Cemiyeti', 1 June 1968, 7 and 'Haftanın
     Sanat Çizelgesi', 27 October 1986, 5.
108 Dietrich, *Deutschsein in Istanbul*, 402–3; Radt, *Teutonia*, 106, 118.
109 Teutonia, 'Über den Sinn unseres Vereins', 1.
110 TAI, 'Undated Letter to Members of Teutonia', approximately 1979, by Arthur Kapps
     and Georg Heuser.

111 Türkiye Cumhuriyet Merkez Bankası, *1979 Yıllık Raporu* (Ankara: TCMB, 30 April 1980), 56.

112 Dietrich, *Deutschsein in Istanbul*, 403.

113 National Archives, 'FO 366/2472 Disposal of Pera Embassy Building and Therapia 1947. This letter formally initiated the question of a possible sale, but the entire file in fact engages the issue.

114 TAI, 'Undated Letter to Members of Teutonia', approximately 1979, by Arthur Kapps and Georg Heuser.

115 'Various outtakes from Milliyet and Günaydın newspapers of 26 and 27 October 1977', 26 and 27 October 1977.

116 New York Times, '4 Days of Fear, Then 7 Minutes for the Rescue', *New York Times*, 17 October 1977, available on the *New York Times* website at: http://www.nytimes .com/1977/10/19/archives/4-days-of-fear-then-7-minutes-for-the-rescue-thursday -oct-13.html (viewed 5 January 2018).

117 TAI, 'Various Outtakes from Milliyet and Günaydın Newspapers of 26 and 27 October 1977', 26 and 27 October 1977.

118 'Prüfungen im Gebäude der Teutonia', 8 May 1979'.

119 Archive of the Foreign Ministry of the Kingdom of the Netherlands, Dep 273631 111, 21A and 25.

120 Çelik Gülersoy, *A Guide to Istanbul* (Istanbul: Yenilik Basımevi, 1969), 221–5.

121 TAI, 'Nutzungsvereinbarung zwischen dem Klub Teutonia und der Bundesrepublik Deutschland', 3 March 1988.

122 TAI, 'Protokoll der Vorstandssitzung', 20 October 1987.

123 TAI, 'Rechenschaftsbericht', 17 March 1988.

124 Beyoğlu Belediye Başkanlığı, *Beyoğlu İçin* (Istanbul, 1984), 1–61.

125 TAI, 'Bericht über Begehungen des Gebäudes des deutschen Vereins 'Teutonia' in Istanbul', 17 December 1984.

126 TAI, 'Rechenschaftsbericht', 17 March 1988.

127 Geser, 'Wir sind im Kleinen', 124; Radt, *Geschichte der Teutonia*, 125–6.

128 TAI, 'Teutonia Statuten', 26 September 1939.

Chapter 3

1 Seda Kula Say, 'Beaux Arts Kökenli bir Mimar Olarak Alexandre Vallaury'nin Meslek Pratiği ve Eğitimciliği Açısından Kariyerinin İrdelenmesi', PhD thesis, Istanbul Technical University, Istanbul, 2014, 11–14. Also known as Alessandro Vallauri (1850–1921), though in the baptismal register of Saint Antoine (at the time a Catholic church still under French protection), his name is registered as Alexander Vallaouri. His father was a migrant from either Pinerolo or Chiusa di Pesio, who was registered at the Sardinian consulate in Smyrna in 1842. Married with Anna Musante from Torino, he spent his years until his death in Istanbul/Constantinople in 1867 with a woman named Hélèna Moro Papadopulo with whom he had six children, Alexandre being the second.

2 Osmanlı Bankası Arşiv ve Araştırma Merkezi, 'Arşivimizden Belgeler – Abraham Paşa'nın İflâsı', http://www.obarsiv.com/ab-abraham-pasa.html, accessed 2 November 2017.

3 Türk Mühendis ve Mimar Odaları Birliği Archive, 'Karar 5899', T.C. Milli Eğitim Bakanlığı Gayrimenkul Eski Eserler ve Anıtlar Yüksek Kurulu Başkanlığı, 13 June 1971.

4 Diken, 'Emek Bizim İnisiyatifi'nden dokuz soruda Emek Sineması'nın yıkım hikayesi', http://www.diken.com.tr/emek-bizim-inisiyatifinden-dokuz-soruda-emek-sinema sinin-yikim-hikayesi/, accessed 2 November 2017 and Radikal, 'Emek yerle bir', http://www.radikal.com.tr/hayat/emek-yerle-bir-1134388/, accessed 2 November 2017.

5 Güventürk Görgülu for Arkitera, 'Emek Sineması ve AVM takıntısı', http://v3.arkitera .com/arsgratiaartis.php?action=displayNewsItem&ID=52146, accessed 5 December 2018.

6 Türkiye Büyük Millet Meclisi, 'Yıpranan tarihi ve kültürel taşınmaz varlıkların yenilenerek korunması ve yaşatılarak kullanılması hakkında kanun', https://www.tbm m.gov.tr/kanunlar/k5366.html, accessed 2 November 2017.

7 Michael Herzfeld, 'Spatial Cleansing: Monumental Vacuity and the Idea of the West', *Journal of Material Culture* 11, no. 2 (2006): 127–49.

8 Ibid., 135. See for instance the website of Grand Pera. Grand Pera, 'About Us', http://www.grandpera.com/en/about-us.aspx, accessed 3 December 2018/ 'Grand Pera is located at the heart of Istiklal Avenue in Beyoğlu, which has been a centre of attraction and a symbol of shopping culture since the nineteenth century. Offering services to the culture, arts, entertainment, fashion, and gastronomic world, Grand Pera is a new-generation lifestyle centre that brought one of Istanbul's most valuable historical buildings, Cercle d'Orient, back to its former glory through quality renovation at world standards and that introduced Emek Cinema to future generations through a sustainable understanding.'

9 Andreas Huyssen, *Present Pasts: Urban Palimpsests and the Politics of Memory* (Stanford, CA: Stanford University Press, 2003), 54.

10 Grand Pera, 'Grand Pera Website', http://www.grandpera.com, accessed 2 November 2017.

11 Sheffield Daily Telegraph, 'The Officials at Yıldız', 30 January 1896, 5.

12 *The Times*, 'The Career of Fehim Pasha', 10 August 1908, 6.

13 Sir George Clerk, 'Istanbul: City of Memories', *The Times*, 9 August 1938, 34.

14 *Daily Telegraph Diplomatic*, 'Eau de Cologne de Constantinople!', 13 August 1926, 9.

15 Orhan Koloğlu, *Cercle d'Orient'dan Büyük Kulüp'e* (Istanbul: Boyut Yayın Grubu, 2005), 136.

16 Ibid., 126–7.

17 Eldem, 'Istanbul as a Cosmopolitan City', 228. Giovanni Scognamillo, *Bir Levantenin Beyoğlu Anıları*, 1st ed. (Istanbul: Metis Kitap, 1990); Atilla Dorsay, *Benim Beyoglum* (Istanbul: Varlik Yayinlari, 1993).

18 Said N. Duhani, Ahmet Parman, and Türkiye Turing ve Otomobil Kurumu, *Eski insanlar eski evler: XIX. yüzyılda Beyoglu'nun sosyal topografisi* (Istanbul: Türkiye Turing ve Otomobil Kurumu, 1984).

19 Koloğlu, *Cercle d'Orient'dan Büyük Kulüp'e*, 133.

20 Ibid., 148.

21 Since the club's current administration has a policy of allowing no one in their archives it was near to impossible to make any serious contributions to the connection of the club's history with the Cercle d'Orient building in the twentieth century. I was also not able to find out whether or not materials were lost during one of the fires. The club's administrator's words followed an unfortunate and seemingly classic adagium historians face when dealing with institutional archives: 'a book has

already written about us, you can use that' (although she also noted that the author of the book, Orhan Koloğlu, was not allowed to use the archives as well).

22 Gönül Dönmez-Colin, *Turkish Cinema : Identity, Distance and Belonging* (London: Reaktion, 2008), 18.

23 Ibid., 18.

24 Özlem Öz and Kaya Özkaracalar, 'Path Dependencies, Lock-In and the Emergence of Clusters: Historical Geographies of Istanbul's Film Cluster', in *The Hidden Dynamics of Path Dependence*, ed. J. Sydow and E. Schuessler (Hampshire, UK and New York: Palgrave Macmillan, 2010), 161–77 and 'What Accounts for the Resilience and Vulnerability of Clusters? The Case of Istanbul's Film Industry', *European Planning Studies* 19, no. 3 (2011): 361–78.

25 Dilek Kaya Mutlu, 'Yeşilçam in Letters: A Cinema Event in 1960s Turkey from the Perspective of an Audience Discourse', PhD thesis, Bilkent University, Ankara, 2002, 129.

26 Ibid., 98; Dönmez-Colin, *Turkish Cinema*, 22.

27 Ibid., 107. Translation by Kaya Mutlu.

28 Öz and Özkaracalar, 'Path Dependencies', 161–77.

29 Mutlu, 'Yeşilçam in Letters', 122.

30 Ibid., 129.

31 Ibid., 129–30.

32 Öncü, 'Istanbulites and Others', 104.

33 Ibid., 105.

34 Ibid.

35 Kaya Mutlu, 'Yeşilçam in Letters', 122.

36 Cumhuriyet Gazetesi, 'Serkldoryan binasının satışı yarın görüşülecek', 1 December 1951, 3.

37 İstanbul Belediyesi, *Güzelleşen İstanbul* (İstanbul: İstanbul Belediye Yayınları, 1943), 55.

38 Ibid.

39 Milliyet, 'Serkldoryan binası dün satılamadı', 25 December 1956, 5 and 'Serkldoryan bloku nihayet satılıyor', 6 January 1957, 1. It should be noted that the value of the Turkish Lira decreased rapidly during the 1950s.

40 Turhan Gürkan for Cumhuriyet Gazetesi, 'Emek Sineması müzikhol oluyor', 17 September 1968, 6.

41 Cumhuriyet Gazetesi, Emek Cinema Advertisement, 4 November 1968, 6.

42 Ibid., 6.

43 Dorsay, *Benim Beyoğlum*, 52.

44 Ibid., 65–6.

45 Mutlu, 'Yeşilçam in Letters', 131.

46 Ibid., 170–1.

47 Ibid., 131.

48 Savaş Arslan, *Cinema in Turkey: A New Critical History* (New York: Oxford University Press, 2011).

49 Zürcher, *Türkey: A Modern History*, 246–58.

50 Arslan, *Cinema in Turkey*, 100.

51 Çağlar Keyder, 'A Brief History of Modern Istanbul', in *The Cambridge History of Turkey*, ed. Reşat Kasaba (Cambridge: Cambridge University Press, 2008), 510.

52 Arslan, *Cinema in Turkey*, 101.

53 Mutlu, 'Yeşilçam in Letters', 132–3.

54 Dönmez-Colin, *Turkish Cinema*, 7–21.
55 Ibid., 48–9; Dilek Kaya Mutlu and Zeynep Koçer, 'A Different Story of Secularism: The Censorship of Religion in Turkish Films of the 1960s and Early 1970s', *European Journal of Cultural Studies* 15, no. 1 (2012): 74.
56 Dönmez-Colin, *Turkish Cinema*, 49.
57 Ibid.
58 Dilek Kaya Mutlu and Zeynep Koçer, 'A Different Story of Secularism', 75. Translation by Mutlu and Koçer.
59 Dönmez-Colin, *Turkish Cinema*, 38.
60 Ibid., 30–1.
61 Arslan, *Cinema in Turkey*, 15–17.
62 Wagstaff, 39.
63 Wagstaff, 29–51.
64 Asu Aksoy, Kevin Robins, and Kaan Çuhacı, *Improvised City – Adil Kebap Dürüm*, Documentary (Istanbul, 2012), https://www.youtube.com/watch?v=Gtw95lZ22dk.
65 Ibid.
66 Yener Süsoy, 'Gazinolar savaşı tekrar başladı', *Milliyet Magazin*, 12 November 1972, 10.
67 Ibid.
68 Mutlu, 'Yeşilçam in Letters', 125–6.
69 Ibid., 126 and Author unknown, 'Bir Filmde Baş Rol Oynayacak Bayanlara Ihtiyaç Vardır', *Perde ve Sahne*, 1954, 15.
70 Dönmez-Colin, *Turkish Cinema : Identity, Distance and Belonging*, 33.
71 Ibid., 118; Arslan, *Cinema in Turkey*, 180.
72 Dönmez-Colin, *Turkish Cinema*, 119–20.
73 Arslan, *Cinema in Turkey*, 186.
74 Ibid., 232 (translation by Savaş Arslan).
75 Atilla Dorsay for Cumhuriyet Gazetesi, 'Sinema ve tiyatro salonları birbiri ardına kapanıyor', 22 January 1976, 6.
76 Ibid.
77 Ibid.
78 Arslan, *Cinema in Turkey*, 101.
79 Ibid., 102.
80 Ibid.
81 Ibid.
82 Ibid., 233.
83 Yalçin Pekşen for Cumhuriyet, 'Beyoğlu'nda "şarap kültürü"nün yerini "bira kültürü" aldı', 13 November 1983, 8.
84 Türk Mühendis ve Mimar Odaları Birliği Archive, Engin Omacan, Cengiz Eruzun, Ratip Kansu, 'Rapor: Serkldoryan Tarihi Yapı Kompleksi Korunmalıdır', 17 January 1995.
85 Türk Mühendis ve Mimar Odaları Birliği Archive, Yavuz Erdem and İsmail Sever, 'Letter from Türkiye Cumhuriyeti Emekli Sandığı İstanbul Mühendisliği to T.C. Kültür ve Turizm Bakanlığı Taşınmaz Kültür ve Tabiat Varlıkları İstanbul Bölgesi Kurulu Müdürlüğü', 2 March 1987.
86 Salim Alpaslan, 'Devletin, Beş Milyonluk İstanbul'daki Tek Sanat Galerisi Kapanma Tehlikesiyle Karşı Karşıyla', *Cumhuriyet*, 29 March 1980, 7.
87 The current number of Mısır Apartmanı is for instance 163, whereas it was 311 in 1983. See: Announcement section, 'Duyuru', *Cumhuriyet*, 12 November 1983, 8.

88 TMMOB, 'Beyoğlu nasıl kurtulur'.
89 Türk Mühendis ve Mimar Odaları Birliği, *Beyoglu nasıl kurtulur?* (Istanbul, year unknown).
90 Mehmet Demirkaya for Cumhuriyet Gazetesi, 'Emek sineması için imza kampanyası', 11 April 1994, 7.
91 Omacan, Eruzun, Kansu, 'Rapor: Serkldoryan Tarihi'.
92 The urban activists' initiative Emek Bizim has been active on social media platforms since 2010; see https://www.facebook.com/emekbizim, accessed 29 January 2019.
93 Rıdvan Akar for Milliyet, 'Beyoğlu için geriye sayım başladı', 4 January 1995, 11.
94 Türkiye Cumhuriyet Merkez Bankası, *1995 Yıllık Raporu* (Ankara: TCMB, 25 April 1995), 80.
95 Akar, 'Beyoğlu için geriye sayım başladı', 11.
96 İclal Dinçer, Zeynep Enlil, Tolga İslam, 'Regeneration in a New Context: A New Act on Renewal and its Implications on the Planning Processes in İstanbul', Bridging the Divide: Celebrating the City. ACSP – AESOP Fourth Joint Congress. July 6–11, Chicago, IL, 2008, 1–10.
97 Ibid., 2.
98 Beyoğlu Belediyesi, 'Emek Sineması Muhteşem', http://www.beyoglu.bel.tr/beyoglu-b elediyesi/haber-detay/Emek-Sinemasi-Muhtesem/300/3993/0, accessed 2 November 2017.

Chapter 4

1 T.C. Galatasaray Lisesi, 'Okul Bilgileri', http://www.gsl.gsu.edu.tr/tr/okul-bilgileri, accessed 20 December 2018.
2 T.C. Galatasaray Üniversitesi, 'Tarihçe', http://www.gsu.edu.tr/tr/universite/genel-bil giler/tarihce, accessed 20 December 2018.
3 T.C. Galatasaray Lisesi, 'Galatasaray Lisesi ve Galatasaray İlköğretim Okulu Yönetmenliği – İkinci Bölüm Madde 6', http://www.gsl.gsu.edu.tr/tr/yonetmelik, accessed 20 December 2018.
4 T.C. Galatasaray, 'Üniversitesi Galatasaray İlkokulu & Ortaokulu, 'İletişim', http:// www.gsi.gsu.edu.tr/iletisim.html, accessed 20 December 2018.
5 Zürcher, *Turkey: A Modern History*, 62.
6 Roderic H. Davison, 'Westernized Education in Ottoman Turkey', *The Middle East Journal* 15, no. 3 (1961): 295.
7 Ibid., 298.
8 Ibid., 299; Fatma Müge Göçek, *Rise of the Bourgeoisie, Demise of Empire: Ottoman Westernization and Social Change* (New York, NY: Oxford University Press, 2011); Selçuk Akşin Somel, *The Modernization of Public Education in the Ottoman Empire, 1839–1908 : Islamization, Autocracy, and Discipline* (Leiden: Brill, 2001); Carter Findley, 'The Tanzimat', in *The Cambridge History of Turkey*, ed. Reşat Kasaba (Cambridge: Cambridge University Press, 2008), 9–37.
9 Findley, 'The Tanzimat', 21–2.
10 Ankara Galatasaray Birliği, 'Gül Baba', *Bitmeyen Mektep* 3 (2015): 3–5. www.galata saraylilarbirligi.org/images/magazine/26-15-19-272bitmeyen%20mektep_3.pdf, accessed 23 February 2019.

11 Fethi İsfendiyaroğlu, *Galatasaray Tarihi*, Vol. 1 (İstanbul: Doğan Kardeş Yayınları, 1952), 50.

12 Ibid., 52.

13 Gülru Necipoğlu, *Architecture, Ceremonial, and Power: The Topkapı Palace in the Fifteenth and Sixteenth Centuries* (Cambridge, MA: The MIT Press, 1991), 111–22.

14 Necipoğlu, *Architecture, Ceremonial, and Power*, 3–30; Halil İnalcik, *The Ottoman Empire: The Classical Age 1300–1600* (London: Phoenix, 2000, 1st ed. 1973), 78–9.

15 Mitler, 'The Genoese in Galata: 1453–1682', 72.

16 Necipoğlu, *Architecture, Ceremonial, and Power*, 3–30.

17 Paul Rycaut, *The Present State of the Ottoman Empire*, 3rd ed. (London: 1670), 26.

18 Ziyad Ebüzziya and Şahir Kozikoğlu (ed.), *1921–1933 Galatasaray Tarihçesi 1933 Mezunları ve 50 yılları* (İstanbul: Yörük Matbaası, 1987*), 11. *Exact year of publication is not provided.

19 Joseph von Hammer, *Constantinopolis und der Bosporos* (Pesth: Hartleben's Verlag, 1822), 128; İsfendiyaroğlu, *Galatasaray Tarihi*, 276.

20 100. Yıl Kutlama Derneği, *Galatasaray Lisesi – Mekteb-i Sultani 1868–1968* (İstanbul: Gün Matbaası 1974), 9–21; Ebüzziya and Şahir Kozikoğlu (ed.), *1921–1933 Galatasaray Tarihçesi*, 370.

21 Vedit İnal, 'The Eighteenth and Nineteenth Century Ottoman Attempts to Catch Up with Europe', *Middle Eastern Studies* 47, no. 5 (2011): 745.

22 Göçek, *Rise of the Bourgeoisie*, 70; Zürcher, *A History of Modern Turkey*, 44.

23 Zürcher, *A History of Modern Turkey*, 43–5, 110–12; Miri Shefer-Mossensohn, *Science among the Ottomans: The Cultural Creation and Exchange of Knowledge*, 1st ed. (Austin: University of Texas Press, 2015), 153. Although Zürcher notes that the attempts towards the end of the nineteenth century to realign the partnerships of the Ottoman Empire away from Great Britain and France and towards the German Empire can be considered as an attempt by state officials to rid the Ottoman Empire of its semi-colonial status, particularly with regard to its economy, these schools should be appreciated in a different fashion. First, the European instructors that were sent to Constantinople came at the invitation of the Ottoman state. Second, one could argue that the leaders from the Ottoman bureaucracy and military, who were the products of these new schools and academies, were at least partially indebted to the exposure to European Enlightenment thinking for developing their own ideas regarding emancipation of the empire and national sovereignty. In the context of urban transformation, Miri Shefer Mossensohn notes that the Ottomans thought of themselves to be part, rather than subject, of European thinking on city making. That is also a consideration worth taking into account in the case of educational reform.

24 Galatasaray Kültür ve Sanat Merkezi, *Bir Numaralı Galatasaraylı Ali Sami Yen* (İstanbul: Galatasaray Spor Kulübü, 2011), 23.

25 Bernard Lewis, *The Emergence of Modern Turkey*, 2nd ed. (London: Oxford University Press, 1968), 122.

26 Göçek, *Rise of the Bourgeoisie*, 70–1.

27 Davison, 'Westernized Education in Ottoman Turkey', 298.

28 Ibid., 299.

29 Lewis, *The Emergence of Modern Turkey*, 122.

30 Ibid., 182.

31 100. Yıl Kutlama Derneği, *Galatasaray Lisesi*, 135–200.

32 Meltem Türköz, 'Surname Narratives and the State – Society Boundary: Memories of Turkey's Family Name Law of 1934', *Middle Eastern Studies* 43, no. 6 (2007): 893–908.

33 Ebru Boyar and Kate Fleet, *A Social History of Ottoman Istanbul* (Cambridge: Cambridge University Press, 2011), 330–1.

34 Vangelis Kechriotis, Maciej Górny and Ahmet Ersoy, 'Haluk's Credo', in *Modernism: Representations of National Culture: Discourses of Collective Identity in Central and Southeast Europe 1770–1945: Texts and Commentaries*, ed. Ahmet Ersoy, Maciej Górny and Vangelis Kechriotis, Vol. III/2 (Budapest: Central European University Press, 2010), 309–12.

35 Ibid.

36 100. Yıl Kutlama Derneği, *Galatasaray Lisesi*, 29–38.

37 Ibid., 21.

38 Ibid., 33.

39 İlhan Akant, *Galatasaray Lisesi: 1936 Yılı Mezunlarının 60. Yılı* (İstanbul: Tanburacı Matbaacılık A.Ş., 1996), 7.

40 Nejat İren, Nuri Efe, Turgut Madenci (eds.), *1922-1934 Galatasaray Tarihçesi 1934 Mezunları ve 50 Yılları* (İstanbul: Galatasaray Eğitim Vakfı/Yenilik Basımevi, 1989), 22.

41 100. Yıl Kutlama Derneği, *Galatasaray Lisesi*, 132–3. Author's own translation.

42 Kerem Öktem, *Angry Nation: Turkey since 1989* (London: Zedbooks, 2011); Taha Parla and Andrew Davison, *Corporatist Ideology in Kemalist Turkey: Progress or Order?* (Syracuse: Syracuse University Press, 2004); Tanıl Bora, 'Nationalist Discourses in Turkey', *South Atlantic Quarterly* 102, no. 2-3 (2003), 437–49.

43 Ebüzziya and Şahir Kozikoğlu (ed.), *1921-1933 Galatasaray* Tarihçesi, 35, 46.

44 Galatasaray Kültür ve Sanat Merkezi, *Bir Numaralı* Galatasaraylı, 13.

45 Ibid. The league initially comprised four clubs, the Moda FC founded by Englishmen, the HMS Imogene FC founded by the crew of the HMS *Imogene*, Elpis FC founded by Greek Istanbulites and Cadi Keuy FC founded by Englishmen as well. Galatasaray SK would become the champion of the league in 1909, 1910, 1911 and 1916. Ali Sami Yen would be the chairman of the club between 1905 and 1918 and briefly again in 1925. Apart from the club he opened the first Galatasaray Museum in Kalamış, which was moved to the premises of the high school when the occupation forces seized the building in 1919. The museum would pave the way for the later Galatasaray Centre for Culture and the Arts in the former Beyoğlu Post Office, right across the gates of the Galatasaray High School.

46 Galatasaray Kültür ve Sanat Merkezi, *Bir Numaralı Galatasaraylı*, 1–30.

47 İren, Efe, Madenci (eds.), *1922-1934 Galatasaray Tarihçesi*, 55.

48 Cüneyd Okay, 'Sport and Nation Building: Gymnastics and Sport in the Ottoman State and the Committee of Union and Progress, 1908-18', *The International Journal of the History of Sport* 20, no. 1 (2003): 153.

49 Ibid.

50 Joep Leerssen, *National Thought in Europe: A Cultural History* (Amsterdam: Amsterdam University Press, 2006), 108.

51 Sudipa Topdar, 'The Corporeal Empire: Physical Education and Politicising Children's Bodies in Late Colonial Bengal', *Gender & History* 29, no. 1 (2017): 179.

52 Vladimir Tikhonov, 'Masculinizing the Nation: Gender Ideologies in Traditional Korea and in the 1890s–1900s Korean Enlightenment Discourse', *The Journal of Asian Studies* 66, no. 4 (2007): 1046–50.

53 Christine Mayer, 'Education Reform Visions and New Forms of Gymnastics and Dance as Elements of a New Body Culture and 'Body Education' (1890–1930)', *History of Education* 47, no. 4 (2018): 523–43.

54 Marion Kant, 'The Moving Body and the Will to Culture', *European Review* 19, no. 4 (2011): 579–94.

55 100. Yıl Kutlama Derneği, *Galatasaray Lisesi*, 101–2. 'Monsieur le Président, (...) nous sommes honorés et fiers de votre visite qui illustre les fêtes du Centenaire de ce Lycée, vieux d'un passé qui s'identifie avec l'histoire même de notre culture. J'ai parlé de modernisation dans le sens occidental, mais pour nous, l'Occident s'identifait à la France. (...) C'est dans la vie intellectuelle et sociale française que les mouvements intellectuels, littéraires, sociaux de notre pays trouvèrent leur raisen [sic] d'être. (....) En raison de son role preponderant dans l'évolution de l'enseignement et des mouvements sociaux en Turquie, notre école fut justement nommée une fenêtre ouverte en Orient sur l'Occident.'

56 Ebüzziya and Şahir Kozikoğlu (ed.), *1921–1933 Galatasaray Tarihçesi*, 22. 'Düşündüm ki Galatasaray, en geç türkleşen Beyoğlu muhitinde, yalnız bir vatan kucağı, millete en nafiz ve kahraman evlâtlar yetiştiren bir irfan ocağı değil, ayni zamanda, türlü dille konuşan insan kütlelerinin, demir parmaklıkları önünden geçerken seslerini alçaltmıya mecbur oldukları kutsî bir ibadet mahalli idi.. Evet, bir ibadet mahalli.. En karışık günlerde, en fecî anlarda orada vatan evlâtları, kalplerindeki duygu ve ateşten hiç bir şey kaybetmeden Türklüğe tapıyorlardı.'

57 Oktay Aras and Taner Saka, *1955'lilerin 50. Yılı 1955/2005 GS Lisesi* (İstanbul: Prizma Advertising Reklam, 2006), 461.

58 Ebüzziya and Şahir Kozikoğlu (ed.), *1921–1933 Galatasaray Tarihçesi*, 359–60.

59 Ibid., 359–60.

60 Ibid.

61 Sadık Doğan Abalıoğlu, *Galatasaray Lisesi 1954–1955 Broşürü* (İstanbul: Yenilik Basımevi, 1955*), 183. *Exact year of publication not provided.

62 Ebüzziya and Şahir Kozikoğlu (ed.), *1921–1933 Galatasaray Tarihçesi*, 127.

63 Aras and Saka, *1955'lilerin 50. Yılı*, 178.

64 Ibid., 67.

65 Ibid., 20.

66 Toygar Bilgin, Koray Tezcan, Selçuk Taylaner, et al., *Galatasaray Lisesi 1958–1959 Mezunları 50 Yıl Sonra* (İstanbul: Yenilik Basımevi, 2009), 114.

67 Güven, *Nationalismus und Minderheiten*, 31–41; Alexandris, *The Greek Minority of Istanbul*, 260–1.

68 Bensiyon Pinto, Tülay Gürler, Nicole Pope, and Leyla Engin Arık, *My Life as a Turkish Jew: Memoirs of the President of the Turkish-Jewish Community, 1989–2004* (İstanbul: Bahçeşehir University Press, 2012), 61. The first time Pinto recounts the word 'Jew' being used in a denouncing fashion was during the 1942 events surrounding the discriminatory wealth tax.

69 Erol Gürel, 'Bir Amerikalı Gözüyle Galatasaray', *Galatasaray Dergisi* 1, no. 3 (1947): 26–7.

70 Ibid., 32.

71 Salih Keramet Nigar, *İnkılâp Şairi Tevfik Fikret* (Istanbul: Kenan Matbaası, 1942), 14.

72 Gürel, 'Bir Amerikalı Gözüyle Galatasaray', 26.

73 Galatasaray Lisesi 1937 Mezunları, *Galatasaray Lisesi Mezunları 1936–1937 Ders Senesi* (İstanbul: Devlet Basımevi, 1937), 42.

74 Galatasaray Lisesi, *100 Galatasaray* (İstanbul: 1968), 60 (1535).

75 Metin Toker, 'Fındık ve Kabuğu', *Galatasaray Dergisi* 3, no. 11 (1949): 1.

76 Aras and Saka, *1955'lilerin 50. Yılı*, 54.

77 GSL '64 Koordinasyon Kurulu, *1964 Mezunları 50. Yıl Anı Kitabı* (İstanbul: 2014), 278–9.

78 Galatasaray Lisesi Broşür Kolu, *1969 Mezunları Yıllığı* (İstanbul: Kıral Matbaası, 1969), 111.

79 Aras and Saka, *1955'lilerin 50. Yılı*, 372.

80 Galatasaray Lisesi Broşür Kolu, *Galatasaray 1957–58* (İstanbul: Öztürk Matbaası, 1958), 45.

81 Aras and Saka, *1955'lilerin 50. Yılı*, 69.

82 Ibid.

83 Ankara Galatasaray Birliği, 'Sultani'nin Sultanları (Galatasaray'da Karma Eğitim)', *Bitmeyen Mektep* 4 (2016): 10, http://www.galatasaraylilarbirligi.org/images/maga zine/bitmeyen%20mektep_4.pdf, accessed 23 December 2018.

84 Ebüzziya and Şahir Kozikoğlu (ed.), *1921–1933 Galatasaray Tarihçesi*, 21.

85 Ibid., 372–3.

Chapter 5

1 I am not mentioning the various other reputable schools of the Ottoman millets here, as well as the Mekteb-i Sultanî, which is currently the Galatasaray High School and is the focus of Chapter 4.

2 Christine Laidlaw, *The British in the Levant: Trade and Perceptions of the Ottoman Empire in the Eighteenth Century* (London: IB Tauris, 2010); Geoff Berridge, *British Diplomacy in Turkey, 1583 to the Present: A Study in the Evolution of the Resident Embassy* (Leiden: Martinus Nijhoff Publishers, 2009).

3 Laidlaw, *The British in the Levant*, 217–24.

4 Edhem Eldem, 'Ottoman Financial Integration with Europe: Foreign Loans, the Ottoman Bank and the Ottoman Public Debt', *European Review* 13, no. 3 (2005): 434.

5 Ibid.

6 Ibid., 441–3.

7 The National Archives, 'The English High Schools in Istanbul – Memorandum', 2, FCO 13/48 English Schools in Turkey 1968.

8 TNA, 'Memorandum', 2.

9 D.E. Thompson, 'The English Highschool for Girls İstanbul', in *Yearbook EHS 1960/ The Wolf and the Crescent*, ed. English High Schools (Istanbul: Ekicigil Matbaası, 1960), 86–7.

10 The National Archives, 'Foundation Deed of Girls School at Constantinople', 1, FCO 13/48 English Schools in Turkey 1968.

11 Edwin Pears, *Forty Years in Constantinople: The Recollections of Sir Edwin Pears 1873–1915* (London: Herbert Jenkins Ltd., 1916), 95–7.

12 Thompson, 'The English Highschool for Girls İstanbul', 86–7.

13 The National Archives, 'Memorandum on the Boys' and Girls' Schools', 2, FCO 13/48 English Schools in Turkey 1968.

14 Nimet Özbek Hadimoğlu, 'Minority Schools, Foreign and International Schools in the New Law on Private Educational Institutions', *Ankara Law Review* 5, no. 1 (2008): 83–4.

15 The National Archives, 'Confidential Notes on Legal Status of EHS', 1, FO 195/2717 English High Schools 1962.

16 The National Archives, 'The English Schools in Istanbul Background – General', 2, FCO 13/48 English Schools in Turkey 1968.
17 The National Archives, 'History of English High School for Girls', 1, FO 924/35 British Schools in Ankara and Istanbul 1944.
18 Thompson, 'The English Highschool for Girls İstanbul', 86–7.
19 The National Archives, 'Letter from British Ambassador Derrek Dodson to Lord Carrington (24-10-1979)', 2, FCO 13/904 EHS Transfer to Turkey 1979.
20 Tamara M.C. van Kessel, 'Cultural Promotion and Imperialism: The Dante Alighieri Society and the British Council Contesting the Mediterranean in the 1930', PhD thesis, University of Amsterdam, Amsterdam, 2011, 7–8, 49–51.
21 Ibid., 52–3.
22 Ibid., 54.
23 Ibid., 57.
24 Thompson, 'The English Highschool for Girls İstanbul', 86–7.
25 The National Archives, 'Letter from Mr Kelly, British Embassy to Mr Gillan, British Council', 1, BW 61/7 English high school for girls.
26 Ibid., 2.
27 George McGhee, *The US-Turkish-NATO Middle East Connection: How the Truman Doctrine Contained the Soviets in the Middle East* (New York: Palgrave Macmillan, 1990), 19–34.
28 Ibid., 21.
29 Ibid., 19–44.
30 The National Archives, 'Progress Report 15-7-1968: British Schools in Istanbul', 2, FCO 13/48 English Schools in Turkey 1968.
31 Ibid., 2.
32 The National Archives, 'Four Years of the British Council in Turkey', 1–3, FO 924/35 British Schools in Ankara and Istanbul 1944.
33 Ibid., 1.
34 Ibid., 4.
35 Kerstin Martens and Sanen Marshall, 'International Organisations and Foreign Cultural Policy: A Comparative Analysis of the British Council, the Alliance Française and the Goethe-Institute', *Transnational Associations* 55, no. 4 (2003): 261–72.
36 TNA, 'Four Years of the British Council in Turkey', 1–7.
37 The National Archives, 'Report: English High Schools, Istanbul – July 1944 (secret)', 4, FO 924/35 British Schools in Ankara and Istanbul 1944.
38 Ibid., 9. The total enrolment in 1944 was 200, with approximately 25 British girls.
39 Ibid., 7 and TNA, 'Memorandum', 1.
40 Ibid., 8.
41 Ibid., 8.
42 Ibid., 7.
43 TNA, 'The English Schools in Istanbul Background – General', 2 and TNA, 'Memorandum', 1.
44 The National Archives, 'British Schools in Turkey (21-9-1962)', 1–2, FO 195/2717 English High Schools 1962.
45 Sarah Davies, 'The Soft Power of Anglia: British Cold War Cultural Diplomacy in the USSR', *Contemporary British History* 27, no. 3 (2013): 297–323.
46 J.M. Lee, 'British Cultural Diplomacy and the Cold War: 1946–61', *Diplomacy and Statecraft* 9, no. 1 (1998): 122.

47 Ibid., 132.
48 James R. Vaughan, "A Certain Idea of Britain': British Cultural Diplomacy in the Middle East, 1945–57', *Contemporary British History* 19, no. 2 (2005): 151–68.
49 Ibid., 164.
50 TNA, 'Report: English High Schools, Istanbul – July 1944 (Secret)', 13.
51 Ibid. 'The Schools would be glad indeed to reduce the period to be devoted to Turkish language and to the teaching of various subjects in Turkish. I have suggested elsewhere that the scientific courses of both Schools need strengthening by means of proper equipment, and I believe that, in the special circumstances prevailing in Turkey, social subjects should be concentrated upon wherever possible.'
52 The National Archives, 'English High School for Girls Foundation – Articles of Constitution', 1, FO 195/2716 English High Schools 1962.
53 TNA, 'Report: English High Schools, Istanbul – July 1944 (Secret)', 16.
54 Ibid., 24.
55 Various alumni of English High School for Girls, English High School for Boys, Beyoğlu Anadolu Lisesi, interview by the author, 13 March 2017, English High Schoollular Derneği, Beyazgül Sokak 81, Arnavutköy, Beşiktaş, Istanbul.
56 BAL English teacher, interview by the author, January 2017, Beyoğlu, İstanbul.
57 The National Archives, 'Extract from Report by Angus Gillan [etc.] Feb–April 1946', BW 61/7 English high school for girls 1944–1946.
58 The National Archives, 'Cypher from Ankara to Foreign Office (2-4-1946)', BW 61/7 English High School for Girls 1944–1946.
59 The National Archives, 'Extract from a Report on a Visit to Istanbul February 13th–19th 1946 by Professor E. Gatenby', BW 61/7 English high school for girls 1944–1946.
60 The National Archives, 'Statement of Accounts of the School for the Year Ended 31st August 1961', 5, FO 195/2718 EHSG Statement of Accounts 1961–1962.
61 The National Archives, 'Letter from Ayhan Unler (lawyer) to Mr Riddle (21-12-1960)', FO 195/2710 English High Schools Istanbul 1960.
62 The National Archives, 'British Schools (from G.M. Michael Warr to Margaret I. Mackie 8-11-1962)', 1–2, FO 195/2717 English High Schools 1962.
63 The National Archives, 'Confidential – British Schools in Istanbul', BW 61/7 English High School for Girls 1944–1946.
64 Zürcher, *Turkey: A Modern History*, 246–54.
65 The National Archives, 'Communication between Cultural Attaché and H.M. Ambassador (8-2-1962)', FO 195/2716 English High Schools 1962.
66 The National Archives, 'English High Schools Istanbul – Minutes of a meeting held at the British Consulate General, Istanbul on Wednesday, 5th December, 1962', 5, FO 195/2717 English High Schools 1962.
67 The National Archives, 'Confidential – Memorandum: Blocked Liras for Culture', 3–4, FO 195/2716 English Schools Istanbul 1962.
68 The National Archives, 'Letter from Sidney Nowill (chairman of EHSG) to L.M. Minford (British Embassy 27-3-1962' and 'Visit to Mr. Hamid Batu (9-2-1962)', FO 195/2716 English Schools Istanbul 1962.
69 The National Archives, 'Confidential from D.F. Duncan', FCO 13/48 English Schools in Turkey 1968.
70 Various alumni of English High School for Girls, English High School for Boys, Beyoğlu Anadolu Lisesi, interview by the author, 13 March 2017, English High Schoollular Derneği, Beyazgül Sokak 81, Arnavutköy, Beşiktaş, Istanbul.

71 EHSG math teacher, interview by the author, 22 March 2017, Alman Kitabevi İstiklal Caddesi 237, Beyoğlu, Istanbul.
72 TNA, 'The English Schools in Istanbul Background – General', 1.
73 Ibid., 2.
74 Ibid., 5.
75 The National Archives, 'Foundation Deed of Girls School at Constantinople (copy of 19th century original)'and 'Foundation Deed of Girls School at Constantinople', 1–7, FCO 13/48 English Schools in Turkey 1968.
76 The National Archives, 'File Note: English High School for Girls Foundation Deed', 1, FCO 13/903 EHS Transfer to Turkey 1979.
77 Gwyneth Petter, 'Letter from the Headmistresss', in *Yearbook EHSG 1971–1972*, ed. EHS Yearbook Committee (Istanbul, 1972), 10.
78 Gwyneth Petter, 'Letter from the Headmistresss', in *Yearbook EHSG 1972–1973*, ed. English High School for Girls (Istanbul, 1973), 14–15.
79 Petter, 'Letter from the Headmistresss' and The National Archives, 'Letter by J.A.L. Morgan (Covering Restricted – 29-11-1974)', 1–3, FCO 13/744 UK High Schools in Istanbul 1974.
80 TNA, 'Progress Report', 3.
81 Ibid., 2.
82 Ibid.
83 EHSG math teacher, interview by the author, 22 March 2017, Alman Kitabevi İstiklal Caddesi 237, Beyoğlu, Istanbul.
84 TNA, 'Memorandum', 4.
85 The National Archives, 'Letter by William Rodgers (From the Parliamentary Under-Secretary (21-2-1968)', 1, FCO 13/48 English Schools in Turkey 1968.
86 The National Archives, 'Letter by A.D.F. Pemberton-Pigott to Cultural Relations Department Foreign Office (20-2-1968)', 1, FCO 13/48 English Schools in Turkey 1968.
87 Ibid.
88 The National Archives, 'The English High Schools in Istanbul (15-2-1968)', 1, FCO 13/48 English Schools in Turkey 1968.
89 The National Archives, 'Letter from British Embassy (9-4-20 to 20-2-1968)', 1, FCO 13/48 English Schools in Turkey 1968.
90 The National Archives, 'The English High Schools, Istanbul', FCO 13/744 UK high schools in Istanbul, Turkey.
91 EHSG math teacher, interview by the author, 22 March 2017, Alman Kitabevi İstiklal Caddesi 237, Beyoğlu, Istanbul.
92 Ibid.
93 Marianne Hirsch and Leo Spitzer, *Ghosts of Home: The Afterlife of Czernowitz in Jewish Memory* (Berkeley and Los Angeles: University of California Press, 2010), 9. Hirsch describes the process as follows: 'When I began to write about my own early memories and about the phenomenon of personal and cultural memory in general, I needed a special term to refer to the secondary, belated quality of my relationship with times and places that I had never experienced or seen, but which are vivid enough that I feel as though I remember them. My "memory" of Czernowitz, I concluded, is a "postmemory."'
94 The National Archives, 'English High Schools – Memorandum on Maarif's Examination of Schools' Financial Position in connection with Applications for Fee Increases', 1, FCO 13/48 English Schools in Turkey 1968.

95 EHSG math teacher, interview by the author, 22 March 2017, Alman Kitabevi
    İstiklal Caddesi 237, Beyoğlu, Istanbul.

96 Ibid.

97 Various alumni of English High School for Girls, English High School for Boys,
    Beyoğlu Anadolu Lisesi, interview by the author, 13 March 2017, English High
    Schoollular Derneği, Beyazgül Sokak 81, Arnavutköy, Beşiktaş, Istanbul.

98 The National Archives, 'Letter from Richard Luce to Keith Stainton (21-11-1979)', 1,
    FCO 13/904 EHS Transfer to Turkey 1979.

99 The National Archives, 'Letter to Keith Stainton (4-11-1979)' 1 and 'Letter from J.A.L.
    Morgan and Gordon Lennox (15-11-1979)', FCO 13/904 EHS Transfer to Turkey 1979

100 TNA, 'Letter to Keith Stainton (4-11-1979)'.

101 TNA, 'Letter from British Ambassador Derrek Dodson to Lord Carrington (24-10-
    1979)', 2.

102 The National Archives, 'English High Schools for Girls Committee – Minutes of
    Meeting Held Jointly with the Boys' School Committee on Monday 25 June 1979', 1,
    FCO 13/903 EHS Transfer to Turkey 1979.

103 EHSG math teacher, interview by the author, 22 March 2017, Alman Kitabevi
    İstiklal Caddesi 237, Beyoğlu, Istanbul.

104 The National Archives, 'English High Schools for Girls Committee – Minutes of
    Meeting', 1.

105 The National Archives, 'Restricted GR1205 (4-7-1979)', 1, FCO 13/903 EHS Transfer
    to Turkey 1979.

106 The National Archives, 'Letter to Norman St John-Stevas M.P. from J.S. Sharland
    (10-5-1979)', 1, FCO 13/903 EHS Transfer to Turkey 1979.

107 TNA, 'Letter from British Ambassador Derrek Dodson to Lord Carrington (24-10-
    1979)', 1.

108 EHSG math teacher, interview by the author, 22 March 2017, Alman Kitabevi
    İstiklal Caddesi 237, Beyoğlu, Istanbul.

109 BAL English teacher, interview by the author, January 2017, Beyoğlu, İstanbul.

110 TNA, 'English High Schools – Memorandum on Maarif's Examination', 1.

111 BAL English teacher, interview by the author, January 2017, Beyoğlu, İstanbul.

112 Ibid.

113 Ibid.

114 Diken, 'Beyoğlu Anadolu'da karma eğitime veda: 'Abartılacak şey değil, orijinaline
    döndü'', *Diken* Website, 15 June 2016, http://www.diken.com.tr/beyoglu-anadoluda
    -karma-egitime-veda-abartilacak-bir-sey-degil-orijinaline-dondu/.

115 Ibid.

Chapter 6

1 Dietrich, *Deutschsein in Istanbul*, 92–6. Gerhard Fricke states it were 24 students:
   Gerhard Fricke, 'Neunzig Jahre Deutsche Schule', in *Festschrift zum neunzigjährigen
   Bestehen der Deutschen Schule Istanbul: 1868–1958*, ed. Deutsche Schule İstanbul
   (Bergisch Gladbach, 1958), 18.

2 Fricke, 'Neunzig Jahre Deutsche Schule', 18.

3 Ulrich Münch, 'Die Anfänge der heutigen Deutschen Schule Istanbul –
   Gründungsjahre der »Deutschen und Schweizer Bürgerschule« von 1867 bis 1874',

in *Daheim in Konstantinopel: deutsche Spuren am Bosporus ab 1850*, ed. Sabine Böhme, Ulrich Münch and Erald Pauw (Nürnberg, Mittelfr: Pagma-Verlag, 2014), 130.

4   Ibid., 138.

5   Ibid., 139. 'eine absolute Nationalitätenlosigkeit zu bewahren und in sich den [östereichisch-ungarischen] Gesamtstaat zu repräsentieren, von jeher nur einzelne Deutsche.'

6   Fricke, 'Neunzig Jahre Deutsche Schule', 17.

7   Geser, 'Wir sind im Kleinen', 149.

8   Ibid., 150.

9   Münch, 'Die Anfänge der heutigen Deutschen Schule', 155–6. 'Hier war zur Konfessionlosigkeit der Boden günstiger als irgendwo anders. In dem Zusammenleben der giesigen Deutschen machen sich die konfesionnelen Unterschiede so wenig geltend und verschwinden bis zu dem Grade, dass manchen von seiner übrigens guten Bekannten nicht weiß, ob sie protestantisch oder katholisch sind, und ich weiß von den Ältern vieler Kinder, die unsere Schule besuchen, nicht, welcher Konfession sie angehören.'

10 Ibid., 159. 'Die bedeutend größere Zahl deutscher Katholiken hier, dient nur den an und für sich alufen Protestanten zum bequemen Deckmantel für ihre Abneigung gegen alle evangelischen Institutionen und Bestrebungen. Nur ja nicht etwas Konfessionelles, deutsch muss alles sein! und so wird das 'deutsch' identisch mit konfessions- d.i. religionslos.'

11 Gerhard Nutsch, 'Skizzen aus der Frühgeschichte der Deutschen Schule in İstanbul', in *125 Jahre Deutsche Schule İstanbul Festschrift*, ed. Deutsche Schule İstanbul (İstanbul, 1993), 73. 'Die wirklich vorhandenem Bedürfnisse der Schulgemeinde hinsichtlich der Ausbildung ihrer Söhne lagen auf einem anderen Gebiet als dem der klassischen Bildung: Handel und Wandel in Constantinopel stellen an jeden der es zu etwas bringen will, die Anforderungen, daß er modern Sprachen, besonders die französische, womöglich aber auch die englische sprechen und schreiben kann.'

12 Nutsch, 'Skizzen aus der Frühgeschichte', 74.

13 Lothar Wittmann, 'Grüßwort des Leiters der Kulturabteilung des Auswärtigen Amtes', in *125 Jahre Deutsche Schule İstanbul Festschrift*, ed. Christa Lippold and Gerhard Nurtsch (İstanbul, 1993), 14.

14 Fricke, 'Neunzig Jahre Deutsche Schule', 18.

15 Nutsch, 'Skizzen aus der Frühgeschichte', 76. 'Wahrlich, es dürfte wenige deutsche Schulen geben, denen eine so herrliche Landschaft in die Fenster hineinlacht.'

16 Geser, 'Wir sind im Kleinen', 74. 'wenig erfreuliche Gebäude der Schule'; 'dass es die Kinder ohne Gefahr für Leib und Leben nicht mehr besuchen können.'

17 Christa Lippold, 'Das erste eigene Gebäude der Deutsche Schule İstanbul', in *125 Jahre Deutsche Schule İstanbul Festschrift*, ed. Christa Lippold and Gerhard Nurtsch (İstanbul, 1993), 94.

18 Fricke, 'Neunzig Jahre Deutsche Schule', 18.

19 Nutsch, 'Skizzen aus der Frühgeschichte', 76.

20 Ibid., 77. 'Will die deutsche Schule in Istanbul auch in Zukunft begründeten Anspruch auf den hohen Reichzuschuß erheben, so muß sie das Schulgeld für nichtdeutsche und nichtchristliche Schüler derart bemessen, dasß dadurch die Ausgaben für diese Schüler voll gedeckt werden.'

21 Ibid. 'Wer da meint daß die fremden Juden durch Besuch der deutschen Schule germanisiert oder wenigstens deutschfreundlich gesinnt werden könnten, kennt

die Eigenschaft der Levantiner Juden nicht, die in nationaler Hinsicht noch weit unzuverlässiger sind als ihre Glaubensgenossen in Mitteleuropa'.

22 Lippold, 'Das erste eigene Gebäude', 97–100.
23 Josef Joraschek, 'Ein kurzer Abriß der Baugeschichte von den ersten Anfängen bis heute', in *125 Jahre Deutsche Schule İstanbul Festschrift*, ed. Christa Lippold and Gerhard Nurtsch (İstanbul, 1993), 103.
24 Lippold, 'Das erste eigene Gebäude', 100.
25 Joraschek, 'Ein kurzer Abriß', 104.
26 Ibid.
27 Dietrich, *Deutschsein in Istanbul*, 227. 'daß sie ihre Mitmenschen als Mensch verstehen und schätzen sollen, über alle Nationen und Religionen hinweg, wie sie es bisher in der Klasse ihre Mitschülern gegenüber auch getan haben.'
28 Aysun Akan, 'A Critical Analysis of the Turkish Press Discourse against Non-Muslims: A Case Analysis of the Newspaper Coverage of the 1942 Wealth Tax', *Middle Eastern Studies* 47, no. 4 (2011): 605–21.
29 Dietrich, *Deutschsein in Istanbul*, 227–49.
30 Ibid., 233.
31 Necla Altınok, 'Beyoğlu Kız Lisesi'nden Alman Lisesi'ne', in *125 Jahre Deutsche Schule İstanbul Festschrift*, ed. Christa Lippold and Gerhard Nurtsch (İstanbul, 1993), 142–3.
32 Politisches Archiv – Auswärtiges Amt (from here onwards PA – AA), B93 41 54–5, '[Übersicht](...), Sammtlicher Schüler in den letzten fünf Jahren'. Muslims are categorized as '*mohammedanisch*'.
33 Alexandris, *The Greek minority of Istanbul*, 258; Örs, 'Beyond the Greek and Turkish Dichotomy', 79–94.
34 Greek Byzantine Catholics recognize the Pope of Rome as the supreme authority in the church, but adhere to the Byzantine Orthodox system of rites. See: Charles Frazee, 'Catholics', in *Minorities in Greece: Aspects of a Plural Society*, ed. Richard Clogg (London: Hurst and Company, 2002), 24–47.
35 Ioan Marius Bucur, 'Justice and Repression in Communist Romania: The Trial of Greek-Catholic Bishop Alexandru Rusu in 1957', *Studia Universitatis Babes-Bolyai – Historia* 58, no. 2 (2013): 113–38.
36 PA – AA, ISTA, KU641.35, 'Der Vorstand des Vereins Zum Betrieb der deutschen Schule – abschrift' (6 April 1957), 7.
37 Ibid., 1. 'angesichts der entscheidenden Wichtigkeit einer wesentlichen Verbreiterung der deutsche Sprachkenntnisse in der Türkei für die kulturellen, besonders aber auch für die wirtschaftlichen deutsch-türkischen Beziehungen, diesem Bedürfnis in tunlichst weitem Masse Rechnung zu tragen.'
38 Robert Hermann Tenbrock, 'Neunzig Jahre Deutsche Schule Istanbul – Stätte türkish-deutscher Begegnung', *Festschrift zum neunzigjährigen Bestehen der Deutschen Schule Istanbul: 1868-1958*, ed. Deutsche Schule İstanbul (Bergisch Gladbach, 1958), 13–14.
39 PA – AA, ISTA, KU641.35, 'Der Vorstand des Vereins', 5. 'die ausgesucht besten Kräfte aus dem weiten anatolischen Hinterland'.
40 PA – AA, ISTA, KU641.35, 'Deutsche Schule Istanbul – Hier: Schaffung von Klassenräumen' (15 May 1957), 2 (Abschrift).
41 PA – AA, B93, 334 55–63, 'Deutsche Schule Istanbul – Hier: Schaffung von Klassenräume' (9 April 1957). 'das Kernstück unserer kulturpolitischen Bemühungen in der Türkei'.

42 PA – AA, B93, 334 55–63, 'Bericht des Generalkonsulats vom 15. Mai 1957 Nr. 326/57' (24 May 1957).

43 Joraschek, 'Ein kurzer Abriβ', 104.

44 PA – AA, B93, 334 55–63, 'Deutsche Schule Istanbul – Hier: Ausbau des Schulgebäudes – Aufstockung' (3 February 1958), 6. 'Es sollte jedoch angestrebt werden, die Deutsche Schule in Istanbul, die augenblicklich in einem sehr wenig schönen Stadtviertel untergebracht ist, zu einem späteren Zeitpunkt an den Bosporus, etwas außerhalb der Innenstad, zu verlegen, wie es vor dem Kriege schon einmal geplant war.'

45 The National Archives, 'British Schools (from G.M. Michael Warr to Margaret I. Mackie 8-11-1962)', 1–2, FO 195/2717. English High Schools 1962.

46 PA – AA, B93, 334 55–63, 'Bericht über die Besprechung des [etc.]' (5 March 1958).

47 PA – AA, B93, 112 58–61, '[Letter from R.H. Tenbrock to Dr. Reimers]' (3 September 1958).

48 PA – AA, B93, 112 58–61, 'Versammlung der Eltern volksschulpflichtiger Kinder in Istanbul' (22 October 1959).

49 PA – AA, B93, 112 58–61, 'Deutsche Schule Istanbul Mit Luftpost!' (4 September 1958). 'allmählich immer mehr bewährte deutsche Richtlinien durch nach unserer Ansicht schlechtere türkische zu ersetzen'.

50 Ibid.

51 Ibid. 'Impact' wegen der in erster Linien kulturpolitischen Auswirkung.'

52 PA – AA, B93, 112 58–61, 'Deutsche Schule Istanbul Mit Luftpost!' (4 September 1958); 'Frage der Anerkennung der Deutschen Schule Istanbul als höhere deutsche Vollanstalt im Ausland' (12 January 1959), 3. 'Begründet wird diese, der heutigen geistigen und politischen Stellung der Türkei keineswegs mehr entsprechende Haltung bei jeder der zahlreichen Demarchen der Botschaft damit, dass es vor allem in Istanbul griechische, armenische, jüdische und sogar eine bulgarische Schule gebe und dass diese natürlich unter Kontrolle gehalten werden müssten, Auf den Einwand, dess es bei den guten deutsch-türkischen Beziehungen keine Bedenken dieser Art Geben dürfe, wird geantwortet: 'Euch Deutschen vertrauen wir, aber wenn wir Euch Erleichterungen gewähren, so kommen sofort auch die englischen, amerikanischen und französischen Schulen mit derselben Forderung und damit bricht unser kulturpolitisches System zusammen.'

53 PA – AA, B93, 75 58–61, 'Die Schwierigkeiten des Unterrichts für die deutschen Kinder in der Deutschen Schule' (no date provided). Zografyon was founded in 1892, Esayan in 1895 and Zapyon Lisesi in 1885. Özel Zografyon Rum Lisesi, 'Okulumuzun Tarihçesi', www.zografyon.com/tarihce.html (accessed 24 December 2018); Özel Esayan Ermeni İlkokulu, Ortaokulu ve Lisesi, 'Okulumuzun Tarihçesi', esayan.k12.tr/tarihce.htm (accessed 24 December 2018); Atilla Yücel and Hülya Hatipoğlu, 'Taksim Square' in Pelin Derviş, Bülent Tanju, Uğur Tanyeli (eds.), *Becoming Istanbul: An Encyclopedia* (İstanbul: Garanti Galeri, 2008), 368–81.

54 PA – AA, B93, 75 58–61, 'Die Schwierigkeiten des Unterrichts für die deutschen Kinder in der Deutschen Schule' (no date provided), and PA – AA, B93, 112 58–61, 'Frage der Anerkennung der Deutschen Schule Istanbul als höhere deutsche Vollanstalt im Ausland' (12 January 1959), 4.

55 Tenbrock, 'Neunzig Jahre Deutsche Schule Istanbul', 13–14; PA – AA, B93, 387 64, 'Sitzung des Ständigen Gemischten Ausschusses zur Durchführung des Deutsch-Türkischen Kulturabkommens' (9 July 1964).

56 Barbaros Çağa, 'Wie sich der Besuch der Deutschen Schule auf mein Leben
    auswirkt', Deutsche Schule İstanbul, *Festschrift zum neunzigjährigen Bestehen der
    Deutschen Schule Istanbul: 1868–1958* (Bergisch Gladbach, 1958), 97–100. '*Die
    Schüler kamen morgens in die Schule und gingen mittags nach Hause.*'
57 Ibid., 98. '*Wir leben in unserer Schule wie eine Familie, und in einer Familie verachtet
    oder Haßt keiner den anderen.*'
58 PA – AA, B93, 334 55–63, 'Deutsche Schule Merkblatt' (Stand Mai 1962).
59 PA – AA, B93, 334 55–63, 'Bericht über den Besuch der Deutschen Schule Istanbul
    vom 8. Bis 10.4.1962' (6-7-1962), 2.
60 PA – AA, B93, 334 55–63, 'Bericht über den Besuch der Deutschen Schule', 3.
61 Ibid., 5.
62 PA – AA, B93, 334 55–63, 'Bericht über den Besuch der Deutschen Schule Istanbul
    vom 8. Bis 10.5.1963' (16 July 1963), 4–6. 'Das Ansehen der Deutschen Schule
    kommt hier ebenso zum Ausdruck wie der Umstand, daß es eine dem Bedarf
    entsprechende Zahl türkischer Gymnasien in Istanbul nicht gibt. Bemerkenswart
    ist, daß die türkischen Eltern, die ihre Söhne und Töchter bei der Deutschen Schule
    Anmelden, durchaus nicht nur den höheren Schichten sondern zu einemen hohen
    Prozentsatz dem Mittelstand angehören. (Das Schulgeld beträgt monatlich 100
    Türkische Pfund = etwa 44,- DM nach dem offiziellen Kurs.).'
63 PA – AA, B93, 334 55–63, 'Bericht über den Besuch der Deutschen Schule Istanbul
    vom 8. Bis 10.5.1963' (16 July 1963), 4–6.
64 PA – AA, B93, 334 55–63, 'Deutsche Schule in Istanbul: Stand der Entwicklung'
    (date not provided).
65 Fatma Gök, 'The History and Development of Turkish Education' in *Education in
    'multicultural' societies: Turkish and Swedish Perspectives*, ed. Marie Carlson, Annika
    Rabo, and Fatma Gök (Stockholm and London: Swedish Research Institute in
    Istanbul & I.B. Tauris, 2007), 247–52.
66 PA – AA, B93, 334 55–63, 'Deutsche Schule Istanbul – hier: Ausbau des
    Schulgebäudes' (17 February 1958), 3.
67 PA – AA, B93, 334 55–63, 'Deutsche Schule Istanbul – hier: Ausbau'. 'ein
    Gesichtspunkt, der nicht nur kulturpolitischer Natur ist.'
68 PA – AA B93, 552 66–7, 'Einrichtung eines Sprachlabors in der Deutschen Schule
    Istanbul' (14 March 1966).
69 PA – AA B93, 552 66–7, 'Bericht über die Lage der Deutschen Schule Istanbul' (7
    February 1966), 9–10.
70 PA – AA, B93 520 66–7, 'Dienstinstruktionen für den neuen deutschen Botschafter
    in Ankara, Herrn Horst Groepper' (18 February 1966), 2.
71 PA – AA, B93 520 66–7, 'Dienstinstruktionen für den neuen deutschen Botschafter', 2.
72 PA – AA, B93 552 66–7, 'Bericht über die Lage der Deutschen Schule Istanbul' (7
    February 1966), 12.
73 PA – AA, B93 552 66–7, 'Bericht über die Lage der Deutschen Schule Istanbul' (14
    February 1967), 10.
74 Ibid.
75 PA – AA, B93 552 66–7, 'Gastschülerstatus für deutsche Schüler der Deutschen
    Schule Istanbul' (7 February 1967), 4.
76 Ibid., 5.
77 Ibid., 3.
78 PA – AA, B93, 552 66–7, 'Gastschülerstatus; hier: Ergebnis der Umfrage' (14 April
    1967).

79   PA – AA, B93, 520 66-7, 'Kulturpolitisches Jahresbericht 1965 aus der Türkei' (25 March 1966). 'Immer deutlicher ergibt sich von Jahr zu Jahr, daß die kulturelle Arbeit in der Türkei sich wirklich lohnt.'

80   Ibid.

81   Ahmet Akgündüz, 'La migration de travail des Turcs en Europe Occidentale Bilan critique des débuts (premières années 60) à l'arrêt du recrutement 1973/74', *Revue européenne des migrations internationales* 11, no. 1 (1995): 154.

82   PA – AA, B93, 520 66-7, 'Kulturpolitisches Jahresbericht 1965 aus der Türkei' (25 March 1966), 10. 'Einsichtige Kritiker dieses Gesetzes wiesen darauf hin, daß die Türkei sich den Luxus eines solchen Verbots angesichts der noch völlig ungenügenden Zahl von Schulen eigentlich nicht leisten könne.'

83   Ibid., 9.

84   Ibid., 13.

85   PA – AA, B93, 769 73-4, 'Internat für schulpflichtige deutsche Kinder in der Türkei' (19 February 1974).

86   Ibid., 2.

87   PA – AA, B93, 841 75-6, 'Bericht über den Besuch der Deutschen Schule (Alman Lisesi) Istanbul vom 30.4. – 4.5.1976 (Juni 1976), 14-15.

88   Ibid., 3.

89   Ibid., 5.

90   Ibid., 4.

91   Ibid., 5. '*Vergleichbares hatte ich auf meinen inzwischen zalhreichen Schulbesuchen noch nicht zu Gesicht bekommen*'.

92   Ibid., 6.

93   PA – AA, B93, 841 75-6, 'Bericht des Lt. Reg-Schuldirektors Becker in der Zentralstelle für das Auslandwesen im Bundesverwaltungsamt Köln zu dem Alman Lisesi und dem Erkek Lisesi' (18 October 1976), 2.

94   Ibid., 3.

95   Ibid. 'Es gibt hier einen erheblich breiteren Mittelstand als in anderen Entwicklungsländern. Aus diesem kommen in der Hauptsache die Schüler des Alman Lisesi, nicht etwa lediglich aus dem Kreis der "Reichen". Diese Kinder des heutigen Mittelstandes rücker aber morgen in die führenden Schichten ein.'

96   Ibid.

97   Ibid., 4. 'Die kulturpolitische Ausstrahlung ist deshalb im wesentlichen aber von dem Studium in Deutschland abhängig.'

98   PA – AA, B93, 841 75-6, 'Schulbesuch im Mai 1976' (20 October 1976), 4.

99   Franz Lippold, 'Die Zeit nach 1968', in *125 Jahre Deutsche Schule İstanbul Festschrift*, ed. Christa Lippold and Gerhard Nurtsch (İstanbul, 1993), 144-9.

100   Ibid., 144. 'Die Begabung zum Sprachenlernen werde zu wenig, eingepauktes Grundwissen zu hoch bewertet'.

101   Franz Lippold, 'Die Deutsche Schule İstanbul, eine Privatschule nach türkischem Recht', in *125 Jahre Deutsche Schule İstanbul Festschrift*, ed. Christa Lippold and Gerhard Nurtsch (İstanbul, 1993), 27-31.

102   Ahmet Akgündüz, 'La migration de travail des Turcs', 156.

103   Lippold, 'Die Deutsche Schule İstanbul', 27-31.

104   Lippold, 'Die Zeit nach 1968', 144-9.

105   Wittmann, 'Grüßwort des Leiters der Kulturabteilung', 14. 'Neben der pädagogischen Aufgabe, Interesse und Freude an der deutschen Sprache zu fördern, wollen wir damit auch ein aktuelles Deutschlandbild vermitteln und die Bindung an unser Land, seine Kultur und seine Menschen vertiefen.'

106 Ibid., 13. 'Viele der türkischen Absolventen des ALMAN LISESI sind unserem Land aufs engste verbunden und tragen häufig an verantwortungsvollen Posten in Politik und Gesellschaft zur Gestaltung der deutsch-türkischen Beziehungen bei.'
107 Die Deutsche Schule İstanbul, 'Hakkımızda', http://www.ds-istanbul.net/hakkimizda/, accessed 24-12-2018.
108 European Commission, 'Erasmus+ – Annual Report 2016/ Statistical Annex', https ://publications.europa.eu/en/publication-detail/-/publication/49350560-0d56-11e8 -966a-01aa75ed71a1/language-en, accessed 27 December 2018. There is no data from post-2016 as of yet.

Conclusion

1 Beyoğlu Belediyesi, 'Altı şeritli Tarlabaşı'ndan geçip Haliç kenarında kahve içeceğiz', *Beyoğlu Aylık Dergi* 1, no. 1 (1986): 2–5. 'Altı şeritli Tarlabaşı'ndan geçip Haliç kenarında kahve içeceğiz. (…) Şimdi bu Tarlabaşı'na baktığımız zaman iki, üç bilemediniz dört katlı dar cepheli binalar görüyoruz. Biz bu bulvar genişliğine uygun olarak 15 kata kadar imar müsadesi vereceğiz. İnşaat izni verilince, patır patır hepsi yıkılıp, en az cephe genişliği on metre olan inşaatler hemen yükselivereçek. Böylelikle o pislik ortadan kalkmış olacak. Yeni bir işmerkezi kurulmuş olacak.'
2 Sakızlıoğlu, 'A Comparative Look at Residents' Displacement Experiences', 163–6.
3 Bartu, 'Who Owns the Old Quarters', 35; Enno Maessen, 'Reading Landscape in Beyoglu and Tarlabasi: Engineering a "Brand New" Cosmopolitan Space, 1980–2013', *International Journal for History Culture and Modernity* 5, no. 1 (2017): 47–67.
4 Beyoğlu Belediyesi, 'Tarlabaşı Bulvarı', *Beyoğlu Aylık Dergi* 2, no. 17 (1987): 5. 'Adnan Menderes ve Turgut Özal'ın hayali gerçekleşiyor.'
5 Çelik, 'Urban Preservation as Theme Park', 84.
6 Beyoğlu Belediyesi, 'Beyoğlu, benim karımdır', *Beyoğlu Aylık Dergi* 1, no. 2 (1986): 10. 'Beyoğlu'na gitmek için bir aynanın karşısına geçerdik. Kravatımız düzgün mü, eldivenlerimiz, şapkamız şık mı, diye bakardık. Karşılaşacağımız kimselere şapka çıkartmak, Lebon Pastanesi'nde bir çay içmek büyük bir olaydı.'
7 Ibid., 11. 'Dünyanın en güzel shopping center'ını yapmak istiyoruz. Dünyanın heryerinde shopping center'lar yarışıyor. (…) Özlediğimiz Beyoğlu, Belediye Başkanımız Sayın Haluk Öztürkatalay'ın ve başkanı bulunduğu derneğin olumlu çabaları ile bir çeki-düzene girecek ve eski güzel haline dönecektir.
8 Zeynep Enlil, 'The Neoliberal Agenda and the Changing Urban Form of Istanbul', *International Planning Studies* 16, no. 1 (2011): 20–2.
9 Eldem, 'Ottoman Galata and Pera Between Myth and Reality', 25.
10 Esra Akcan, 'The "Occupy" Turn in the Global City Paradigm: The Architecture of AK Party's Istanbul and the Gezi Movement', *Journal of the Ottoman and Turkish Studies Association* 2, no. 2 (2015): 359–78.
11 Föllmer and Smith, 'Urban Societies in Europe since 1945', 475–91.
12 Eldem, 'Ottoman Galata and Pera between Myth and Reality', 26–7.
13 Ibid., 19–36.
14 Dökmeci and Lale Berköz, 'Transformation of Istanbul', 198.
15 Kerem Eksen, 'Reinventing the Spirit of Istanbul', (Unpublished Conference Paper – 3 November 2017), 1–7.
16 Daniel Atkinson and Denis Cosgrove, 'Urban Rhetoric and Embodied Identities: City, Nation, and Empire at the Vittorio Emanuele II Monument in Rome, 1870–1945', *Annals of the Association of American Geographers* 88, no. 1 (1998): 30.

BIBLIOGRAPHY

Published primary sources

Abalıoğlu, Sadık Doğan. *Galatasaray Lisesi 1954–1955 Broşürü*. İstanbul: Yenilik Basımevi, 1955*. *Exact year of publication not provided.

Akant, İlhan. *Galatasaray Lisesi: 1936 Yılı Mezunlarının 60. Yılı*. İstanbul: Tanburacı Matbaacılık A.Ş., 1996.

Akar, Rıdvan for Milliyet. 'Beyoğlu için geriye sayım başladı'. 4 January 1995, 11.

Ankara Galatasaray Birliği. 'Gül Baba'. *Bitmeyen Mektep* 3 (2015): 3–5. www.galatasaray lilarbirligi.org/images/magazine/26-15-19-272bitmeyen%20mektep_3.pdf.

Ankara Galatasaray Birliği. 'Sultani'nin Sultanları (Galatasaray'da Karma Eğitim)'. *Bitmeyen Mektep* 4 (2016): 10. www.galatasaraylilarbirligi.org/images/magazine/bi tmeyen%20mektep_4.pdf.

Aras, Oktay, and Taner Saka. *1955'lilerin 50. Yılı 1955/2005 GS Lisesi*. İstanbul: Prizma Advertising Reklam, 2006.

Beyoğlu Belediyesi. 'Altı şeritli Tarlabaşı'ndan geçip Haliç kenarında kahve içeceğiz'. *Beyoğlu Aylık Dergi* 1, no. 1 (1986): 2–5.

Beyoğlu Belediyesi. 'Beyoğlu, benim karımdır'. *Beyoğlu Aylık Dergi* 1, no. 2 (1986): 10–11.

Beyoğlu Belediyesi. 'Tarlabaşı Bulvarı'. *Beyoğlu Aylık Dergi* 2, no. 17 (1987): 5–8.

Beyoğlu Belediye Başkanlığı. *Beyoğlu İçin*. Istanbul, 1984.

Bilgin, Toygar, Koray Tezcan, Selçuk Taylaner, Edis Adoran, Bener Akbaş, Ender İkiışık, Bilsel Bakay, Ersin Üner, Şükrü Kaya Çatal, Aykut Güven and Oktay Sunam. *Galatasaray Lisesi 1958–1959 Mezunları 50 Yıl Sonra*. İstanbul: Yenilik Basımevi, 2009.

Deutsche Schule İstanbul. *Festschrift zum neunzigjährigen Bestehen der Deutschen Schule Istanbul: 1868–1958*. Bergisch Gladbach, 1958.

Dorsay, Atilla. *Benim Beyoglum*. Istanbul: Varlik Yayinlari, 1993.

Duhani, Said. *Vielles Gens Vieilles Demeures: Topograhie sociale de Beyoğlu au XIXième siècle*. Istanbul: Touring et Automobile Club de Turquie, 1947.

Duhani, Said, Ahmet Parman, and Türkiye Turing ve Otomobil Kurumu. *Eski insanlar eski evler : XIX. yüzyilda Beyoglu'nun sosyal topografisi*. Istanbul: Türkiye Turing ve Otomobil Kurumu, 1984.

Ebüzziya, Ziyad, and Şahir Kozikoğlu (ed.) *1921–1933 Galatasaray Tarihçesi 1933 Mezunları ve 50 yılları*. İstanbul: Yörük Matbaası, 1987*. *Exact year of publication is not provided.

EHS Yearbook Committee. *Yearbook EHSG 1971–1972*. Istanbul, 1972.

English High Schools. *Yearbook EHS 1960: The Wolf and the Crescent*. Istanbul: Ekicigil Matbaası, 1960.

English High School for Girls. *Yearbook EHSG 1972–1973*. Istanbul, 1973.

Galatasaray Kültür ve Sanat Merkezi. *Bir Numaralı Galatasaraylı Ali Sami Yen*. İstanbul: Galatasaray Spor Kulübü, 2011.

Galatasaray Lisesi. *100 Galatasaray*. İstanbul: 1968.

Galatasaray Lisesi 1937 Mezunları. *Galatasaray Lisesi Mezunları 1936–1937 Ders Senesi.* İstanbul: Devlet Basımevi, 1937.

Galatasaray Lisesi Broşür Kolu. *Galatasaray 1957–58.* İstanbul: Öztürk Matbaası, 1958.

Galatasaray Lisesi Broşür Kolu. *1969 Mezunları Yıllığı.* İstanbul: Kıral Matbaası, 1969.

GSL '64 Koordinasyon Kurulu. *1964 Mezunları 50. Yıl Anı Kitabı.* İstanbul: 2014.

Gülersoy, Çelik. *A Guide to Istanbul.* Istanbul: Yenilik Basımevi, 1969.

Gürel, Erol. 'Bir Amerikalı Gözüyle Galatasaray'. *Galatasaray Dergisi* 1, no. 3 (1947): 24–5, 32.

Hachette. *Les Guides Blues Illustrés: Istanbul et ses Environs.* Paris: Hachette, 1958.

Hachette. *Les Guides Bleus: Turquie.* Paris: Hachette, 1969.

Hammer, Joseph von. *Constantinopolis und der Bosporos.* Pesth: Hartleben's Verlag, 1822.

İren, Nejat, Nuri Efe, Turgut Madenci (eds.) *1922-1934 Galatasaray Tarihçesi 1934 Mezunları ve 50 Yılları.* İstanbul: Galatasaray Eğitim Vakfı/Yenilik Basımevi, 1989.

İsfendiyaroğlu, Fethi. *Galatasaray Tarihi.* Vol. 1. İstanbul: Doğan Kardeş Yayınları, 1952.

İstanbul Belediyesi. *Güzelleşen İstanbul.* Istanbul, 1943.

Koçu, Reşat Ekrem. *'Barlar' İstanbul Ansiklopedisi.* İstanbul: Tan Matbaası, 1960.

Koloğlu, Orhan. *Cercle d'Orient'dan Büyük Kulüp'e.* Istanbul: Boyut Kitapları, 2005.

Lippold, Christa, and Gerhard Nurtsch (eds.) *125 Jahre Deutsche Schule İstanbul Festschrift.* İstanbul, 1993.

Nigar, Salih Keramet. *İnkılâp Şairi Tevfik Fikret.* Istanbul: Kenan Matbaası, 1942.

Özdemir Arkan. *Beyoğlu: Kısa Geçmişi, Argosu.* Istanbul: İletişim, 1988.

Pears, Edwin. *Forty Years in Constantinople: The Recollections of Sir Edwin Pears 1873–1915.* London: Herbert Jenkins Ltd., 1916.

Perde ve Sahne. 'Bir Filmde Baş Rol Oynayacak Bayanlara Ihtiyaç Vardır'. *Perde ve Sahne* 2 (1954): 15–26.

Pinto, Bensiyon, Tülay Gürler, Nicole Pope, and Leyla Engin Arık. *My life as a Turkish Jew: memoirs of the president of the Turkish-Jewish community, 1989–2004.* İstanbul: Bahçeşehir University Press, 2012.

Rycaut, Paul. *The Present State of the Ottoman Empire.* 3rd edn. London: J. Starkey and H. Brome, 1670.

Schmidt, Thilo. 'Deutschland Radio Kultur Länderreport: Ich bin dann mal weg'. https://www.deutschlandfunkkultur.de/ich-bin-dann-mal-weg-pdf.media.a33f5cf360e3b097f12fa68557eddbd4.pdf, accessed 17 August 2011.

Scognamillo, Giovanni. *Bir Levantenin Beyoğlu Anıları.* Istanbul: Metis Kitap, 1990.

Toker, Metin. 'Fındık ve Kabuğu'. *Galatasaray Dergisi* 3, no. 11 (1949): 1.

Türkisch – Deutsche Wohltaetigkeitsgesellschaft Teutonia. 'Ein Rückblick'. *Teutonia Mitteilungsblatt* 1, no. 1 (1956): 2–3.

Türkisch – Deutsche Wohltaetigkeitsgesellschaft Teutonia. 'Über den Sinn unseres Vereins'. *Teutonia Mitteilungsblatt* 1, no. 2 (1956): 1–2.

Türkisch – Deutsche Wohltaetigkeitsgesellschaft Teutonia. 'Hauptversammlung der Teutonia am 29 März 1957'. *Teutonia Mitteilungsblatt* 1, no. 12 (1957): 4–6.

Türkisch – Deutsche Wohltaetigkeitsgesellschaft Teutonia. '1. Juni 1847 – 1. Juni 1857'. *Teutonia Mitteilungsblatt* 2, no. 14 (1957): 1–2.

Türkisch – Deutsche Wohltaetigkeitsgesellschaft Teutonia. '110 Jahre "Teutonia"'. *Teutonia Mitteilungsblatt* 2, no. 15 (1957): 5–6.

Türkisch – Deutsche Wohltaetigkeitsgesellschaft Teutonia. 'Hauptversammlung am 25. März 1958'. *Teutonia Mitteilungsblatt* 2, no. 24 (1958): 4–5.

Türkisch – Deutsche Wohltaetigkeitsgesellschaft Teutonia. 'Der Neue Badeplatz in Fenerbahce'. *Teutonia Mitteilungsblatt* 26 (1958): 6.

Türkisch – Deutsche Wohltaetigkeitsgesellschaft Teutonia. 'Veranstaltungen der Teutonia'. *Teutonia Mitteilungsblatt* 8, no. 76 (1963): 15–16.
Türkisch – Deutsche Wohltaetigkeitsgesellschaft Teutonia. 'Zeichen und Wunder: Zum Umbau und zur Renovierung des Teutonia-Gebäudes'. *Teutonia Mitteilungsblatt* 9, no. 80 (1964): 1–2.
Türkisch – Deutsche Wohltaetigkeitsgesellschaft Teutonia. 'Ordentliche Generalversammlung der Teutonia am 29. März 1965'. *Teutonia Mitteilungsblatt* 10, no. 82 (1965): 1–3.
Türkisch – Deutsche Wohltaetigkeitsgesellschaft Teutonia. 'Generalversammlung der Teutonia am 17. März'. *Teutonia Mitteilungsblatt* 11, no. 83 (1966): 2–3.
Türkiye Cumhuriyet Merkez Bankası. *1979 Yıllık Raporu*. Ankara: TCMB, 30 April 1980.
Türkiye Cumhuriyet Merkez Bankası. *1995 Yıllık Raporu*. Ankara: TCMB 25 April 1995.
Yüzüncü Yıl Kutlama Derneği. *Galatasaray Lisesi – Mekteb-i Sultanî 1868–1968*. İstanbul: Gün Matbaası, 1974.

Interviews

Alumni of English High School for Girls, English High School for Boys, Beyoğlu Anadolu Lisesi, interview by the author, 13 March 2017, English High Schoollular Derneği, Beyazgül Sokak 81, Arnavutköy, Beşiktaş, Istanbul.
BAL English teacher, interview by the author, January 2017, Beyoğlu, İstanbul.
EHSG math teacher, interview by the author, 22 March 2017, Alman Kitabevi İstiklal Caddesi 237, Beyoğlu, İstanbul.
Sanver, Remzi, interview by the author, 16 January 2017, Bilgi University Santral Kampüsü, Eyüp, İstanbul.

Newspapers

Alpaslan, Salim. 'Devletin, Beş Milyonluk İstanbul'daki Tek Sanat Galerisi Kapanma Tehlikesiyle Karşı Karşıyla'. *Cumhuriyet*, 29 March 1980, 7.
Cumhuriyet Gazetesi. 'Serkldoryan binasının satışı yarın görüşülecek'. 1 December 1951, 3.
Cumhuriyet Gazetesi. 'Türk Alman Hayır Cemiyeti'. 1 June 1968, 7 and 'Haftanın Sanat Çizelgesi'. 27 October 1986, 5.
Cumhuriyet Gazetesi. 'Emek Cinema Advertisement'. 4 November 1968, 6.
Daily Telegraph Diplomatic. 'Eau de Cologne de Constantinople!'. 13 August 1926, 9.
Demirkaya, Mehmet, for Cumhuriyet Gazetesi. 'Emek sineması için imza kampanyası'. 11 April 1994, 7.
Dorsay, for Cumhuriyet Gazetesi. 'Sinema ve tiyatro salonları birbiri ardına kapanıyor'. 22 January 1976, 6.
Gürkan, Turhan for Cumhuriyet Gazetesi. 'Emek Sineması müzikhol oluyor'. 17 September 1968, 6.
Milliyet. 'Serkldoryan binası dün satılamadı'. 25 December 1956, 5 and 'Serkldoryan bloku nihayet satılıyor'. 6 January 1957, 1.
Milliyet. 'Beyoğlu çekidüzen veriliyor'. 9 June, 1984, 3.
Pekşen, Yalçin for Cumhuriyet. 'Beyoğlu'nda "şarap kültürü"nün yerini "bira kültürü" aldı'. 13 November 1983, 8.

Sheffield Daily Telegraph. 30 January 1896, 5.
Süsoy, Yener, 'Gazinolar savaşı tekrar başladı'. *Milliyet Magazin*, 12 November 1972, 10.
The New York Times. 'The Turkish Minorities'. 17 September, 1943, 20.
The Times. 'The Career of Fehim Pasha'. 10 August 1908, 6.

Web Sources

Arango, Tim. 'On Istiklal, Istanbul's Champs-Élysées, Symbols of a City's Malaise'. *The New York Times*, 20 September 2016, https://www.nytimes.com/2016/09/21/world/europe/is tiklal-istanbul-turkey.html.
Aksoy, Asu, Kevin Robins, and Kaan Çuhacı. 'Improvised City - Adil Kebap Dürüm'. *Documentary*, Istanbul, 2012, https://www.youtube.com/watch?v=Gtw95lZ22dk.
Beyoğlu Belediyesi. 'Emek Sineması Muhteşem'. http://www.beyoglu.bel.tr/beyoglu-b elediyesi/haber-detay/Emek-Sinemasi-Muhtesem/300/3993/0, accessed 2 November 2017.
Beyoğlu Belediyesi. 'Devlet güzel sanatlar galerisi'. 26 February 2018, http://www.beyoglu .bel.tr/beyoglu-belediyesi/detay/DEVLET-GUZEL-SANATLAR-GALERISI/185/1215 /0.
Die Deutsche Schule İstanbul. 'Hakkımızda'. http://www.ds-istanbul.net/hakkimizda/, accessed 24 December 2018.
Diken. 'Beyoğlu Anadolu'da karma eğitime veda: 'Abartılacak şey değil, orijinaline döndü''. *Diken*, 15 June 2016, http://www.diken.com.tr/beyoglu-anadoluda-karma-egitime -veda-abartilacak-bir-sey-degil-orijinaline-dondu/.
Diken. 'Emek Bizim İnisiyatifi'nden dokuz soruda Emek Sineması'nın yıkım hikayesi'. http://www.diken.com.tr/emek-bizim-inisiyatifinden-dokuz-soruda-emek-sinema sinin-yikim-hikayesi/, accessed 2 November 2017 and Radikal. 'Emek yerle bir'. http:// www.radikal.com.tr/hayat/emek-yerle-bir-1134388/, accessed 2 November 2017.
European Commission. 'Erasmus+ – Annual Report 2016: Statistical Annex'. https://pu blications.europa.eu/en/publication-detail/-/publication/49350560-0d56-11e8-966a -01aa75ed71a1/language-en, accessed 27 December 2018.
Görgülü, Güventürk for Arkitera. 'Emek Sineması ve AVM takıntısı'. http://v3.arkitera .com/arsgratiaartis.php?action=displayNewsItem&ID=52146, accessed 5 December 2018.
Grand Pera. 'Grand Pera Website'. http://www.grandpera.com/, accessed 2 November 2017.
Grand Pera. 'About Us'. http://www.grandpera.com/en/about-us.aspx, accessed 3 December 2018.
New York Times. '4 Days of Fear, Then 7 Minutes for the Rescue'. *New York Times*, 17 October 1977, http://www.nytimes.com/1977/10/19/archives/4-days-of-fear-then -7-minutes-for-the-rescue-thursday-oct-13.html, accessed 5 January 2018.
Osmanlı Bankası Arşiv ve Araştırma Merkezi. 'Arşivimizden Belgeler - Abraham Paşa'nın İflâsı'. http://www.obarsiv.com/ab-abraham-pasa.html, accessed 2 November 2017.
Özel Esayan Ermeni İlkokulu, Ortaokulu ve Lisesi. 'Okulumuzun Tarihçesi'. esayan.k12.tr/ tarihce.htm, accessed 24 December 2018.
Özel Zografyon Rum Lisesi. 'Okulumuzun Tarihçesi'. www.zografyon.com/tarihce.html, accessed 24 December 2018.

T.C. Galatasaray Lisesi. 'Galatasaray Lisesi ve Galatasaray İlköğretim Okulu Yönetmenliği – İkinci Bölüm Madde 6'. http://www.gsl.gsu.edu.tr/tr/yonetmelik, accessed 20 December 2018.

T.C. Galatasaray Lisesi. 'Okul Bilgileri'. http://www.gsl.gsu.edu.tr/tr/okul-bilgileri, accessed 20 December 2018.

T.C. Galatasaray Üniversitesi Galatasaray İlkokulu & Ortaokulu. 'İletişim'. http://www.gsi .gsu.edu.tr/iletisim.html, accessed 20 December 2018.

T.C. Galatasaray Üniversitesi. 'Tarihçe'. http://www.gsu.edu.tr/tr/universite/genel-bilgiler/ tarihce, accessed 20 December 2018.

T.C. Kültür ve Turizm Bakanlığı Güzel Sanatlar Genel Müdürlüğü. '9.Şefik Bursalı Resim Yarışması Şartnamesi 2009'. accessed 26 February 2018.

T.C. Milli Eğitim Bakanlığı. 'Website Beyoğlu Anadolu Lisesi'. accessed 19 December 2018, http://beyogluanadolu.meb.k12.tr/.

Türkiye Büyük Millet Meclisi. 'Yıpranan tarihi ve kültürel taşınmaz varlıkların yenilenerek korunması ve yaşatılarak kullanılması hakkında kanun'. https://www.tbmm.gov.tr/k anunlar/k5366.html, accessed 2 November 2017.

Archives of the Ministry of Foreign Affairs of the Netherlands, The Hague

Dep 273631 – 21A.
Dep 273631 – 25.
Dep 273631 – 111.

The National Archives, Kew – London

BW 61/7 English High School for Girls 1944–1946.
FCO 13/48 English Schools in Turkey 1968.
FCO 13/744 UK high schools in Istanbul, Turkey.
FCO 13/903 EHS Transfer to Turkey 1979.
FCO 13/904 EHS Transfer to Turkey 1979.
FO 195/2710 English High Schools Istanbul 1960.
FO 195/2716 English High Schools 1962.
FO 195/2717 English High Schools 1962.
FO 195/2718 EHSG Statement of Accounts 1961–1962.
FO 924/35 British Schools in Ankara and Istanbul 1944.

Politisches Archiv Auswärtiges Amt, Berlin

PA – AA B93 41 – 54–55.
PA – AA B93 75 58–71.
PA – AA B93 112 58–61.
PA – AA B93 334 – 55–63.
PA – AA B93 387 – 64.
PA – AA B93 520 66–67.

PA – AA B93 552 66–67.
PA – AA, B93, 769 73–74.
PA – AA, B93, 841 75–76.
PA – AA, ISTA, KU641.35.

Teutonia Archives

Internal and external correspondence.
Member lists.
Minutes from board meetings 1950–1990.
Minutes from member meetings 1950–1990.
Türkisch – Deutsche Wohltaetigkeitsgesellschaft Teutonia, Teutonia Mitteilungsblatt (see published primary sources).
Unpublished history on the Teutonia club by Franz von Caucig.

Türk Mühendis ve Mimar Odaları Birliği,
İstanbul Büyükkent Şubesi, Istanbul

Emek Sineması Dosyası.
Serkldoryan Dosyası.
Türk Mühendis ve Mimar Odaları Birliği. *Beyoglu nasıl kurtulur?*. Istanbul, year unknown.

Secondary literature

Adalet, Begüm. *Hotels and Highways: The Construction of Modernization Theory in Cold War Turkey*. Stanford: Stanford University Press, 2018.
Agnew, John. 'Space: Place'. In *Spaces of Geographical Thought*, edited by Paul Cloke and Ron Johnston, 81–96. London: Sage, 2005.
Akan, Aysun. 'A Critical Analysis of the Turkish Press Discourse against Non-Muslims: A Case Analysis of the Newspaper Coverage of the 1942 Wealth Tax'. *Middle Eastern Studies* 47, no. 4 (2011): 605–21.
Akcan, Esra. 'The "Occupy" Turn in the Global City Paradigm: The Architecture of AK Party's Istanbul and the Gezi Movement'. *Journal of the Ottoman and Turkish Studies Association* 2, no. 2 (2015): 359–78.
Akgündüz, Ahmet. 'La migration de travail des Turcs en Europe Occidentale Bilan critique des débuts (premières années 60) à l'arrêt du recrutement 1973/4'. *Revue européenne des migrations internationales* 11, no. 1 (1995): 153–77.
Akpınar, İpek. 'The Rebuilding of Istanbul after the Plan of Henri Prost 1937–1960: From Secularisation to Turkish Modernisation'. PhD thesis, University of London, 2003.
Aksoy, Asu, and Kevin Robins. 'Changing Urban Cultural Governance in Istanbul: The Beyoğlu Plan'. *KPY Working Paper* 1 (2011): 1–20.
Aktar, Ayhan. *Varlık Vergisi ve "Türkleştirme" Politikaları*. İstanbul: İletişim, 2000.

Aktar, Ayhan. "'Turkification" Policies in the Early Republican Era'. In *Turkish Literature and Cultural Memory*, edited by Catharina Duft, 29–62. Wiesbaden: Harrassowitz Verlag, 2009.

Aktar, Ayhan. 'Conversion of a 'Country' into a 'Fatherland': The Case of Turkification Examined, 1923–1934'. In *Nationalism in the Troubled Triangle: New Perspectives on South-East Europe*, edited by A. Aktar, N. Kızılyürek and U. Özkırımlı, 21–35. London: Palgrave Macmillan, 2010.

Alexandris, Alexis. *The Greek Minority of Istanbul and Greek-Turkish Relations, 1918–1974*. Athens: Centre for Asia Minor Studies, 1992.

Altaban, Özcan, and Murat Güvenç. 'Urban Planning in Ankara'. *Cities* 7, no. 2 (1990): 149–58.

Anderson, Benedict. *Imagined Communities: Reflections on the Origin and Spread of Nationalism*, Revised edn. London New York: Verso, 2006.

Arslan, Savaş. *Cinema in Turkey : A New Critical History*. New York: Oxford University Press, 2011.

Atkinson, Daniel, and Denis Cosgrove. 'Urban Rhetoric and Embodied Identities: City, Nation, and Empire at the Vittorio Emanuele II Monument in Rome, 1870–1945'. *Annals of the Association of American Geographers* 88, no. 1 (1998): 28–49.

Bahar, Izzet. 'German or Jewish Humanity or Raison d'Etat: The German Scholars in Turkey, 1933–1952'. *Shofar: An Interdisciplinary Journal of Jewish Studies* 29, no. 1 (2010): 48–72.

Bartu, Ayfer. 'Who Owns the Old Quarters? Rewriting Histories in a Global Era'. In *Istanbul: Between the Global and the Local*, edited by Çağlar Keyder, 31–46. Lanham: Rowman and Littlefield Publisher, 1999.

Baruh, Lorans Tanahtar. 'The Transformation of the 'Modern' Axis of Nineteenth-Century Istanbul: Property, Investments and Elites from Taksim Square to Sirkeci Station'. PhD thesis, Boğaziçi University, 2009.

Batuman, Bülent. 'City Profile: Ankara'. *Cities*, 31 (2013): 578–90.

Batur, Afife. 'Galata and Pera: A Short History, Urban Development Architecture and Today'. *ARI: The Bulletin of the İstanbul Technical University* 55, no. 1 (2002): 1–10.

Baykan, Ayşegül, and Tali Hatuka. 'Politics and Culture in the Making of Public Space: Taksim Square, 1 May 1977, Istanbul'. *Planning Perspectives* 25, no. 1 (2010): 49–68.

Berridge, Geoff. *British Diplomacy in Turkey, 1583 to the Present: A Study in the Evolution of the Resident Embassy*. Leiden: Martinus Nijhoff Publishers, 2009.

Bilsel, Cana. 'Remodelling the Imperial Capital in the Early Republican Era: The Representation of History in Henri Prost's Planning of Istanbul'. In *Developing EU-Turkey Dialogue, A Cliohworld Reader*, edited by Guomundur Halfdanarson, Hatice Sofu, 249–69. Pisa: University of Pisa Press, 2010.

Bora, Tanıl. 'Nationalist Discourses in Turkey'. *South Atlantic Quarterly* 102, no. 2/3 (2003): 433–51.

Borie, Alain, Pierre Pinon, and Stéphane Yerasimos. *L'occidentalisation d'Istanbul au XIXe siècle, Rapport de synthèse, septembre 1996*. Paris: École d'Architecture de Paris La Défense, Bureau de la Recherche Architecturale, 1996.

Boyar, Ebru, and Kate Fleet. *A Social History of Ottoman Istanbul*. Cambridge: Cambridge University Press, 2011.

Boym, Svetlana. *The Future of Nostalgia*. New York: Basic Books, 2002.

Bozdoğan, Sibel. *Modernism and Nation Building: Turkish Architectural Culturel in the Early Republic*. Seattle: University of Washington Press, 2001.

Bozdoğan, Sibel, and Esra Akcan. *Turkey: Modern Architectures in History*. London: Reaktion Books, 2012.

Bromberger, Christian. 'Towards an Anthropology of the Mediterranean'. *History and Anthropology* 17, no. 2 (2006): 91–107.

Bucur, Ioan Marius. 'Justice and Repression in Communist Romania: The Trial of Greek-Catholic Bishop Alexandru Rusu in 1957'. *Studia Universitatis Babes-Bolyai – Historia* 58, no. 2 (2013): 113–38.

Burawoy, Michael. 'Reconstructing Social Theories'. In *Ethnography Unbound: Power and Resistance in the Modern Metropolis*, edited by M. Burawoy, A. Burton, Arnett Ferguson, et al., 8–28. Berkeley: University of California Press, 1991.

Çalış, Şaban Halis. *Turkey's Cold War: Foreign Policy and Western Alignment in the Modern Republic*. London: I.B. Tauris, 2017.

Çelik, Zeynep. *The Remaking of Istanbul*. Berkeley and Los Angeles: University of California Press, 1993.

Çelik, Zeynep. 'Urban Preservation as Theme Park: The Case of Soğukçeşme Street'. In *Streets Critical Perspectives on Space*, edited by Zeynep Çelik, Diane Favro and Richard Ingersoll, 83–94. Berkeley and Los Angeles: University of California Press, 1994.

Cerasi, Maurice. 'The Formation Of Ottoman House Types: A Comparative Study In Interaction With Neighboring Cultures'. *Muqarnas* 15, no. 1 (2008): 116–56.

Conermann, Stephan. 'Die Lage jüdischer deutscher Hochschullehrer und die Einschränkung wissenschaftlichen Arbeitens während der NS-Zeit'. In *Istanbuler Texte und Studien 12*, edited by Christopher Kubaseck and Günter Seufert, 49–66. Würzburg: Ergon-Verlag, 2016.

Çoruk, Ali Şükrü. 'Cumhuriyet Devri Türk Romanında Beyoğlu (1924–1980)'. MA Thesis, Istanbul University, Istanbul, 1993.

Cosgrove, Denis. *Social Formation and Symbolic Landscape*. Madison, WI: The Wisconsin University Press, 1998, first published: 1984.

Cosgrove, Denis. 'Landscape and Landschaft'. *GHI Bulletin* 35 (2004): 57–71.

Daniels, Stephen, and Denis Cosgrove. 'Introduction: Iconography and Landscape'. In *The Iconography of Landscape*, edited by Denis Cosgrove and Stephen Daniels, 1–10. Cambridge: Cambridge University Press, 1988.

Davies, Sarah. 'The Soft Power of Anglia: British Cold War Cultural Diplomacy in the USSR'. *Contemporary British History* 27, no. 3 (2013): 297–323.

Davison, Roderic H. 'Westernized Education in Ottoman Turkey'. *The Middle East Journal* 15, no. 3 (1961): 289–301.

Dawidowicz, Lucy S. (ed.) *A Holocaust Reader*. West Orange: Behrman House Inc., 1976.

Della Dora, Veronica. 'The Rhetoric of Nostalgia: Postcolonial Alexandria between Uncanny Memories and Global Geographies'. *Cultural Geographies* 13, no. 2 (2006): 207–38.

Deringil, Selim. "'There is No Compulsion in Religion': On Conversion and Apostasy in the Late Ottoman Empire: 1839–1856'. *Comparative Studies in Society and History* 42, no. 3 (2000): 547–75.

Dietrich, Anne. *Deutschsein in Istanbul: Nationalisierung und Orientierung in der deutschsprachigen Community von 1843 bis 1956*. Opladen: Leske+Budrich, 1998.

Dinçer, İclal, Zeynep Enlil, Tolga İslam. 'Regeneration in a New Context: A New Act on Renewal and its Implications on the Planning Processes in İstanbul'. Bridging the Divide: Celebrating the City. ACSP – AESOP Fourth Joint Congress. July 6–11, Chicago IL, 2008, 1–10.

Dökmeci, Vedia, Ufuk Altunbaş, and Burcin Yazgı. 'Revitalisation of the Main Street of a Distinguished Old Neighbourhood in Istanbul'. *European Planning Studies* 15, no. 1 (2007): 153–66.

Dökmeci, Vedia, and Lale Berköz. 'Transformation of Istanbul from a Monocentric to a Polycentric City'. *European Planning Studies* 2, no. 2 (1994): 193–205.

Dökmeci, Vedia, and Hale Çiraci. 'Pera: A Threatened Historic European City Within Istanbul'. *Ekistics* 55, no. 333 (1988): 359–70.

Dönmez-Colin, Gönül. *Turkish Cinema: Identity, Distance and Belonging*. London: Reaktion, 2008.

Driessen, Henk. 'Mediterranean Port Cities: Cosmopolitanism Reconsidered'. *History and Anthropology* 16, no. 1 (2005): 129–41.

Dumont, Paul. 'Freemasonry in Turkey: A By-product of Western Penetration'. *European Review* 13, no. 3 (2005): 481–93.

Eksen, Kerem. 'Reinventing the Spirit of Istanbul'. Unpublished Conference Paper – 3 November 2017, 1–7.

Eldem, Edhem. *A History of the Ottoman Bank*. Istanbul: Ottoman Bank Historical Research Center, 1999.

Eldem, Edhem. *Bankalar Caddesi: Osmanlı'dan Günümüze Voyvoda Caddesi – Voyvoda Street from Ottoman Times to Today*. Istanbul: Osmanlı Bankası, 2000.

Eldem, Edhem. 'Ottoman Financial Integration with Europe: Foreign Loans, the Ottoman Bank and the Ottoman Public Debt'. *European Review* 13, no. 3 (2005): 431–45.

Eldem, Edhem. 'Galata-Pera between Myth and Reality'. In *From 'mileu de memoire' to 'lieu de memoire': The Cultural Memory of Istanbul in the 20th Century*, edited by Ulrike Tischler, 18–36. Munich: Peter Lang, 2006.

Eldem, Edhem. 'Istanbul as a Cosmopolitan City: Myths and Realities'. In *A Companion to Diaspora and Transnationalism*, edited by Ato Quayson and Girish Daswani, 212–30. Malden, Oxford: Blackwell Publishing Ltd, 2013.

Eldem, Edhem, Daniel Goffman, and Bruce Masters. *The Ottoman city between East and West: Aleppo, Izmir, and Istanbul*. Cambridge: Cambridge University Press, 2005.

England, Kim. 'Getting Personal: Reflexivity, Positionality, and Feminist Research'. *The Professional Geographer* 46, no. 1 (1994): 80–89.

Enlil, Zeynep. 'The Neoliberal Agenda and the Changing Urban Form of Istanbul'. *International Planning Studies* 16, no. 1 (2011): 5–25.

Ergun, Nilgün 'Gentrification in Istanbul'. *Cities* 21, no. 5 (2004): 391–405.

Findley, Carter. *Ottoman Civil Officialdom: A Social History*. Princeton, NJ: Princeton University Press, 1989.

Findley, Carter. 'The Tanzimat'. In *The Cambridge History of Turkey*, edited by Reşat Kasaba, 9–37. Cambridge: Cambridge University Press, 2008.

Fogu, Claudio. 'We Have Made the Mediterranean: Now We Must Make the Mediterraneans'. In *Critically Mediterranean: Temporalities, Aesthetics, and Deployments of a Sea in Crisis*, edited by Elhariry Yasser, and Edwige Tamalet Talbayev, 181–98. Cham: Palgrave MacMillan, 2018.

Föllmer, Moritz. 'Cities of Choice: Elective Affinities and the Transformation of Western European Urbanity from the Mid-1950s to the Early 1980s'. *Contemporary European History* 24, no. 4 (2015): 577–96.

Föllmer, Moritz, and Mark B. Smith. 'Urban Societies in Europe since 1945: Toward a Historical Interpretation'. *Contemporary European History* 24, no. 4 (2015): 475–91.

Frazee, Charles. 'Catholics'. In *Minorities in Greece: Aspects of a Plural Society*, edited by Richard Clogg, 24–47. London: Hurst and Company, 2002.

Fregonese, Sara, and Adam Ramadan. 'Hotel Geopolitics: A Research Agenda'. *Geopolitics* 20, no. 4 (2015): 793–813.

Fuhrmann, Malte. 'Istanbul, die Deutschen und das 19. Jahrhundert – Wege, die sich kreuzen'. In *Daheim in Konstantinopel / Memleketemiz Dersaadet: Deutsche Spuren am Bosporus ab 1850 / 1850'den İtibaren Boğaziçi'ndeki Alman İzleri*, edited by Erald Pauw, 23–38. Neurenberg: Pagma Verlag, 2014.

Geser, Marcel. '"Wir sind im Kleinen, was das Vaterland im Großen": Der deutsche Kindergarten in Istanbul von 1850 bis 2007'. In *Facetten internationaler Migration in die Türkei: Gesellschaftliche Rahmensbedingungen und persönliche Lebenswelten*, Istanbuler Texte und Studien 13, edited by Barbara Push and Tomas Wilkoszewski, 111–28. Istanbul: Orient-Institut Istanbul, 2016.

Girardelli, Paolo. 'Architecture, Identity and Liminality: On the use and meaning of Catholic spaces in late Ottoman Istanbul'. *Muqarnas: An Annual on the Visual Culture of the Islamic World*, XXII (2005): 233–64.

Girardelli, Paolo. 'Sheltering Diversity: Levantine Architecture in Late Ottoman Istanbul'. In *Multicultural Urban Fabric and Types in the South Eastern Mediterranean*, edited by M. Cerasi, A. Petruccioli, A. Sarro and S. Weber, 113–40. Istanbul: Orient Institut, 2008.

Girardelli, Paolo. 'The Renovation of the Società Operaia Italiana di Mutuo Soccorso (SOI), in İstanbul (1908–1910)'. In *Değişen Zamanların Mimarı - The Architect of Changing Times, Edoardo de Nari (1874–1954)*, edited by Baha Tanman, 122–7. Istanbul: İstanbul Araştırma Enstitüsü, 2012.

Goffman, Erving. *The Presentation of Self in Everyday Life*. 1st edn. 1959. London: Penguin Books, 1990.

Göçek, Fatma Müge. *Rise of the Bourgeoisie, Demise of Empire: Ottoman Westernization and Social Change*. New York, NY: Oxford University Press, 2011.

Göçek, Fatma Müge. *Denial of Violence: Ottoman Past, Turkish Present, and Collective Violence against the Armenians, 1789-2009*. Oxford: Oxford University Press, 2015.

Gök, Fatma. 'The History and Development of Turkish Education' in *Education in 'Multicultural' Societies: Turkish and Swedish Perspectives*, edited by Marie Carlson, Annika Rabo, and Fatma Gök, 247–55. Stockholm and London: Swedish Research Institute in Istanbul & I.B. Tauris, 2007.

Grabow, Sven. 'The Santiago De Compostela Pilgrim Routes: the Development of European Cultural Heritage Policy and Practice From a Critical Perspective'. *European Journal of Archaeology* 13, no. 1 (2010): 89–116.

Gül, Murat. *The Emergence of Modern Istanbul: Transformation and Modernisation of a City*. London: I.B. Tauris, 2012.

Güven, Dilek. *Nationalismus und Minderheiten: die Ausschreitungen gegen die Christen und Juden der Türkei: 6/7 September 1955*. München: Oldenbourg, 2012.

Hadimoğlu, Nimet Özbek. 'Minority Schools, Foreign and International Schools in the New Law on Private Educational Institutions'. *Ankara Law Review* 5, no. 1 (2008): 53–100.

Hamadeh, Shirine. *The City's Pleasures: Istanbul in the Eighteenth Century*. Seattle: University of Washington Press, 2008.

Hamadeh, Shirine. 'Invisible City: Istanbul's Migrants and the Politics of Space'. *Eighteenth-Century Studies* 50, no. 2 (2017): 173–93.

Hanıoğlu, Şükrü. *The Young Turks in Opposition*. New York and Oxford: Oxford University Press, 1995.

Hanley, Will. 'What Ottoman Nationality Was and Was Not'. *Journal of the Ottoman and Turkish Studies Association* 3, no. 2 (2016): 277–98.

Herzfeld, Michael. 'Practical Mediterraneanism: Excuses for Everything, from Epistemology to Eating'. In *Rethinking the Mediterranean*, edited by W.V. Harris, 45–63. Oxford: Oxford University Press, 2005.

Herzfeld, Michael. 'Spatial Cleansing: Monumental Vacuity and the Idea of the West'. *Journal of Material Culture* 11, no. 2 (2006): 127–49.

Hirsch, Marianne, and Leo Spitzer. *Ghosts of Home: The Afterlife of Czernowitz in Jewish Memory*. Berkeley and Los Angeles: University of California Press, 2010.

Hobsbawm, Eric, and Terence Ranger. *The Invention of Tradition*. Cambridge: Cambridge University Press, 1983.

Huisman, Frank, Joris Vandendriessche, and Kaat Wils. 'Introduction: Blurring Boundaries: Towards a Medical History of the Twentieth Century'. *BMGN – Low Countries Historical Review* 132, no. 1 (2017): 3–15.

Huyssen, Andreas. *Present Pasts: Urban Palimpsests and the Politics of Memory*. Stanford CA: Stanford University Press, 2003.

İnal, Vedit. 'The Eighteenth and Nineteenth Century Ottoman Attempts to Catch Up with Europe'. *Middle Eastern Studies* 47, no. 5 (2011): 725–56.

İnalcik, Halil. *The Ottoman Empire: The Classical Age 1300–1600*. 1st edn. 1973. London: Phoenix, 2000.

Işık, Ayhan. 'The Emergence, Transformation and Functions of Paramilitary Groups in Northern Kurdistan (Eastern Turkey) in the 1990s'. PhD Thesis, Utrecht University, Utrecht, 2020.

Jerram, Leif. 'Space: A Useless Category for Historical Analysis?'. *History and Theory* 52, no. 3 (2013): 400–19.

Kant, Marion. 'The Moving Body and the Will to Culture'. *European Review* 19, no. 4 (2011): 579–94.

Kasbarian, Sossie. 'The Istanbul Armenians: Negotiating Coexistence'. In *Post-Ottoman Coexistence: Sharing Space in the Shadow of Conflict*, edited by Rebecca Bryant, 207–37. New York: Berghahn Books, 2016.

Kaya Mutlu, Dilek, 'Yeşilçam in Letters: A Cinema Event in 1960s Turkey from the Perspective of an Audience Discourse' PhD thesis, Bilkent University, Ankara 2002.

Kazancıgil, Aykut, Uğur Tanyeli, and İlber Ortaylı. 'Niye Geldiler, Niye Gittiler? Kimse Anlamadı'. In *Cogito-Türkiye'nin Yabancıları*, edited by Ayşe Erdem and Enis Batur, 119–32. Istanbul: Yapı Kredi Yayınları, 2000.

Kechriotis, Vangelis. 'Greek-Orthodox, Ottoman Greeks or Just Greeks? Theories of Coexistence in the Aftermath of the Young Turk Revolution'. *Études balkaniques* 1 (2005): 51–72.

Kechriotis, Vangelis, Maciej Górny, and Ahmet Ersoy. 'Haluk's Credo'. In *Modernism: Representations of National Culture : Discourses of Collective Identity in Central and Southeast Europe 1770–1945/ Texts and Commentaries*, edited by Ahmet Ersoy, Maciej Górny and Vangelis Kechriotis, Vol. III/2, 309–12. Budapest: Central European University Press, 2010.

Kessel, Tamara M.C. van. 'Cultural Promotion and Imperialism: The Dante Alighieri Society and the British Council Contesting the Mediterranean in the 1930'. PhD thesis, University of Amsterdam, Amsterdam, 2011.

Keyder, Çağlar. 'The Setting'. In *Istanbul: Between the Global and the Local*, edited by Çağlar Keyder, 3–28. Lanham: Rowman and Littlefield Publisher, 1999.

Keyder, Çağlar. 'A Brief History of Modern Istanbul'. In *The Cambridge History of Turkey*, edited by Reşat Kasaba, 504–23. Cambridge: Cambridge University Press, 2008.

Keyder, Çağlar, and Ayşe Öncü. 'Globalization of a Third-World Metropolis: Istanbul in the 1980's'. *Review (Fernand Braudel Center)* 17, no. 3 (1994): 383–421.

Kezer, Zeynep. *Building Modern Turkey: State, Space, and Ideology in the Early Republic*. Pittsburgh, PA: University of Pittsburgh Press, 2016.

Kim, Hoi-eun. 'Made in Meiji Japan'. *Geschichte und Gesellschaft* 41, no. 2 (2015): 288–320.

King, Charles. *Midnight at the Pera Palace: The Birth of Modern Istanbul*. Norton & Company: New York, 2014.

Knapp, Bernard, and Wendy Ashmore. 'Archaeological Landscapes: Constructional, Conceptualized, Ideational'. In *Archaeologies of landscape: Contemporary Perspectives*, edited by Wendy Ashmore and Bernard Knapp, 1–30. Malden, MA and Oxford: Blackwell Publishers, 1999.

Konuk, Kader. *East West Mimesis: Auerbach in Turkey*. Stanford: Stanford University Press, 2010.

Kuban, Doğan. *Istanbul: An Urban History – Byzantion, Constantinopolis, Istanbul*. 2nd edn. İstanbul: İş Bankası Kültür Yayınları, 2010.

Laidlaw, Christine. *The British in the Levant: Trade and Perceptions of the Ottoman Empire in the Eighteenth Century*. London: IB Tauris, 2010.

Lane, Jeremy F. *Jazz and Machine-Age Imperialism: Music, "Race," and Intellectuals in France, 1918–1945*. Ann Arbor: The University of Michigan Press, 2013.

Lee, J. M. 'British Cultural Diplomacy and the Cold War: 1946–61'. *Diplomacy and Statecraft* 9, no. 1 (1998): 112–34.

Leerssen, Joep. *National Thought in Europe: A Cultural History*. Amsterdam: Amsterdam University Press, 2006.

Leerssen, Joep. 'Nationalism and the Cultivation of Culture'. *Nations and Nationalism* 12, no. 4 (2006): 559, 578.

Leerssen, Joep. *Spiegelpaleis Europa: Europese cultuur als mythe en beeldvorming*. 2nd edn. Nijmegen: Vantilt, 2011.

Leerssen, Joep. 'German Influences: Choirs, Repertoires, Nationalities'. In *Choral Societies and Nationalism in Europe*, edited by Krisztina Lajosi and Andreas Stynen, 14–32. Leiden, Boston: Brill, 2015.

Lewis, Bernard. *The Emergence of Modern Turkey*. 2nd. edn. London: Oxford University Press, 1968.

Martens, Kerstin, and Sanen Marshall. 'International Organisations and Foreign Cultural Policy: A Comparative Analysis of the British Council, the Alliance Française and the Goethe-Institute'. *Transnational Associations* 55, no. 4 (2003): 261–72.

Massey, Doreen. *Space, Place, and Gender*. Minneapolis: University of Minnesota Press, 1994.

Mayer, Christine. 'Education Reform Visions and New Forms of Gymnastics and Dance as Elements of a New Body Culture and 'Body Education' (1890–1930)'. *History of Education* 47, no. 4 (2018): 523–43.

McGhee, George. *The US-Turkish-NATO Middle East Connection: How the Truman Doctrine Contained the Soviets in the Middle East*. New York: Palgrave Macmillan, 1990.

Meyer-Schlichtmann, Carsten. *Von der Preussischen Gesandtschaft zum Doğan-Apartmanı: 130 Jahre Geschichte eines Grundstückes und Hauses in Beyoğlu – Istanbul*. Istanbul: Istanbul Kitaplığı, 1992.

Mitler, Louis. 'The Genoese in Galata: 1453–1682'. *International Journal of Middle East Studies* 10, no. 1 (1979): 71–91.

Münch, Ulrich. 'Die Anfänge der heutigen Deutschen Schule Istanbul – Gründungsjahre der "Deutschen und Schweizer Bürgerschule" von 1867 bis 1874'. In *Daheim in Konstantinopel / Memleketemiz Dersaadet: Deutsche Spuren am Bosporus ab 1850 / 1850'den İtibaren Boğaziçi'ndeki Alman İzleri*, edited by Erald Pauw, 127–64. Neurenberg: Pagma Verlag, 2014.

Mutlu, Dilek Kaya, and Zeynep Koçer. 'A Different Story of Secularism: The Censorship of Religion in Turkish Films of the 1960s and Early 1970s'. European Journal of Cultural Studies 15, no. 1 (2012): 70–88.

Necipoğlu, Gülru. Architecture, Ceremonial, and Power: The Topkapı Palace ın the Fifteenth and Sixteenth Centuries. Cambridge, MA: The MIT Press, 1991.

Nye, Joseph S. 'Soft Power'. Foreign Policy 80 (1990): 153–71.

Okay, Cüneyd. 'Sport and Nation Building: Gymnastics and Sport in the Ottoman State and the Committee of Union and Progress, 1908–18'. The International Journal of the History of Sport 20, no. 1 (2003): 152–6.

Öktem, Kerem. Angry Nation: Turkey since 1989. London: Zedbooks, 2011.

Öncü, Ayşe. 'Istanbulites and Others: The Cultural Cosmology of Being Middle Class in the Era of Globalism'. In Istanbul: Between the Global and the Local, edited by Çağlar Keyder, 95–120. Lanham: Rowman & Littlefield, 1999.

Örs, İlay Romain. 'Beyond the Greek and Turkish Dichotomy: The Rum Polites of Istanbul and Athens'. South European Society and Politics 11, no. 1 (2006): 79–94.

Ortaylı, İlber. İkinci Abdülhamit Döneminde Osmanlı İmparatorluğu'nda Alman Nüfuzu. Ankara: Ankara Üniverstesi Basımevi, 1981.

Öz, Özlem, and Kaya Özkaracalar. 'Path Dependencies, Lock-In and the Emergence of Clusters: Historical Geographies of Istanbul's Film Cluster'. In The Hidden Dynamics of Path Dependence, edited by J. Sydow and E. Schuessler, 161–77. Hampshire, UK and New York: Palgrave Macmillan, 2010.

Öz, Özlem, and Kaya Özkaracalar. 'What Accounts for the Resilience and Vulnerability of Clusters? The Case of Istanbul's Film Industry'. European Planning Studies 19, no. 3 (2011): 361–78.

Parla, Taha, and Andrew Davison, Corporatist Ideology in Kemalist Turkey: Progress or Order?, Syracuse: Syracuse University Press, 2004.

Pauw, Erald, Sabine Böhme, Ulrich Münch. 'Vorwort'. In Daheim in Konstantinopel / Memleketemiz Dersaadet: Deutsche Spuren am Bosporus ab 1850 / 1850'den İtibaren Boğaziçi'ndeki Alman İzleri, edited by Erald Pauw, 5–12. Neurenberg: Pagma Verlag, 2014.

Radt, Barbara. Geschichte der Teutonia: Deutsche Vereinsleben in Istanbul 1847–2000. Istanbul: Orient Institut d. Deutschen Morgenländischen Gesellschaft, 2001.

Rigney, Ann. 'Embodied communities: Commemorating Robert Burns, 1859'. Representations 115 (2011): 71–101.

Rüsen, Jörn. 'Holocaust Memory and Identity Building: Metahistorical Considerations in the Case of (West), Germany'. In Disturbing Remains: Memory, History, and Crisis in the Twentieth Century, edited by Michael S. Roth and Charles G. Salas, 252–70. Los Angeles: Getty Research Institute, 2001.

Sakızlıoğlu, Bahar. 'A Comparative Look at Residents' Displacement Experiences: The Cases of Amsterdam and Istanbul'. PhD thesis, Utrecht University, Utrecht, 2014.

Say, Seda Kula, 'Beaux Arts Kökenli bir Mimar Olarak Alexandre Vallaury'nin Meslek Pratiği ve Eğitimliği Açısından Kariyerinin İrdelenmesi'. Istanbul Technical University, 2014.

Schwartz, Joan M., and Terry Cook. 'Archives, Records, and Power: The Making of Modern Memory'. Archival Science 2, no. 1–2 (2002): 1–19.

Seyhan, Azade. 'German Academic Exiles in Istanbul: Translation as the Bildung of the Other'. In Nation, Language, and the Ethics of Translation, edited by Sandra Bermann and Michael Wood, 274–88. Princeton and Oxford: Princeton University Press, 2005.

Shaw, Standford J. 'The Population of Istanbul in the Nineteenth Century'. International journal of Middle East studies 10, no. 2 (1979): 265–77.

Shaw, Stanford J. 'The Ottoman Census System and Population, 1831–1914'. *International Journal of Middle East Studies* 9, no. 3 (1978): 325–38.

Shefer-Mossensohn, Miri. *Science among the Ottomans: The Cultural Creation and Exchange of Knowledge*. 1st edn. Austin: University of Texas Press, 2015.

Somel, Selçuk Akşin. 'Die Deutschen an der „Pforte der Glückseligkeit": Kulturelle und soziale Begegnungen mit Istanbuler Türken zwischen 1870 und 1918. Almanlar Dersaadet'te: 1870–1918 Devresi İstanbul'unda Almanlarla Osmanlıların Kültürel ve Toplumsal Buluşma Deneyimi'. In *Boğaziçi'ndeki Almanya / Deutsche Praesenz am Bosphorus*, edited by Matthias von Kummer, 35–65. Istanbul: Generalkonsulat der Bundesrepublik Deutschland, 2009.

Tikhonov, Vladimir. 'Masculinizing the Nation: Gender Ideologies in Traditional Korea and in the 1890s–1900s Korean Enlightenment Discourse'. *The Journal of Asian Studies* 66, no. 4 (2007): 1029–65.

Tischler, Ulrike. 'Microhistorical Views of the Sociocultural Phenomenon of Pera Society in the Post-Ottoman Period'. In *From 'mileu de memoire' to 'lieu de memoire': The Cultural Memory of Istanbul in the 20th Century*, edited by Ulrike Tischler, 156–69. Munich: Peter Lang, 2006.

Topdar, Sudipa. 'The Corporeal Empire: Physical Education and Politicising Children's Bodies in Late Colonial Bengal'. *Gender & History* 29, no. 1 (2017): 176–97.

Türeli, İpek. 'Heritagisation of the "Ottoman/Turkish House" in the 1970s: Istanbul-based Actors, Associations and their Networks'. *European Journal of Turkish Studies* 19 (2014): 1–32.

Türeli, İpek, Istanbul. *Open City: Exhibiting Anxieties of Urban Modernity*. New York: Routledge, 2018.

Türkoğlu Önge, Sinem. 'Spatial Representation of Power: Making the Urban Space of Ankara in the Early Republican Period'. In *Developing EU-Turkey Dialogue – A Cliohworld Reader*, edited by Guðmundur Hálfdánarson and Hatice Sofu, 233–57. Pisa: Pisa University Press, 2010.

Türköz, Meltem. 'Surname Narratives and the State—Society Boundary: Memories of Turkey's Family Name Law of 1934'. *Middle Eastern Studies* 43, no. 6 (2007): 893–908.

Üngör, Uğur. *The Making of Modern Turkey*. Oxford: Oxford University Press, 2012.

Uzun, C. Nil, 'The Impact of Urban Renewal and Gentrification on Urban Fabric: Three Cases in Turkey'. *Tijdschrift voor Economische en Sociale Geografie* 94, no. 3 (2003): 363–75.

Vaughan, James R. '"A Certain Idea of Britain": British Cultural Diplomacy in the Middle East, 1945–57'. *Contemporary British History* 19, no. 2 (2005): 151–68.

Volait, Mercedes. 'The reclaiming of "Belle Époque" Architecture in Egypt (1989–2010): On the Power of Rhetorics in Heritage-Making'. *ABE Journal* 3, no. 1 (2013): 1–36 (paragraphs).

Woodall, Carole. '"Awakening a Horrible Monster": Negotiating the Jazz Public in 1920s Istanbul'. *Comparative Studies of South Asia, Africa and the Middle East* 30, no. 3 (2010): 574–82.

Wyers, Mark David. 'Selling Sex in Istanbul'. In *Selling Sex in the City: A Global History of Prostitution, 1600s–2000s*, edited by Magaly Rodríguez García, Lex Heerma van Voss, and Elise van Nederveen Meerkerk, 278–305. Leiden: Brill, 2007.

Wyers, Mark. *Wicked Istanbul: The Regulation of Prostitution in the early Turkish Republic*. Istanbul: Libra Kitap, 2012.

Yorulmaz, Naci. *Arming the Sultan: German Arms Trade and Personal Diplomacy in the Ottoman Empire before World War I*. London and New York: I.B. Tauris, 2014.

Yücel, Atilla, and Hülya Hatipoğlu. 'Taksim Square'. In *Becoming Istanbul: An Encyclopedia*, edited by Pelin Derviş, Bülent Tanju, Uğur Tanyeli, 368–81. İstanbul: Garanti Galeri, 2008.

Yumul, Arus. '"A Prostitute Lodging in the Bosom of Turkishness": Istanbul's Pera and its Representation'. *Journal of Intercultural Studies* 30, no. 1 (2009): 57–72.

Zürcher, Erik-Jan. *Türkey: A Modern History*. 3rd edn. London and New York: I.B. Tauris, 2004.

INDEX

www.ingramcontent.com/pod-product-compliance
Lightning Source LLC
Chambersburg PA
CBHW050442280326
41932CB00013BA/2209